BIKE TRIP MEMOIRS

Cycling Six Continents

MAY 1, 2018

RELEASE 1.0.0

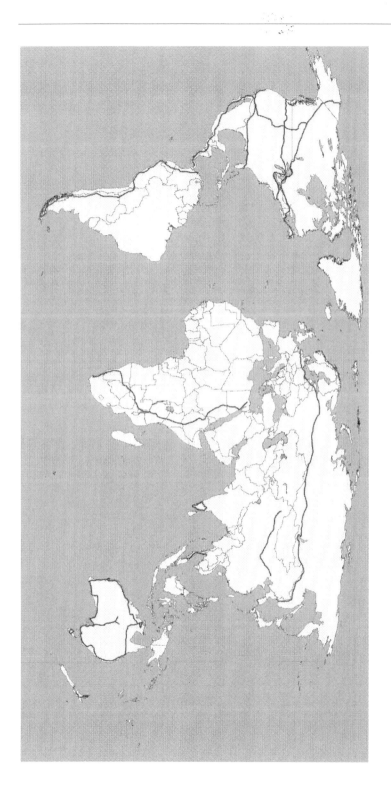

Revision 1.0.0 – May 2018

Contents

Introduction

1st trip to Cape Cod

Fully working brakes can't be that important. After the brakes slow you down enough, then you put your feet down to reach a complete stop. It was with this logic that I set off on my first overnight bicycle trip at age 19.

Our plan was simple: follow the Claire Saltonstall Bikeway[1] from Brookline, a suburb of Boston, to the tip of Cape Cod. The bikeway was 135 miles in a combination of bike paths and secondary roads that connected Boston with Provincetown (P-town). From P-town there was an afternoon ferry that returned to Boston. We took our tents with the plan to ride at least half the distance Saturday and the rest on Sunday. I had organized the ride for half a dozen college friends, though this was my first overnight bicycle trip.

Fewer than ten miles into the trip, disaster struck. Our route crossed a park, went down a small hill and then around a bend. My bicycle had gone down the hill, but I was going too fast and missed the bend. I rode off the edge of the path and then my bicycle stopped. I went flying over the handlebars and did a full summersault, landing flat on my back. My day pack took the brunt of the impact. However, on my lower right side below the pack, a rock stuck into my side and scraped my back.

A reasonable, sensible thing to do would have been to turn back and take care of my injury. However, I was 19, male and invincible. Besides, I was the leader. So, my friends found a nearby drugstore and purchased some large bandages. We taped up the wound and continued on our trip.

That afternoon it was hot, and it hurt as I sweat into the wound. I had a lack of energy until we found a spot to buy a banana for some fuel. What really perked me up, though, was seeing the first sign of Sagamore Bridge in the distance. The Sagamore crossed the Cape Cod Canal and was a sign that we had arrived at the Cape. Hooray!

Not much farther, in Barnstable, Massachusetts, we found a church that let us camp on their front lawn, "as long as we were packed up in time for

---

[1] Claire Saltonstall bikeway - http://www.masspaths.net/bikeways/ccbw/

Sunday services." This was not a problem, as we planned to get on the road early to finish riding to P-town. No rain was forecast, so we could lay out the ground sheets without tents. It still hurt, however, when my friends carefully changed the dressing on my wound.

Next morning, we had a beautiful ride through the Cape on sections of bike path as well as smaller roads. We arrived in P-town with time to spare and mingled with different crowds, looking at shops but also resting from our ride.

After a ferry ride to Boston, I felt triumphant cycling through downtown Boston to Brookline on Sunday afternoon. We had made it and completed the trip! Even with the fall, I had finished the ride.

A job, a bicycle, and a girlfriend

It was during summers at MIT that I first developed my love for bicycle touring. I had grown up in Colorado, been active in Boy Scouts and done a lot of camping, hiking, and backpacking. I enjoyed my time in the urban environment of Boston and kept busy with my studies during the school year. It was during those long summer days that I really enjoyed getting away from the city and out into nature. I didn't own an automobile, and bicycle travel was inexpensive. Relative to Colorado, New England seemed small and compact. Cycling all day from Longmont, Colorado, you might reach Laramie, Wyoming (Laramie is a fine place but not the world's most exciting destination). Cycling from Brookline, Massachusetts, you could easily reach Rhode Island, Connecticut, New Hampshire and even Maine or Vermont.

Three things that most influenced my cycle touring were a job, a bicycle, and a girlfriend.

My sophomore year I applied for and was fortunate to be selected into MIT's 6-A program. This internship program matches Electrical Engineering and Computer Science students with companies on a five-year plan to earn both Bachelor of Science and Master of Science degrees. Students work for the company for three summers and one more semester while writing a thesis based on work at the company.

My match was the Large Computer Group (LCG) at Digital Equipment Corporation, located in Marlboro, Massachusetts. Marlboro was only 26 miles from Brookline via U.S. 20 or 30 miles via Route 30. There was a van pool that made round trips during the work week from nearby Boston. Rather than take the van, I figured out that I could also ride my bicycle, as it only took two hours each way for the ride. That first summer I ended up cycling approximately 60% of the time and taking the van roughly 20% of the time. The rest of the time I would stay out in the Marlboro area. I had a tent and a sleeping bag in my work cubicle and would either sleep in the woods nearby or in my cube. There were showers at work. On a few occasions, the security guards or I would surprise each other, but my boss didn't say anything, and nobody else seemed to mind a co-op student sleeping in his cubicle.

As my cycling increased, I looked for and found a new touring bicycle, a Lotus Odyssey model. It had a triple crank up front, which allowed for a wide range of gears. It also had a front rack, so I could carry things in both front and rear panniers. It was a great bicycle for touring and let me put in many miles. Some weekends rather than cycling back to Boston, I would ride the other direction, going as far as western Massachusetts and Vermont as well as up to Maine.

Cape Cod continued to be a favorite destination. There were multiple youth hostels that provided inexpensive accommodation. The ferry from P-town allowed for a one-way trip back from the tip of the Cape and the ferries to Nantucket and Martha's Vineyard enabled me to visit those islands as well. I still felt a real sense of serenity in reaching and then crossing the bridges onto the Cape. I organized trips with friends in successive summers and made many trips on my own as well.

Mary and I met during my senior year, her freshman year, when we both lived in the same coed Brookline fraternity. We were friends while in the house but didn't start dating until the spring of my graduate year when we both no longer were living in the fraternity. I was smitten. We spent all the time we could together that summer. Our relationship and my need to finish my thesis meant that I did a lot less bicycle touring that summer.

After graduation I moved back to Colorado to start a job with Hewlett-Packard. Mary and I continued a long-distance relationship over the next two years before marrying the day after she graduated from MIT. We spent our honeymoon on a bicycle trip, riding from Brookline to Rochester, Minnesota. It was a great trip filled with its own adventures. However, both before and after that point, I did a lot less bicycle touring than I had as an undergraduate student.

It wouldn't be until our relationship fell apart and we separated that I would jump back into bicycle touring with both feet (wheels?), leading to my first bicycle trip across the U.S.A. in 1992. I followed that bicycle trip with further long trips in 1997, 2001, 2007, 2013 and 2016.

This book is the story of those six long bicycle tours:

- A bicycle ride across America in 1992
- A bicycle ride across Canada in 1997
- A bicycle ride around Australia, across America, through New Zealand and India in 2001
- A bicycle ride across Europe and Asia (mostly Russia) and through China and Thailand in 2007
- A bicycle ride across Africa in 2013
- A bicycle ride across North and South America in 2016

I have found a long trip is somewhat magical in that it allows you to travel day by day, experiencing the small things, as well as to have a sense of accomplishment in completing a larger goal like crossing a continent.

For the last five of these six trips, I kept a mostly daily blog with photos and descriptions. These blogs are still available online and listed with each chapter. Bicycle touring is by nature repetitious, and it is good that most of the time nothing too exciting happens. However, this also makes the blogs a bit more repetitious (I awoke. I cycled. I stopped. It was hot and the road was busy. The next day, I awoke. I cycled. It wasn't as hot, but the road was still busy....). What I have tried to do in this book is step back a bit and describe some of my overall experiences and perceptions as well as some of the more interesting things that happened along the way. I did this by consulting my blogs, and thus I describe my 1992 trip in less detail than the later ones, which are also more recent in memory.

I don't know how well I have succeeded in my goals but would appreciate any feedback, including corrections.

1992 - Tales from across America

URL: http://www.bike1992.com

Plans

I wonder what is on the other side of that hill? After I cycled up and over Seven Cross Hill and saw more hills ahead, I wondered what was beyond those as well. I was riding Colorado 14 east of Fort Collins on a trip that would take me all the way to Chicago. I ended up covering 1000 miles in nine glorious days of riding before I took Amtrak back to Denver. Along the way I had some great days in the saddle following the pioneer trails along the Platte River across Nebraska and an only slightly hillier ride across Iowa, where people asked me if I was training for RAGBRAI[2]. However, what I liked most was just being on the bike, observing the scenery and noticing subtle changes along the plains. It also planted more firmly seeds of an idea to bicycle across America.

Some of the seeds had been there for a while. However, the ten years since I had graduated from high school had also been a time of change. I had graduated from MIT with a Master's Degree and started a job with Hewlett-Packard, where I had worked the past five years. I had gotten married, and we had bought a house. A year before cycling to Chicago, the foundation of the marriage had crumbled, and we had separated. Even if in hindsight some of the cracks were apparent earlier, it was still a big shock.

One of the ways I had worked through our relationship troubles had been to turn back to bicycling. When we divided our property, I told Mary to keep our automobile as well as an antique '49 Chrysler she had brought into the marriage. I would ride my bicycle. At first it was somewhat of a challenge to see if I could ride through the Colorado winter. I told friends that there would probably only be 6-10 days of weather bad enough that I

---

[2] RAGBRAI is the Register's Annual Great Bike Ride Across Iowa, http://www.ragbrai.org.

would wish I had a car. I was happy when my count that winter stayed on fingers of one hand. While there were some cold mornings and I needed to watch for icy patches, it didn't require any different clothing than if one went cross country skiing.

I also became more active in a local bicycle advocacy group, Choice City Cycling Coalition (C4) and with a recreational riding group, Peoples Effort to De-emphasize Automobiles in Loveland (PEDAL[3]). Many weekends I was out riding on a PEDAL ride, which was great both for being outdoors and for the social interaction with other riders.

However, my ride to Chicago was the first week-long ride I had done in a while. I wasn't completely sure if I would make it all the way to Chicago, so I plotted out a route not too far from the Amtrak lines. If it turned out to be slower than I anticipated, I could catch the train in Omaha or other points along the way. This turned out to be unnecessary. It was a great ride and nice reminder of some of the intense rides I had done the summers in college. I also started to think more seriously about a ride across America.

A friend of mine had taken an organized trip across America with Adventure Cycling[4]. That always sounded like a great adventure, and I enjoyed learning more about it. I knew that if I could ride to Chicago in a long week, then I could also do a ride across America on my own and started to dream and scheme how I might make such a ride.

This was days before the world wide web (WWW), Google Maps and even Windows 3.1. However, I did follow some internet news groups and had a program named Automap. Automap ran on my PC and, as the title suggests, would allow you to pick cities along a route and tell you of possible routes. I explored different possibilities as well as preferences, deciding that I wanted to ride through the Columbia River Gorge, avoid Yellowstone, stay in the U.S.A and abide by several other constraints. It was a fun exercise as I approached my second winter in Colorado without an automobile.

---

[3] PEDAL club, http://pedalclub.org/

[4] Adventure Cycling, https://www.adventurecycling.org/

While I did end up buying a car in November, I didn't abandon cycling or my idea about riding across America. Plans also became firmer once Mary and I decided not to reconcile in January 1992 and filed our papers for divorce. There is an official three-month waiting period before a decree is issued. Less than a month after our divorce was final, I was on the road on my first cycle trip across America.

Columbia River Gorge, tire troubles

I had subtitled my trip "Portland to Portland." However, it really made the most sense to start the trip by dipping the rear wheel in the Pacific and finishing with the front wheel in the Atlantic Ocean. I rented an automobile at the Portland airport to take my bike and gear to Astoria, at mouth of the Columbia River and then cycled out to Fort Stevens State Park. Here I did my obligatory dip of my rear wheel and camped in the park for an early departure the following morning.

On my first full day cycling, I had the first of several tire troubles that would plague me on the trip. I had a new Cannondale T-1000 touring bicycle that took nice wide 700x35 tires. Michelin made a good tire, so I had two new tires on the bike as well as a foldable spare with me. Cycling on the way back to Portland, my rear tire developed a half-inch cut. First, I tried to put a piece of rubber (a boot) in the gap but eventually swapped it for the spare tire instead. Not to worry, I was able to pick up another spare tire in Walla Walla two days later.

Another four days later, as I was climbing up MacDonald Pass in Montana, the rear sidewall of this tire blew out. I swapped it for the spare. It was a Saturday afternoon, and by time I would reach Helena, bike shops would close until Monday morning. Furthermore, I wasn't quite sure when I might cross next town large enough to have spare tires. I called my parents and had them send out a new tire express to the U.S. post office in Miles City, Montana, 300 miles ahead on my route. I crossed my fingers and, fortunately, made it to Miles City without troubles. After that I traveled with two spare tires. I had one more tire blowout in Wisconsin, but it all worked to get me across America.

Other than tire troubles, my ride up the Columbia River Gorge went well. I had good tailwinds in part of the gorge and otherwise cycled long days.

Lewiston, Idaho, was my first chance for a breather when I cycled *only* 70 miles and hence stopped well before dark. From Lewiston it was a scenic but remote ride up the river canyon and over Lolo Pass into Montana.

On other side of Montana were Adventure Cycling offices in Missoula. I stopped by, but the office didn't have the maps I was seeking. From Missoula it was a few longer days of cycling the "Big Sky country" of Montana to the eastern plains to reach Baker. This area reminded me a bit of Colorado, where I had grown up with similar corn crops and small farms.

Riding 207 miles with tailwinds

Early to bed and early to rise— I am a morning person, and on the bike trip I was often in bed by 8:30 p.m. and up at first light. On the morning of June 4th, I was up at 5 a.m. and ready to go soon thereafter.

There was a strong wind blowing across the prairies, and fortunately it was a tailwind. The twelve miles to the North Dakota border went quickly and wind continued to blow me on to Bowman at forty-five miles. My pattern was to ride for a few hours and then stop for breakfast, so time to stop in Bowman. After a leisurely breakfast, I was happy the wind was still strong. This cycling was a lot easier than most days.

Often when riding I will have a "target" destination or two picked out in the morning. This gives me several alternatives to pick from depending on how the day progresses. My target for the day had been Lemmon, South Dakota, just over 100 miles from Baker. However, I was almost at Lemmon by noon, and it seemed to be a shame to stop and let the tailwind go to waste.

The issue was that not long after Lemmon was Standing Rock Indian Reservation. Finding accommodations on a reservation is sometimes difficult and camping without permission is a "no no," so I needed to either stop in Lemmon or plan to ride all way across the reservation. It was early enough in the day that I decided to try riding across the reservation.

By time I reached 156 miles, near McIntosh, I came to what turned out to be twenty miles of road construction. The pavement was gone, and I was riding on hard-packed dirt road. Some sections also had loose gravel scraped over the top, into which my back wheel would slide. Other sections had a wide berm scraped in the middle that directed traffic first to one side and then to the other. There was a three-mile section of red mud, where they had poured water on the surface to make a muddy paste. The red splatter got over everything. Overall, it was a bit like an obstacle course and became a bit surrealistic.

Not long after the construction zone, the wind stopped. There were half a dozen successive hills where the road would climb up ~200 feet to a crest then drop into a drainage area and then repeat the process again. There wasn't a good spot to stop in the Indian Reservation in either the construction zone or the hilly region, so I kept going. Fortunately, I made it to Mobridge, South Dakota, before dark, after having cycled 207 miles. To this day, 207 miles is the longest distance I have cycled in a day on either a loaded or unloaded touring bicycle.

A few days of riding farther to reach Minneapolis/St Paul Minnesota ensued. I had ridden more than 1800 miles in sixteen days and hence could afford to take a rest day here with friends of the family in a suburb of Cottage Grove.

Wisconsin, Michigan, and the Midwest

After a nice rest day in the Twin Cities, including an interview for a story in the local newspaper, I was back on the road. I lost one more tire in Wisconsin, but it was otherwise uneventful riding. There had been several routing choices in which I decided to keep my riding "all in the U.S.A." but also go along the Upper Peninsula (UP) of Michigan. This meant riding down across the UP, crossing the Straights of Mackinac and then continuing through Ohio south of Lake Erie.

Bicycles are prohibited on the Mackinac Bridge. I solved that issue by taking a ferry from the UP to Mackinac Island, spending an easy day on the island and taking another ferry to the Lower Peninsula the next morning. The island was interesting, since few if any automobiles are allowed, so bicycle travel is the common method used. By now I had ridden ~2/3 of my intended distance and felt that I was "ahead" of schedule.

Coming down through Michigan, near Livonia, I had one stormy afternoon with ominous clouds. I found a motel early and the power went out for a while. I learned later that there had been several sightings of tornadoes. Otherwise, it was mostly long days in the saddle as I crossed more urban areas of Ohio and Pennsylvania south of Lake Erie.

After New York I was in familiar ground, following the Erie Canal across New York, crossing several hilly bits in Vermont and riding on to Brookline. I stayed with friends here before finishing my "Portland to Portland" trip by riding up to Portland, Maine. This was my chance to dip the front wheel in the Atlantic Ocean, and the trip was complete.

Overview and thoughts on the trip

I completed my first ride across America in just over five weeks, with just one rest day and one or two short days included. It was an intense ride with many hours in the saddle and not a lot of time for sightseeing or socializing with locals in towns I crossed. This gave me time to reflect on my recently ended relationship as well as what might come next. I stayed mostly in motels with just a few nights camping in the tent.

Other cycle tourists often find one of the most enjoyable times is interacting with locals or visiting small town America. I had my share of kind interactions, but often it was stopping in at a convenience store for quick snack. In the evenings I found a motel and was quick to sleep, so I didn't meet as many people as if I had camped or found lodging with locals. However, I also don't have regrets on missing this, as it was like other "gonzo "rides I had done and matched my expectations.

The largest mechanical issue I had was tire failures. The Michelin tires either popped off the rims or developed sidewall failures. I continued to ride Michelin tires for several years after that, but eventually I switched to other tire brands.

I had a real sense of accomplishment after the trip and was glad that I had taken time off to complete what otherwise had been a dream that seemed impractical.

Epilogue: A walk across the Mackinac Bridge

In my first ride across America, there had been one small part I missed: the Mackinac Bridge, where bicycles were prohibited. Normally, I am not that much of a "purist" to have to ride every single inch, but the idea of going back to walk across the bridge still appealed to me.

The first weekend of September, Labor Day, there is an annual walk across the bridge[5], so I decided to return in 1992 to walk the missing link. I rented a car and drove up to the area.

Labor Day is traditional kickoff for the U.S. election season, and 1992 was an election year. The day before the walk, I drove up to Sault-Sainte Marie and saw a parade in which President George H. W. Bush went past in the presidential motorcade. I found it exciting, as it was first time I had seen a president in person.

Each year approximately 50,000 people come for the bridge walk. Early in the morning, there is a large convoy of school buses that provide transportation from south to north across the bridge. The walk itself kicks off at 7 a.m. and for a while it is only pedestrians on the bridge. After a while they reopen lanes on one side to let school buses convoy people from south to north again. After 11 a.m., no new pedestrians can start walking the bridge, and when the last pedestrian finishes the five-mile walk, the bridge reopens for normal traffic.

I had a motel on the south side of the bridge, and early in the morning I took the shuttle to the north. Almost everyone else I met was from Michigan. Some of them were with local health clubs promoting walking. Others had vests with patches to commemorate each of many annual walks they had done. It felt like a Michigan event.

At an election year, President Bush and family had decided to also make the bridge walk a campaign stop. That added to the circus. There were protestors with anti-Bush signs when I left the bus. Bush himself flew in via helicopter to an enclosed area to start the walk. Near where the helicopter landed was a speaking podium, and the Secret Service had

---

[5] Mackinac Bridge Walk, http://www.mackinacbridge.org/annual-bridge-walk-2/

metal detectors to screen those allowed past. The Secret Service also confiscated any signs (which were mostly anti-Bush). Near the podium campaign staff handed out a new set of (pro-Bush) signs. Someone looking at the TV coverage of the event would see a crowd of ~50,000 people and near the podium a large set of pro-Bush signs with no anti-Bush signs.

I thought this was deceptive and a "made for TV" campaign event. Pretty much most everyone I met had come to walk the bridge and not really to be part of a campaign event, either pro- or anti-Bush. Some were impatient to start the walk, and the campaigning delayed a normal 7 a.m. start. However, soon enough the Bushes started walking across the bridge, followed by several black Secret Service limos and a lot of campaign staff. A little later everyone else was allowed on the bridge, and we completed our walk.

While I wasn't as much of a purist to walk every single inch, it was still an interesting experience to complete this missing link from my ride across America.

Epilogue: Work changes and dreams of another trip

On November 6th, four months after my cross-America ride, our group at Hewlett-Packard was called to a conference room. There was an ominous feel as our management chain was all there, along with managers from other organizations on the Fort Collins site. There was even a woman with a big button saying "employee assistance program, EAP."

Our lab manager spent what seemed like eternity describing the great things our group had done and what talented people we were, before getting to the "but" part of the equation--. in particular, "but, tomorrow we would all be doing different work." Hewlett-Packard was consolidating efforts, and our work was moving to either California or Massachusetts. We might be able to move to follow the work, but more likely other groups on site had open jobs for which we could apply.

It was both a shock and a surprise as I liked my work and had put a lot of energy into my work projects. Intuitively, I knew things would be OK, but it was disconcerting to look for another job again. I wasn't alone, as a team with gallows humor put together a cardboard sign or two saying "will program for food".

Somehow, in all this change, I drew strength from the bike trip I had taken the preceding summer. Part of it was a swagger, "I rode across America, so I can solve this too..." and a confidence that came with it. I also felt very fortunate and grateful that I had completed this ride before the shutdown, since now it would have been more difficult with a new job. It was important to take these opportunities when I could. As part of that idea, I vowed to myself to take another long bike trip "in five years or so." While I didn't know where I might ride, this planted the earliest seeds for my next cross-continental bicycle ride.

1997 - Tales from across Canada
URL: http://www.bike1997.com

Plans
Why Canada? The idea started with the Alaska Highway and expanded from there. Also, the trip worked well with my work plans.

After my cross-U.S.A. trip, I went back to a pattern of less frequent cycling vacations and shorter distances. In 1993, I cycled 1440 km around the small country of the Netherlands, visiting family and going all throughout the small 300 x 250 km country. In 1994, I rode an organized "Ride the Rockies" trip in Colorado. In 1995, I did five shorter cycling tours that, when placed end-to-end, traveled the Atlantic coast from Key West, Florida, to Halifax, Nova Scotia. It was on my Atlantic coast ride that I started to think more seriously about the next big trip and the lure of Alaska Highway as a destination.

I worked for Hewlett-Packard in Massachusetts, having moved there in 1993 after our lab was shut down. I had taken a job to lead a new team that inherited the product I previously worked on in Colorado. Our project had gone through multiple phases: building a team, stabilizing the old product and then planning, designing, and building an entire new replacement product. I found my job fulfilling and the work challenging. I also enjoyed my new role as manager of a team rather than as an individual contributor.

However, I was also reaching a point where our new product had been built and I wasn't learning or growing as quickly with new skills. It seemed like a good time to look for additional challenges to keep myself learning and growing. As I discussed things with my managers, an idea took shape: a "rotation" to our California offices. Our lab was a small organization that worked closely with a much larger lab in Silicon Valley. While I couldn't see myself moving permanently to California, it was appealing to work in that California organization for several years before returning to Massachusetts.

Approximately 18 months before my trip, I discussed things with my bosses and worked through rough ideas. This gave me time to put everything into good order, including discretely training my successors. The team members wouldn't learn of changes until shortly before my departure. I was grateful to Hewlett-Packard and particularly my management that they were willing to support me with this job rotation.

Structuring my absence as part of a job rotation also gave me flexibility on the exact duration. I had to wrap up my old assignment before departure and couldn't start a new assignment until I arrived in California (and as it turned out, that assignment changed during my trip as well). I updated my plans to include not only the Alaska Highway but also continuing east from there across Canada. I set an overall time budget of three months-- twice as much time as my first cross-continental ride but not quite twice the distance.

Trip start in Alaska and Yukon Territory

The Princess Hotel was located next to the Chena River in Fairbanks. I looked out to see many ice floes drifting in the river. Breakup! An eagerly awaited sign of spring, the ice had broken and river had started flowing just two days before. A prize of $300,000 was split amongst multiple winners who had correctly guessed April 30th as the date.

I went back to my bicycle for a personal mission. Our divorce decree had been issued almost exactly five years prior. I had with me a "temporary" engagement ring I had made by epoxying a 741 operational amplifier computer chip to a silver band. This was the placeholder we used until Mary could select a real ring and yet have a ring to show those who asked. I had made two copies and believe both Mary and I ended up with one. I tossed the ring onto a waiting ice floe and let it drift headed towards the Yukon River. I would never see it again. I paused briefly to reflect on the symbolism and went back to start my ride.

The next four days I cycled in Alaska. As I went farther upstream, I came to areas where the rivers were frozen again. My trip started on May 2nd and was early in the season, as tourist services on the Alaska Highway weren't fully open for summer yet. On these first parts in Alaska and Yukon Territory, I visited several historic lodges.

The lodges seemed to be a cross between a guest house and a more traditional motel. There wasn't always room to bring in my bicycle. At

Cherokee Lodge near Delta Junction, I found a room with the water heater, since my bedroom was otherwise too small. That evening was a prom celebration from the nearby high school and students came in their tuxes and fancy dresses. The next morning before departure I helped take down prom decorations.

In the settlement of Koidern, the first day riding past the Canadian border, both motels were closed for the season. It was another 17 miles to next motel, and the road ahead turned to gravel. I had my tent with me, but it was cold and I wanted to find a warm place inside if I could. I knocked on the door of nearby fishing lodge. I am still not certain if they were really open for the season or just taking pity on a cold-looking cyclist, but they told me they had a room. The room still had other things in it, as if someone's bedroom more than a formal hotel room, but it was a warm place for the night.

The next morning, I was ready to tackle the gravel road. It was 33 degrees Fahrenheit and there was a hint of snow flurries. The gravel gave extra friction, and I tried to cycle in smoothest part of the lane. In one or two spots, mud got up into my fenders and I had to stop and remove it. At around the five-mile mark, I encountered a "road construction" sign. The flagger told me to be careful of large construction trucks, as they were reconstructing about a mile of road. In the next section I both walked and cycled past a dozen large construction vehicles. At 17 miles, I reached my first destination for breakfast, the closed Pine Valley motel/café. Oops, so much for breakfast. The kind owner was nice enough to refill my water bottles though.

There was a pay phone at Pine Valley and I called to check the 1-800 number from work. There was an "urgent" message at the top of the inbox. It was telling people that the monthly meeting was in a new conference room. The sender marked the message "urgent" since the meeting was in a few hours. I sat beside my bicycle next to a closed motel in Pine Valley, amused at these messages that were urgent just a month or two ago. I briefly considered dialing into the monthly meeting later from a pay phone farther down the road and realized there wasn't much point. Our work world would go on without my need to check in for these urgent phone calls.

The gravel continued for another 13 miles past Pine Valley to the Donjek River. This 30-mile stretch was the longest unpaved section I cycled for the entire trip. However, there were numerous other short sections or "gravel patches" on the Alaska Highway. Otherwise, the road had good surfaces and gentle gradients. The highway was built in 1942 as a winter road, opened to the public in 1948 and fully paved in 1960. In the 50 plus years of existence, some sections had been under continuous construction and improvement, but by 1997 it was an easy road to travel by bicycle.

I cycled the Alaska Highway again in 2016 as part of my Across the Americas ride. I found it interesting to see that most of the lodges I had stayed at were still standing. However, almost none of them were still tourist accommodations. What was also interesting was that some areas under road construction in 1997 were again (still?) under road construction in 2016. Apparently, there are permafrost and unstable soils, particularly north of the Donjek River, that make road building difficult.

 It was a dozen cycling days to Watson Lake, where I visited the "Signpost Forest." This collection of 20,000 signs came from throughout the world. I had fun wandering through to look for signs from familiar places. The visitor center also had a mock-up of a P-39 fighter with Russian markings. The route for the Alaska Highway was selected to go past airfields that were used to stage lend-lease planes during the second world war. Both Watson Lake and earlier areas had a lot of historical pieces that I learned reading "The Milepost." The Milepost[6] was a road guide that gave mile-by-mile descriptions of the route, including services, and hence was valuable to a cycle tourist, particularly as this was before I had a cell phone (or much cell coverage) or internet to look up locations.

Rim troubles, bears, and hot springs
I left Watson Lake on my thirteenth day cycling. It turned out to be an unlucky day.

---

[6] The Milepost, http://www.themilepost.com/

My rear wheel had developed a slight wobble a few times in the first twelve days, and I had tightened up my spokes the night before to bring it back to true. My bicycle rode well when I left town.

A little past 9 a.m., it started raining, a slow steady rain that would continue for most of the rest of the day. Not much later I came to my first gravel section for the day, five miles to Iron Creek Lodge, where I stopped for a mid-morning snack.

The terrain after Iron Creek was still "old road" and had numerous descents and climbs. The grades were steep enough that I walked up an occasional hill. The rain was steady and miserable. I am sure it would have been beautiful scenery, but I was concentrating on keeping dry and warm.

Slowly the miles counted down. I had another four miles of gravel before the rain eventually stopped for the day, and I even saw a rainbow. I had traveled 90 miles already and was looking for an afternoon cheeseburger. My rear wheel had started wobbling again, but figured I would sort it out at Coal River, just ten miles down the road.

At Coal River, there were three pieces of bad news. The most significant was that my rear rim was tearing apart. The rim was cracked and there wouldn't be a way to true it up again. It was only a matter of time before it collapsed. It was frustrating, since I had had this wheel built especially for the trip, and it had only had 470 miles on it before the 900 miles I had ridden in the past two weeks.

The second piece of bad news was that Coal River Lodge, café and campground weren't yet open for the season—nothing like cycling 100 miles to find a closed campground. There was someone working on opening things up, but he was unhelpful and unfriendly. He also didn't want me camping in the yard, so, with a sigh, I hit the road again.

The owner of the Coal River Lodge told me the third piece of bad news, another dozen miles of gravel road. It was around 6 p.m., but I decided I would try continuing as far as I could to Liard River, 37 miles away. If necessary, I would camp and cycle the rest before breakfast. I figured it was only a matter of time before the rim collapsed, but each mile would bring me closer to Fort Nelson, likely the next town with a bicycle shop or at least a sports store.

I made it 129 miles before the rim collapsed. I was going down a small hill and heard a "pow!" followed by a hiss as the tire jammed against the chain stay and then deflated. There was no point in fixing the tire since the problem would happen again. So, I started walking. I had another 8 miles to Liard River, but perhaps I might get a ride.

A little over a mile farther, I saw black bear ambling across the road. Uh oh! The bear looked up at me with a curious look. Not quite certain what to do, I decided to yell, "Hey bear! Hello there bear!" and whistle. The bear looked at me even more curiously and decided to eventually gallop across the road and hide in the bushes. The bear was still looking at me curiously as I walked by.

A little over a mile later, a truck stopped by. Folks were kind enough to load the bicycle and me in the truck and drive to Liard River Lodge. It had been a long day, with almost 130 miles of cycling, road construction, mechanical failure, rain and bears, and I was happy to be back at a point of civilization.

There was a pay phone at the lodge and next morning I looked in the Yellow Pages and called Griffen Sports, in Fort St. John. They agreed to get a rim and build a bicycle wheel, but it would take 3-4 days to arrive. They would send it up via Greyhound Bus.

Liard River is the site of nearby hot springs. This gave me several days of relaxation, reading and a chance to visit the hot springs. It was a nice restful stay. As the time to leave neared, I called Griffen Sports again, but the person who answered knew nothing about my wheel. I called the next day and eventually decided to also call CMP Sports in nearby Fort Nelson. CMP Sports had a wheel pre-built that they could send up on the bus right away! I cancelled the wheel delivery from Griffen Sports. When I eventually cycled through Fort St John, I visited their store and am not sure they ever really started my order.

The wheel from Fort Nelson arrived on evening Greyhound Bus. The afternoon before, I had the cook from Liard River Lodge drop me off where I had stopped walking so I could walk the missing miles to the lodge. Overall, it was an unplanned six-day intermission waiting for a wheel. If I had to break down, the Liard River Hot Springs were a beautiful place to stay.

Finish the Alaska Highway and on to the plains

Six days at Liard Hot Springs and I was eager to get back on the road. I swapped out the wheel in evening. Early the next morning, I said goodbye to staff and to the friendly lodge cat and was back on the road. This next section was scenic but also rugged riding as I crossed over the continental divide. However, I was also slowly getting to more "civilized" regions.

The replacement wheel was a 32-spoke regular cycling wheel instead of a 36-spoke touring wheel. Several factors increase strength of a wheel, including having a double-walled rim as well as more spokes. This one had neither. A bigger problem was that the spokes were working themselves loose, and the wheel was starting to wobble. I had one particularly challenging descent into Buckinghorse River. I squeezed the rear brakes on the descent and sped up. Apparently, the rear wheel was wobbling enough that closing the brakes part way made the wheel track straighter and faster. That evening I tightened more than half the spokes. The wheel was better after that, though I was still nervous.

It snowed at Buckinghorse River. It was a late spring storm with several centimeters of snow in Buckinghorse River and 10 centimeters in Edmonton. Fortunately, I had enough warm clothes, and the next day it was dry and warmer again. A day or two later, I made it to Fort St. John. I stopped in Griffin Sports bike shop to have them true up my rear wheel. I also asked about that original wheel they were going to send to Liard Hot Springs, but the mechanic wasn't in, so I still didn't quite know if it was ever ordered. One day later was Dawson City and the official end to the Alaska Highway.

I crossed into Alberta and, after three long days riding, reached the big city of Edmonton. In Edmonton, I found a bike shop and acquired a proper touring wheel with 36-spokes and double rims for my bike. The 32-spoke lightweight wheel had gotten me several hundred miles and while not durable was still OK as an emergency backup. I tied it up on back of my paniers and sleeping bag as a spare.

The trip from Fairbanks to Edmonton had taken almost exactly a month, or one third of my allotted time, including six days waiting for the wheel. It wasn't quite a third of the planned distance so I knew I would need to ride slightly longer rides.

Riding across the prairies

I knew I was on the great plains when a local on the street was warning me about the "big hill" that was coming ahead. This sounded serious so asked a bit more. It turned out this hill was another 50 km away at a spot where the Yellowhead Highway descended to a river and then climbed up the other side. While there was a little climbing involved, it paled in comparison to the hillier parts I had just completed on the Alaska Highway.

In contrast, not much more than a week before, I had asked a local about the route to the next town of Wonowon. They told me, "There is one big hill, no maybe two or perhaps three." As I had cycled along, my count was up to six reasonable sized hills before I reached the town. In the plains, a single hill, 50 km away, stands out, whereas in the forested areas, locals driving automobiles stopped noticing and paying attention to hills.

In contrast, the winds on the prairies were a larger concern than hills. I had one wonderful day riding in Saskatchewan with strong tailwinds where I rode 240 km before deciding to stop for the day. The next day the winds shifted, and I struggled to barely make 65 km against a strong headwind. This was the first of several days with headwinds. While the wind slows you down, I found the psychological effects at least as big. Try to get up early to beat the wind, only to have it already blowing and rushing past your ears all day.

After a particularly trying day fighting the wind, I had a "how are you doing" type conversation with a local where I mentioned, "Great, if it weren't for this wind." They looked quizzically before thinking and saying, "Yes, I guess there is some wind today." It was that contrast between hills and winds that stuck out for me on the prairies.

I followed a route known as Yellowhead Highway that also paralleled one of the early railroad lines across Canada. Every 7.5 miles there used to be a silo and perhaps a settlement to bring crops to the train. Some of these settlements had since become abandoned ghost towns, but with exception of the wind, there was a nice rhythm to riding on the plains.

Local news and Canadian politics

1997 was an election year in Canada. I would read the local papers and try to figure out how the politics worked. I also used it as an excuse to read the Canadian Constitution as well as learn some of the history. In the evenings I might turn on TV in motel and catch some news.

One thing that struck me was the regional differences between provinces that I observed. Roughly speaking, my impressions included the following:

- Yukon Territory and far northern parts of BC didn't have many people and areas I visited were focused on the tourist industry. There were also First Nations areas, though my contact with them was minimal.
- Alberta was in the midst of an energy boom. Jobs were plentiful and advertised in Newfoundland as well as other places. The politics seemed more conservative, with a "reform" party picking up a big share of votes. There also seemed to be a backlash on the "bilingual" aspects of Canada. For example, I had locals point out to me that it seemed to be strange to require food packaging in French as well as English when there were few French speakers in Alberta.
- Saskatchewan and Manitoba were traditional strongholds of the NDP and did well that year as well.
- Ontario was part of the original Canadian Confederation. People I talked with were proud of that confederation and some equated Ontario with Canada. In contrast to farther west, it was important that Canada was bilingual and that Quebec as well as Ontario was part of the original confederation.
- Quebec was Quebec, with a referendum on separation not too many years before. Canada Day (July 1st) was decidedly quiet in Quebec, and I saw at least one half of a Canadian flag being flown.
- Canadian Maritimes were struggling at times economically. Tourism was still a draw,, particularly in Nova Scotia and PEI. However, I also got the sense that the support from the rest of Canada was important to this area.

- Newfoundland also struggled economically, with a declining population and depleted fisheries. Tourism wasn't as robust as in Nova Scotia and PEI. I got the sense support from the rest of Canada was at least as important as in the Maritimes.

Against that backdrop, it was interesting to see election results that resulted in the ruling Liberal Party picking up almost every riding in Ontario but failing to expand their base in other provinces. It was interesting to see the traditional conservative party struggle while Reform was stronger in the west. Meanwhile, NDP and Bloque Quebecois each picked up key regional constituencies. To some extent, this mirrored what I also noticed talking with locals as well as following the news.

Around the Great Lakes

Near Portage La Prairie, Manitoba, I came to two important changes. The most significant was the tree line and the start of forested regions. This made a big difference to the wind. The second change was that the Yellowhead Highway joined up with the Trans-Canada route.

After these came together, I crossed the larger city of Winnipeg and was on my way to Kenora, Ontario, when I noticed tell-tale signs of a wobble in my rear wheel. Just my luck, the wheel had cracked and the spokes were starting to pull it apart. I cycled carefully to Kenora and came into the first bike shop I found.

Fortunately, the fix was quicker this time. The bike shop ordered a new rim from Winnipeg, built up the wheel and got me back on my way with only a day of downtime--much better news than before.

In 1997 the main road from Kenora across to Thunder Bay was a notorious "black spot," meaning a dangerous road. Shoulders were narrow, and there were many trucks and winding curves. Based on this information, I decided to take a slightly roundabout route to first go south to Fort Francis and then across to Thunder Bay.

During my 1992 cross-U.S.A. trip, I had stayed entirely inside the U.S.A. In 1997, I made a similar choice to stay entirely within Canada. These were still early internet days, so I had one or two mail drops, including Sault-Sainte Marie, where I had mail sent "general delivery" to retrieve at the post office. I did learn on this trip that mail sent across the U.S./Canada border incurred extra delays and almost missed a letter or two since they didn't arrive in time.

After crossing over Lake Huron, I took a ferry to Manitoulin Island and then rode almost to Toronto before taking ring roads to the north and east to come to the north side of Lake Erie. My parents came out to meet me one day just as I was crossing from Ontario into Quebec.

Overall, it took a second month to ride from Edmonton to Quebec City. On average, my distances of 90-miles per day were longer than those of the first month. However, with exception of headwinds, the riding wasn't as difficult. Often, I would be on the road by 6 a.m. and finish in early afternoon. This would give me time to relax, look around town and get to bed early to repeat this schedule the next morning.

Quebec

I entered Quebec just a few days before Canada Day (July 1st). Canada Day celebrates the union of the provinces of Canada (Ontario and Quebec) with New Brunswick and Nova Scotia as a federation of four provinces. As I cycled through Ontario, flags were already out in anticipation of the holiday.

Crossing into Quebec, it suddenly became a much more subdued holiday, including on Canada Day itself. Quebec flags outnumbered Canadian flags about 2:1. I saw one place flying only half of a Canadian flag, but otherwise saw many more banners celebrating a Quebec historical event 325 years prior (1672) than celebrating Canada Day.

My high school French seems to have deserted me. Fortunately, in most shops where I wanted to purchase things or in places to stay, it was simple enough to work things out. I stopped through the town of Riviere-Du-Loop to pick up another mail drop, though I had to wait for the post office to open. If I do this trip again, I will make my mail drops on the U.S. border cities and briefly cross.

Atlantic Canada

My time in the maritime provinces of New Brunswick, Prince Edward Island and Nova Scotia went quickly, with just a few days spent in each province. The Confederation Bridge linking PEI with New Brunswick had just opened that year. Cyclists were prohibited from riding across the bridge, but there was a free shuttle bus (pickup truck) that took my bicycle. This was not a bad deal since the automobile toll was $35 Canadian. From other end of PEI, I took the ferry on to Nova Scotia. A few days with nice tailwinds and I was in North Sydney and the ferry to Newfoundland.

In hindsight, Newfoundland was one of my favorite provinces I cycled. I took the ferry to Port-Aux-Basques and followed the trans-Canada highway across the island to St. Johns. It was a large ferry, and my boat included a convoy of 36 air-stream trailers, all from a touring group.

Tourism in Newfoundland seemed less developed than in Nova Scotia or PEI. For example, in Nova Scotia there were all sorts of pamphlets describing "trails" one could follow with convenient links to accommodations and other tourist services. PEI had a large tourist office near the Confederation Bridge where one could look up various tourist facilities. Newfoundland may have had a tourist office, but the big event in 1997 seemed to be a second sailing of the Cabot. John Cabot "discovered" the coast of North America in 1497, just five years after Christopher Columbus. There is speculation about Vikings and earlier discoveries, but the 500th anniversary of Cabot's voyage was important in Newfoundland that summer. In 1997, there was a re-enactment of Cabot's voyage, landing first at Cape Bonavista and then circling major cities on the coast.

Newfoundland had struggled economically, particularly after the collapse of cod fisheries. Some of the younger people had left. When I looked through local papers, perhaps a third of the job advertisements were outside the province, e.g. oil field jobs in Alberta. I also noticed postings of "homecoming weeks." The idea was that if your relatives came back to visit, then it would be nice to coordinate with other returnees so all could see each other as well.

Several of the towns I passed through, including Deer Lake and Gander and Stephenville, were important airfield sites from an earlier era when trans-Atlantic aircraft had a shorter range. Apparently, in 1938, the Gander Airfield was the largest and busiest in the world. There was also an airplane museum in Gander that I visited. When I was there,

Stephenville still had flights from former east-bloc countries, e.g. the Czech Republic, with a stop in Newfoundland before crossing to Cuba.

Weather in Newfoundland was volatile. My first day riding, I cut out early due to an intense rain storm. Almost as quickly and severely as it came up, it also faded, and next day was a good cycling day again. However, I wasn't as lucky with the wind. In the Saint Lawrence River valley, I was spoiled with tailwinds, but now I had a little of everything: cross winds, tail winds, and headwinds.

Crossing the town of Corner Brook, I looked down and noticed a wobble in the back wheel again. Uh oh. Fortunately, Corner Brook and Gander were both towns with bike shops before St. Johns. I rode to the Corner Brook bike shop and got a diagnosis. The rim that had brought me from Edmonton was now falling apart. They didn't have a suitable replacement rim. There was a reason I had been carrying that spare rim that I first got on the Alaska Highway! So, we swapped back to my 32-spoke rim. I was, however, still a bit nervous, so I also took a new spare – a 32-spoke metal wheel the bike shop had available.

On July 22nd, I reached my destination of St. Johns after a short detour to Cape Spear, the easternmost-point. My rims and wheels had lasted! I bought my airline tickets back and then had two and a half days to spend as a tourist exploring the city.

Overview and thoughts on the trip

I took three months for my second ride across North America. Including my rest days, my pace averaged 85 miles per day. It wasn't as intense a ride as my crossing of the U.S.A. five years earlier, though I did spend most of my time on the bike.

Cycle tourists sometimes ask about favorite places to ride, including a cross-continental trip. I think there is a lot of value in riding your own country or area first, for example, Americans cycling across the U.S.A., Canadians cycling across Canada, or Europeans cycling their own countries and nearby European countries. With that said, Canada had a lot to recommend. My favorite places were still the "edges," including the far north in Yukon Territory or the other edge in Newfoundland. However,

Canada has a bonus in the variety of landscapes, terrain and, to some extent, outlooks of people in different provinces.

The biggest mechanical issue I had was rims. I lost the first near Liard Hot Springs on the Alaska Highway, the second near Kenora, Ontario, and the third near Corner Brook, Newfoundland. After the trip, I talked with mechanics at a local bike shop, and they recommended trying a 48-spoke rim, often used for tandem bicycles. They also suggested using a hub used by "Phil Woods." Hence, after this trip, on later tours I switched to these rims.

I was grateful to Hewlett-Packard both for providing me the time off and being able to do it during a transition as a rotation to a new assignment. This meant I was finished with old assignments and didn't need to start figuring out new ones until after the trip. I was also happy I had taken this time and that the rough "in five years" plan had worked.

I had spent almost three months cycling to reach a destination, and it still felt like an accomplishment to reach the endpoint. I was now fired up and ready to go back to work.

Epilogue: Work changes

On November 6th, three months after starting my rotational assignment in California, I learned unfortunate news. In a few months the site in Massachusetts would close. My rotation had now become a one-way trip. There was no more idea of working two years and then perhaps cycling on the way back.

My new management was supportive and even offered to let me rotate to Colorado instead. However, I had just started this assignment, was new to California and didn't feel as if I had fully experienced things, so I declined. Instead, I threw myself into a newer assignment, helping to pick up pieces from my colleagues in Massachusetts and rebuilding those project teams in California with some support also going to India. I had worked through the Colorado lab shutdown and now used that same experience to help with the Massachusetts shutdown. It was a busy time.

At the same point, I reflected again that I felt happy that I had again taken time to do the cross-Canada trip the preceding summer. If I had not taken that time, I would likely have been in Massachusetts when my work disappeared. I wasn't quite certain when or where, but vowed to myself to again take time for another long cycle trip, perhaps in five years or so. This would give me some time to contribute well at work and some time to dream and explore possibilities for a future trip.

2001 - Tales from around Australia

URL: http://www.bike2001.com

Plans

Blame it on National Geographic and on HR policies.

In December 1997, February 1998 and April 1998, National Geographic magazine had a three-part series by Roff Smith describing a 10-month trip he had taken counter-clockwise around the perimeter of Australia. Wow! He also published a book, Cold Beer, and Crocodiles[7], about the time I departed. I had read the articles some months after their original publication and they and Richard Allen's book, Shimmering Spokes[8], planted a seed that I explored by further reading other accounts of cyclists riding Australia.

While 1999 was still early to be restless in regard to my original, "I will tour in five years" plan, it wasn't too early to get ideas. One key point was how long a HR policy allowed a leave of absence. I was pleasantly surprised to discover that Hewlett-Packard policies included up to one year on a personal leave of absence. While there was no job guarantee (unlike military leave or maternity), it would rely on your relationship with your bosses to approve a leave and later determine if there was a job after you returned. I had good relations with my bosses and started to explore possibilities in 2000. It was easier to ask for a long period up front and shorten the time than the other way around. Hence, I first asked for a leave of a year.

One year was sufficient time, so I started to dream of a combination of trips I might take by bicycle:

- Start with a two-month "warmup ride" across the U.S.A. to make sure bike and equipment were all fine before going overseas.

---

[7] Cold Beer and Crocodiles, https://www.amazon.com/Cold-Beer-Crocodiles-Australia-Adventure/dp/0792263650

[8] Shimmering Spokes, https://www.amazon.com/Shimmering-Spokes-One-Australians-Odyssey/dp/1864365218

- The main event would be a ride around Australia. I roughly budgeted eight months: two months to ride from Sydney to Darwin, two months from Darwin to Perth, two months from Perth to Sydney and the remaining time either for miscalculations or further meanderings, with perhaps a side trip to New Zealand.
- Finish the trip cycling through South India.

There was much more published on the internet than a few years before, and this let me plan and dream as I explored further to see what others had done for their trips.

A custom bike

A nice shiny new bike for a big trip? With the exceptions of tires and rims, Cannondale had served me adequately for my 1992 and 1997 trips. However, I found the idea of a special custom bike attractive for the next trip. Custom bikes have exact sizing, with enough mounts for water bottles, panniers, and other gears. There were several custom bike makers in the market in 2001, and I decided to look further at a small shop located in Bend, Oregon.

The bike builder, Robert, had made his name mostly with specialized custom panniers but also had a semi-recent line of custom bikes advertised. Reviews I could find on the internet seemed favorable. On Memorial Day weekend 2000, I drove up to Bend to talk to Robert in person. I saw his shop as well as his bicycles and panniers. In addition to hand-crafted, sized fully lugged frame, Robert could build a bike with sturdy 26" wheels, four water bottle mounts, an integrated rack and many other goodies. We took my measurements, and I placed an initial order.

Memorial Day was ten months before my planned departure date, and the bike would take some time to build. I didn't want to depart on a brand-new bike so some months of trial riding would be good. We agreed on "Thanksgiving" as a target time to receive the bike. I could then drive back to Oregon, pick up the bike and do some shorter winter tours with it before departure.

As Thanksgiving approached and I made contact to come back for the bike, I learned that there were problems at his frame builder, and it might not be ready by Thanksgiving. While not the best news, Robert helped by suggesting perhaps Christmas. Unfortunately, the frame builder issues continued as the date slid further towards mid-February. There was a serious risk the bike would not be ready for the start of my trip, so I got my Cannondale prepared for start of the trip. I owned two bikes at this point, the other also a Cannondale, but it would remain behind.

I still wanted the new bike, but once the trip date came upon me, I realized I would need to start with my Cannondale again. I changed the delivery address for the bike to my parents' home and requested delivery as soon as possible.

Robert delivered the bike at the end of April, when I was nearly two months into my trip on my warmup ride across the U.S. At this point, the Cannondale was riding fine, and I decided I would continue with it rather than try a brand-new, untested bike right at the start in Australia. As a result, I didn't actually try my new custom bike until the trip was over.

In hindsight, that turned out to be a wise decision, since as soon as I placed the seat tube in the frame, the brackets in the rear started to tear out. Wow! I contacted Robert, and he indicated that most likely his frame builder had not followed his specifications and offered to replace it under warranty. So, I mailed the bike back to Oregon for Robert to fix and send back to me. It arrived a few months later, but I never fully trusted that bike again and didn't take it for my subsequent long tours.

I learned a valuable lesson about attraction to that custom bike. While in many cases, things turn out OK, there can also be a higher risk that you end up with a problem. For that reason I also didn't consider a custom bike again for my later trips.

Warmup ride across America (again)

I took my car keys and placed them under the floor mat and left the door unlocked. I had sold the car to a friend for reasonable price. I might not be back again for a full year, so it made more sense to sell a 10-year-old car than keep it stored away until my return.

I almost finished packing up my condominium. I condensed my belongings into one bedroom of the two-bedroom condominium. I rented the rest of a condominium to another friend. Our agreement was that she would screen my mail to toss junk mail and forward more important items to my parents in Colorado. In return, the rent was lower than it would otherwise be for one bedroom condominium in the Bay Area near top of the dot-com boom.

Everything was ready. My packed bike was leaning against a wall in an otherwise empty room. My brother came by with pastries for breakfast. A friend, John, also arrived, as we would cycle these first few days together. Our initial route was by now familiar terrain: over to Monterrey and then down the Pacific Coast. A little north of San Diego, I would cut inland and then follow a route known as the "Southern Tier" all the way across to Florida.

It was a pretty and at times wet ride, the first four days along Big Sur and then to San Luis Obispo, where my friend John left via train. I was now on my own and cycled just a bit farther to Pismo Beach. It rained heavily overnight but looked clear enough for departure, so I cycled from Pismo Beach farther south. I came to multiple flooded areas, including four road closures, but could get through and settled in Lompoc for the night. It continued to rain heavily enough that I decided to take a rainy daybreak.

Overall, the local papers reported that Lompoc had received 6.82 inches of rain in this storm. Signs closed Highway One to all traffic south of Lompac. After my rest day, the sun was back, and I decided to try cycling on the closed road. While an automobile wouldn't have been able to cross, I was able to walk my bike past a huge sinkhole on side of the road. This got me farther down the road and along the coast. Three more days brought me down and across the busy metro Los Angeles area to Oceanside, California, where I would now start heading east.

Oceanside is at sea level, and Julian is at 4200 ft. It was a slow day riding up the hill. It started overcast and dry and ended up with some wet snow when I reached Julian. Fortunately, it didn't stick to the road much, and this was last snowfall I had on my warmup ride.

The following three weeks were uneventful cycling as I crossed the arid West and made my way into Texas. Along the way the route climbed over 6000 ft. in New Mexico and hence I had some chilly mornings camping. I also had a mixture of winds: some tail winds but also an ugly day of headwinds coming into Marathon, Texas. I crossed the Pecos River, a traditional dividing line between East and West and soon found myself with more vegetation, including trees, again.

Texas took 16 days of riding and had some of my most varied terrain and landscapes. What surprised me was that I could find "West Texas BBQ" even in the heart of what should have been east Texas. I particularly enjoyed coming across fields of wildflowers in the Texas Hill Country as I skirted south of Austin. The hills were sharp, but eventually Adventure Cycling stopped printing elevation profiles on their maps and, correspondingly, there was less need.

Once in Louisiana, I spotted what looked like a shortcut on the maps. The normal Adventure Cycling route from Opelousas to St. Francisville was 110 miles, and my maps showed a possibility of using Louisiana Route 10 that was nearly 50 miles shorter. My state maps did show a five-mile segment with markings not listed in the legend, gravel perhaps? I asked several locals, who told me there had been construction several years ago but now this was a good road. Hence, I set off down this road through rural back areas of Louisiana.

When I reached the town of Melville, I got a surprise none of the locals had told me about: a broad wide channel of the Afchafalaya, with huge barges and ships. The good news was that there was a ferry landing and crossing. The bad news was the ferry operating hours were 5 a.m. to 8 a.m. and 4 p.m. to 9 p.m. It was now 10 a.m., so I faced a six hour wait until the next ferry.

Just a little way north, there was a railroad bridge across the channel. Even more interesting, there was a narrow pedestrian walkway along those tracks. I contemplated using the walkway to cross the bridge and then started walking. I passed a small building on the bridge, and just after that a head poked out and yelled at me. "Uh oh, busted," I thought. The attendant called me back and told me a train was coming. We pulled my bike into the little building and chatted as we waited for the train to pass. I learned that I was far from the first cyclist to try this shortcut. The train took its time coming, and once it was past, I proceeded.

As I walked on the bridge, I considered what would have happened if I had been on the bridge at the same time as a train. There probably was enough room for me to lean out of the way to avoid the speeding train. However, there is also a good chance I would have had to drop my bike into the waters below. In any case, I felt relieved on the other end. There was some gravel road here, but eventually I made my way across one more ferry and to St. Francisville. I now also knew why Adventure Cycling had chosen their route.

I crossed Baton Rouge and departed from the Adventure Cycling route as I passed along the Gulf Coast. This was several years before Hurricane Katrina came through the same area, and I later recognized some of the areas from storm coverage. Six days of cycling across Florida, and I reached the Atlantic coast at St. Augustine. My training ride was now complete, and I just needed to get back to Los Angeles, where I had a flight to Australia to start the main event.

I rode Amtrak on a three-day ride from Jacksonville to Los Angeles. The route paralleled many areas I had cycled, and it was a faster motion rewind of my trip. I stayed north of LA with friends I had met in a bike mechanic school. My parents and two older brothers came to California as well, and we had a mini-family reunion in the area for a few days. I went through my equipment and finalized what to take with me. On May 1st, I packed everything up and boarded the flight for Sydney.

Australia at last, up the coast to Townsville

They drive on the left in Australia, a fact that is obvious to anyone who understands the heritage of this former British colony. However, it still was an adjustment after an overnight flight, minimal sleep, and my arrival in an airport for a city of four million. I also switched my mindset from miles to kilometers.

The airport is 10 km south of the center of the city. My first exercise was to find the Sydney Opera House, my chosen start line. Traffic wasn't too bad, but I ended up walking the last few bits. After that, I rode another 35 km headed "outbound" on my way starting out of the city. After this first hectic but shorter day, riding became easier as I could find the Pacific Highway and follow it north along the coast.

The population of Australia was approximately 20 million, so in that first day I mostly crossed where 20% of the people live. Australia is surprisingly urban, with ~2/3 of the population living in or near the capital cities (Sydney, Melbourne, Perth, Brisbane, Adelaide, Hobart, Darwin, Canberra) and less than 5% of the population living in the Outback. However, I spent very little of my time in the big cities and a majority in the outback areas. As a result, I found my descriptions of cycling in Australia didn't always match those of a more "typical" Australian cyclist, who was most often in an urban area riding each day.

It took three weeks to cycle up the coast to Townsville. This area had large cities of Sydney and Brisbane as well as the populated Gold Coast. Otherwise, there was a sequence of smaller towns and agricultural lands. Until Brisbane it was the Pacific Highway, and after that it was the Bruce Highway. These were well-surfaced and most often two lane roads with sections of four lane highway in more urban areas.

In Brisbane, I stayed with friends of friends, but otherwise I found hotel accommodations most every night along the way. Cycling wasn't extremely difficult, with no huge hills to climb. I did have a few minor glitches with my rear cassette falling apart and a wheel that went out of true. However, since I was riding close enough past bike shops, I could get them sorted out quickly.

Along the way I crossed the Tropic of Cancer and saw my first road trains. These trucks with three or sometimes four trailers would come past making lots of noise. Fortunately, there was usually plenty of warning and plenty of room on the road, so they weren't much trouble.

Once I reached Townsville, I was ready for my first rest day. I had been paralleling the Great Barrier Reef for several hundred kilometers, and at Townsville it was 90 kilometers off the coast. I booked a tourist day trip. It took us about two and a half hours on a fast catamaran to reach the reef. We anchored and could choose between a trip on a fishing boat, scuba diving, snorkeling and a trip on a glass-bottom boat. I picked up snorkeling gear and swam around the reef looking at coral, fish, jellyfish, clams, sea snakes, sea cucumbers, anemone, and other creatures. I was particularly enchanted by listening to parrot fish crunching coral and by the giant clams with little fish swimming inside. After lunch I went on another snorkeling trip, and then I took a ride in the glass-bottom boat while listening to a marine biologist explain what we observed. Late in the afternoon we returned to Townsville.

Queensland and into the Outback

From Townsville my route now took me westward and into the Outback. While it would have been possible to keep cycling north to Cairns and then along the Gulf of Carpentaria, in 2001 this route wasn't yet all paved. Instead, I followed the main route across to Mount Isa. This route started with small towns situated roughly a day apart. It took me a week to ride from Townsville to Mount Isa.

At one point a van pulled alongside as I was cycling along. About eight young adults were inside, and the van pulled a cargo trailer behind it. It turns out they were Christian evangelists on tour. They asked if they could do a blessing. I said, "Sure," and they gave a brief blessing of myself and my bike trip. Shortly thereafter, someone yelled, "Road train!" and off the van zoomed.

The landscapes slowly changed from wooded areas with eucalyptus to more grassy areas as it became dryer. I crossed the Great Dividing Range, but even here hills weren't a big consideration. Instead, I paid more attention to winds, which, fortunately, were as often tailwinds as headwinds.

Mount Isa, population 20,000, was the largest town along the way. This was also the site of a large mine that once was the largest producer of silver and lead in the world and also in the top ten for zinc and copper. They offered mine tours, and I took a rest day to learn more. The mine itself was underground up to a depth of 1800 meters. There were a total of 5000 people employed, with 800 miners continuously underground. Overall, the mine tour showed well how ores were first crushed, mechanically separated, chemically separated, and then sent to smelters for lead, copper, and zinc.

After Mount Isa, I knew the route would become even more remote, as towns roughly a day apart now became "road houses." The road houses weren't always a cycling day apart, so I would camp along the road. I had a guide, originally intended for those towing caravans, that listed roadsiderest areas where one could pull off along the highway and camp. This next part of Australia turned out to include my favorite cycling parts of the trip.

Northern Territory and up to Darwin

The first two days from Mount Isa were long rides: 188 km the first day and 215 km the second. The first day was a case where I reached my intended destination, a roadside rest area, around midday. It didn't look inviting to spend the entire afternoon in rather bleak surroundings, however, and if I kept going, I could make it to a small settlement of Camooweal, which had a motel. Hence, I kept going. This area had low scrub brush that helped with the wind.

Shortly after Camooweal I crossed into the Northern Territory (NT). The entire population of NT was 200,000, but most of these lived in or near Darwin. It became more important to pay attention to water availability. Fortunately, I had guides from the internet that suggested likely water points. While I had been carrying ~5 liters of water in Queensland, I slowly increased this to eight liters split between a camelback in my knapsack, bottles on the bike and extra bottles as well.

My guides told me of a store approximately 168 km from my start in Camooweal. I saw some rough buildings, but no activity or cars, so I figured it would be over the next hill. Approximately 10 km later, I realized I must have passed the store. My guides now told me the next water would be at 221 km at a roadside rest area. I kept going, but it was late afternoon, and dark came quickly. Hence, I made it 215 km on what would have been my longest day. I found a wide space in the road and set up my tent.

Next morning I went for another symbolic event I had in my plans for a while. The previous New Year's Eve had been the much awaited "Y2K" event. Our company, like many, had elaborate response plans to respond to any customer issues that might arise. Part of the plan included having two members from each team be "on call" and carry a beeper. We never received any real calls but only our test messages as well as wrong number calls from previous uses of the beepers. I wasn't too excited about assigning my team members beeper duty and ended up with one of them for much of the period. However, I still despised that extra beeper duty.

I had carried with me to Australia one of our team beepers. Now that I was in outback Australia and one of the farther points from civilization, it was time to get rid of it. I got up from camp and found a nearby culvert tunnel under the road and chucked that beeper as far away as I could. Done!

The next morning, I cycled off and passed the roadside rest area 6 km later. I had not quite realized how close I was, or I would likely have ridden to it the previous day. Another 40 km farther brought me to Barkley Homestead, one of the first remote roadhouses I had on the trip. Barkley had services a traveler might need, including gasoline, ten motel rooms, a restaurant and a camping area. Diesel generators provided power as this area was off the grid. I counted 35 caravans parked overnight as well as several road trains.

Over the next months I would often stay at road houses like Barkley as I came past them. Other nights I would camp in my tent beside the road, most often in one of the designated pullout areas. At these pullout areas, I met many Australians touring with their caravans pulled behind. The caravan drivers would tell their cyclist stories and were also part of my "bush telegraph," from which I might learn of other cyclists some days ahead or behind. I even met one of these cyclists, a French rider who had been three days behind me in Townsville but had now caught up by cycling longer distances each day.

It was two days cycling from Barkley to the junction with the primary north-south road known as Three Ways. By now my front tire was showing a lot of wear, with the tread worn away along half the circumference and threads showing underneath. It was another 500 km to Katherine, the next town with a bike shop, so I replaced my tire with my spare and hoped I wouldn't get other tire troubles.

The route to Katherine was along a historic area with airfields built during the second world war. Bombers had hit the town of Darwin, and it was potentially on the front lines. There was a railroad to carry men and material to Alice Springs in the middle of Australia, but from there north only simple tracks to ferry goods by truck. Eventually those tracks made it a bit farther north, as did a sequence of small airstrips to fly aircraft north to Darwin. I stayed close to several of these airfields, including one at a pub known as Daly Waters. Daly Waters pub, established in 1930, had accumulated a lot of different knickknacks on the walls from tourists and other visitors. There was a rugby match on the television and a lively crowd of spectators.

In the time I visited, a new railway line was under construction between Darwin and Adelaide. Construction was completed several years later, in 2004, and I saw reports in the news.

The town of Katherine, population 9000, was the largest town I had come to for nearly two weeks and a good spot for another rest day. I visited a bike shop and replaced two well worn tires. I also took a tour to visit nearby Katherine Gorge, cycling some 60 km on one of my rest days for the trip. There were crocodiles here, mostly freshies, but I also started to hear about salties as well. I was now in an area known as "the top end."

After Katherine I took a more relaxed pace as I had two weeks before a planned flight back to the U.S.A. to attend my 20th High School Reunion. Two days cycling brought me to Cooinda and Kakadu National Park, where I took two rest days to explore. I started with a sunrise cruise on the Yellow Waters. It was dry season, when the waters were up to five meters lower than in the wet summer. We saw five salt water crocodiles, two boars, herons, egrets, kingfishers, whistling ducks, jabiru, and many other birds. In the winter, they tend to concentrate into smaller areas.

I also took a day tour to Jim Jim and Twin Falls. Our 4WD vehicle picked us up in the morning and brought us 50 km along a rough road to the falls. Water was coming from 205 meters high and dropping into a deep plunge pool. Most declined to swim at Jim Jim, partially due to cold waters but more likely because of the large saltwater crocodile traps nearby. We did, however, take a nice swim at Twin Falls, where we stayed for several hours.

After Kakadu I completed my cycling up to Darwin and considered the first third of the circumnavigation complete. I explored the town and took an adventure tour to Litchfield Park along with five other tourists from the

U.K. We hiked, we swam, we camped and we learned more about the aboriginal owners in this area. After coming back from Litchfield, I dropped my bike off for service, stored my bags at a hotel and then boarded flights back to the U.S.A. for my reunion.

Outback reflections: Britz, backpackers, gray nomads, and others

One thing I found particularly interesting about the Outback were different types of tourists that visited as well as their common modes of transportation. For much of the Outback, I didn't see many U.S. or Japanese tourists, who tended to concentrate in areas such as Uluru and perhaps a few in Darwin. My fellow travelers included the following:

- Gray nomads, a name adopted by Australians often in their 50's and 60's who were traveling through the outback towing a caravan behind their vehicle. As in the U.S.A., there are also "snowbirds" who go north in search of a warmer climate during the winter. What made the gray nomads different was that they wouldn't stay in one place, but perhaps spread their journey by staying in one place for a week, driving a few hundred kilometers and staying in the next place.

  Their average pace sometimes matched mine, because we might camp at the same roadside area one night, and then several days later they would come past, and then we would leapfrog. It often included a friendly afternoon conversation. I met people who had immigrated to Australia in the aftermath of the second world war as refugees.

  At the time I was there, Australia had a new influx of refugees, many setting off from Indonesia in not-always-seaworthy craft in hopes of reaching the shore and applying for asylum. There was a well-publicized event that year when such a boat, the MV Tampa, carrying mostly Afghan refugees, ran into troubles. A Norwegian went to rescue the craft. As they approached Christmas Island, the Australian government refused to let it land. I heard many different opinions from Australians, including former refugees, about what should have happened.

Gray nomads would occasionally stop on the road when we passed and a few even offered a "cuppa" tea. They were often a good source for the "bush telegraph" to tell me when other cyclists were also on the road a few days ahead or behind.

- Backpackers, from many countries but particularly from the UK. Apparently, the UK had a program known as a "gap year," where young people could take a year between high school and college education to travel. In Australia they could also get work permits. Many backpackers I met didn't have a lot of funds and would work for a while to earn enough to travel to the next part of their trip. We inevitably shared some inexpensive accommodations. Several of my fellow travelers on the Litchfield trip were backpackers and busy figuring out how they could survive spending minimal amounts on food.

I didn't see as many backpackers outside of small outback towns, e.g. camping beside the roads. I expect they were more likely to take a bus or hitchhike, though I did meet a few who had purchased an inexpensive automobile for their travels.

- Britz customers. Britz was a company that rented out small campervans. They must have excellent marketing in German-speaking countries, including Germany, Switzerland, and Austria, as inevitably when I met travelers in a Britz campervan, they were often German-speaking. These travelers were spending many weeks or sometimes months and using the campervan to slowly explore different outback areas. As a result, we sometimes camped in the same areas.
- Americans, included in the list but I rarely met them in the Outback. Instead, a more typical "see Australia" package that I found Americans using would include (a) several days in Sydney (b) several days in Melbourne (c) visit to Uluru (d) perhaps visit to Cairns and the Great Barrier Reef and (e) one more location, such as Perth or Darwin – a total of perhaps three weeks to "see all of Australia."

Americans were rare enough in the Outback that after I started adopting some Australian words, such as "brekky" or "sealed roads," I found myself noticing this only after I ran into American travelers later. When other travelers tried to guess my nationality, they guessed I came from Canada at least as often as from the U.S. They tell me it is partially since they didn't expect Americans to be traveling these areas and partially because Canadians mistaken for Americans can take offense while Americans mistaken for Canadians are more often amused.

- <u>Japanese</u>, not really seen in outback areas other than Uluru. However, some gray nomads would have their "crazy Japanese" traveler stories, sometimes about a cyclist who would go during sweltering wet season and cycle many long distances, perhaps in cyclones.

I also met French, other Europeans and a few Chinese among travelers, but most common it was gray nomads, Britz travelers and backpackers that I met in the Outback. It was interesting to understand their perspectives on Australia, current politics including asylum seekers, the "sorry" campaign and aborigines. It was also helpful to get travel tips and information about the road ahead.

Western Australia to Broome, wheel troubles

After a nice trip back to the U.S.A. and some restful weeks, I was back in Darwin and ready to start the next leg of my trip, ~1800 km of riding through remote regions to Broome. A Darwin bicycle shop had replaced my worn drive train and lubed and checked everything.

My first order was to ride back to Katherine, a three-day trip this time as I took a more direct route. In Katherine, I took a tour of the Katherine School of the Air. This school serves an attendance area approximately three times the area of the UK. There are 300 students organized in grades one through seven. They mail much of the instruction materials to the students and use radio time to give the teacher on-air interaction with the class. Teachers also visit the students once per year, and there are also some occasions when students can visit the school.

The section from Darwin to Perth had some of the largest gaps between known water stops. I had a guide from the internet in which someone had listed all the water tanks, road houses and other places to get water and followed it closely. I had figured a rough rule of thumb for my water usage: one liter for each 20 kilometers and two liters for an overnight. There weren't too many times I needed to go overnight without water, so typically I was carrying eight or nine liters of water. At a maximum in Australia I carried 16 liters (four gallons), but that was a bit farther, leaving Broome.

This area had mostly one paved road. It also coincidentally was a place where I encountered several other cyclists. There was a Japanese couple along with their five-year-old riding on the back of the father's bicycle with a coloring book. There was an older couple from Port Macquarie, NSW, who each year rode a different segment around Australia. I met one gentleman who had just finished a tough stretch across unsealed roads in the Outback. I also started to hear more about two cyclists from NSW named Brendan and Wendy. Brendan and Wendy had left two months before my start in Sydney and were still ahead, but eventually I met up with them near Broome and then later multiple times after that.

One interesting part was that the "bush telegraph" worked particularly well on this stretch with one sealed road. I kept leapfrogging with different caravan drivers, and they typically would also tell me of other cyclists a few days ahead and behind.

A few days after leaving Katherine, I crossed into Western Australia (WA). The state of WA is 3.6x times larger than the U.S. state of Texas, with only 10% of the population. Around 80% of those people live in or near Perth, so this means a lot of empty lands. When I passed an area known as 80-mile beach, tourists told me that Australia had a rocket range in South Australia and fired missiles to the northwest – I figured there would be only one paved road the missiles crossed. To give an equivalent in U.S. geographic terms, this would be equivalent to firing missiles from Louisiana to the U.S./Canadian border in Montana all while only crossing one paved road.

In the WA border, they also checked agricultural products. The ants had gotten most of my produce, and I had eaten the rest, so I had no big worries there. Western Australia was also time to reset my watch by 90 minutes from Northern Territory time.

Have you seen the bungles? After crossing into WA, I came to a small place formerly known as Turkey Creek and now known by the aboriginal name Warmun. The claim to fame for Warmun was as a jumping off point to see the Bungle Bungles. This is an area of 30 kilometers by 25 kilometers uplifted 200 meters from surrounding plains and then eroded in interesting ways. There were long striped "bungles," as well as deep narrow canyons such as Echidna Canyon. I took a rest day to take a guided trip along with six other tourists. We saw bungles striped in a distinctive gray/red pattern. The red was iron oxide and the gray was blue-green algae coating. These were also known as beehives. We also saw Echidna Chasm, as well as Cathedral Gorge. It was a fascinating place, and I was glad I took some time to see it.

After Warmun were several small, mostly aboriginal towns. Some of these had a strange feel to them, particularly one night in a motel surrounded by a high fence topped with barbed wire and locks on the gates.

A little past the Fitzroy crossing, I made an alarming discovery. My rear tire was developing multiple stress cracks coming from the spoke holes. I had seen something similar before crossing Canada. Eventually these holes would widen and rip out, causing the wheel to collapse. This was a 48-spoke wheel with a good Phil Woods hub. I had gotten more distance from the wheel, though I supposed eventually it might stress too. I was still around 280 kilometers from the next substantial town of Broome, so I hoped the wheel would last. In the worst case I would have to hitch a ride from a caravan driver.

Three days cycling and I made it to Broome—and my wheel did too! I met Brendan and Wendy at the turnoff into Broome and had a nice hour chat comparing our respective around-Australia trips. After that I went into Broome to find a bike shop and sort out my options.

Broome has a population of just under 15,000 people and is the largest town around. I stopped first at the tourist center and next at the bike shop. It was a Monday afternoon. The bike shop had an arrangement with a wheel builder in Perth. They could build a new 36-spoke wheel in Perth on Tuesday/Wednesday and send it up by truck. It would take two days for the truck to arrive in Broome, and this meant, hopefully, I would have a new wheel on Friday. This also meant some "Broome time" as I waited for a replacement wheel.

I took my rest days to see the sights in Broome. This area was best known for the pearl industry. Prior to plastic buttons, this area once provided 75% of the world's mother of pearl. There is a historical museum that explains the entire history. Local history included a large Chinatown area, and Broome was also a site for Japanese bombing during the second world war.

I took an organized bus trip to a place known as Windjana Gorge and Tunnel Creek. There were twelve of us on tour: ten Australians, one Swiss and me. The gorge was impressive—60-meters-high and carved from limestone. At Tunnel Creek, a small creek goes underneath the limestone through a tunnel for 750 meters. We waded through the water carrying torches (flashlights) as it became dark in the middle--an interesting experience. In total we traveled nearly 800 km by bus that day to see these sights.

On Friday, the replacement wheel arrived! I wanted to save my old 48-spoke hub, so I set off to take the old wheel apart while the bike shop installed the new wheel. As you will read later, I should have paid more attention to their efforts. However, all looked well and let me make a stop by the post office to mail away the hub.

The next morning, I started down the road again towards Perth.

Outback reflections: aborigines

After riding through the Northern Territory and more than 1000 kilometers of Western Australia, I came through many areas now controlled by aboriginal tribes. I observed things and read several books about the history of aboriginals in Australia. The following are my perceptions as I had written in my journal:

First some history. Until about thirty years ago, the early history of Australia mostly described convicts, settlement and exploration. It was as if the continent were empty and thus the inhabitants who had lived there for thousands of years before were ignored. These inhabitants had a spoken and written language, e.g. rock art, were nomadic and survived in harsh country. While settling Australia, Europeans were sometimes brutal in their conquest of aborigines, sometimes hunting them like animals. Many died from new diseases. History also includes events such as "the lost generation," children taken from aboriginal homes and forcibly assimilated into foster families.

I couldn't help but draw parallels with experiences of the Native Americans, where there is both positive history (think of Pilgrims and Indians sharing Thanksgiving) and negative history (think of buffalo and Indian hunters on the plains). However, unlike Native Americans, they didn't force aboriginals onto reservations. Some perished, some were displaced and some stayed on their historical lands.

In the Outback, a sometimes-symbiotic relationship existed for a while at some stations. Aboriginals lived around the station, worked during peak times, and were fed or paid. This stopped in the mid-1970's, when courts ruled that fair wages must be paid. As a result, many aboriginals moved closed to these small outback towns or into their own communities. Places where I saw large concentrations of aboriginals included Camooweal, Elliott, Katherine, Kununurra, Halls Creek and Fitzroy Crossing. Typically, I would see small groups along the streets either walking or sitting. I saw a few working in shops, but even in these aboriginal-dominant towns, almost all the workers were white.

As history has been rediscovered, the Australian government put more money into supporting aboriginal needs such as legal help, health clinics and schools. I did, however, observe one aboriginal gentleman hunting through the trash for food.

That extra money for aboriginal causes also caused some backlash. I heard parents in the town of Larimah remark that if their children were aboriginal, there would be a school or clinic in that town. There were also some Australian politicians with more extreme views. Overall, Australia had a "whites only" policy on immigration for many years and still have some nativist political movements taking advantage of it. However, my sense was this was a fringe movement without a wide following.

A very visible cause for resentment is alcohol abuse amongst aboriginals. Where many aboriginals are out on the streets, it is visible if there is a drinking problem. Towns such as Katherine or Mount Isa have stories and letters about how to control this, such as having specific drinking zones. In Fitzroy Crossing, the motel was right next to a lively bar with many aboriginals around. It seems like a mixed bag here, as I have also seen many aboriginal communities policing themselves with "no alcohol" rules prominently posted.

In the last twenty years, Australia's high courts have ruled on land claims. These claims were filed in accordance with historical British common law to show that "traditional owners" didn't abandon the land, but instead have a recorded history of settlement and ownership of certain lands. Not all those claims have been reasonable (e.g. claims for 1/3 of NSW, including choice parts of Sydney), but many have gone through and are going through the courts, with mineral rights a particularly tough issue. A few areas of claims, such as Kakadu, are leased back to the government for use as parks.

Australian politics were still working through a "reconciliation" between white and aboriginal Australians. Included are such issues as whether a "sorry" is due and the nature of this reconciliation. Here are some observations and perceptions I made while cycling in this area:

- I never felt threatened in areas with many aborigines around. The bicycle seems to be a good leveler. I rode past, gave a smile and wave and got smiles back. My 1:1 encounters were also positive (In slight contrast to experiences in the U.S.A. walking into a bar on an Indian reservation to refill water bottles, spandex seemed out of place there...also in contrast to riding through south Chicago).
- Some of the gray nomads I talked with were still sorting things out. There was genuine sympathy for the history. There was discomfort in areas with many aborigines. Folks don't want to appear racist but felt discouraged by stereotypes of drunken aborigines. Some resentment of the amount of money spent on the aborigines was evident also. There was a visible fringe, e.g. a

politician named Hansen, but this was a small minority. More were sorting things out.

- Outback roadhouses and towns sometimes had a garrison feel to them, with locks, barbed wire, chains, and gates. The classic example was in Fitzroy Crossing, where lively bar is right next to the motel. It took me a while to find my way out a gate, past the dogs in early morning. It seems as though there had been enough theft and vandalism to justify this lockup mentality.
- Aborigines weren't necessarily going back to a pre-European state, but somewhere in between, with trucks, houses, and stores, but also some traditional culture preserved. Some tourism is picking up. (Aboriginal groups share some history, but there are also differences in language/culture/outlook amongst these groups). Land claims will continue to be an important issue going forward.
- There may be extra money spent, but it does not mean things are equal. For example, a disproportionate number of prisoners in NT were aboriginal (like an analogous situation in the U.S. with blacks, one can argue how much is biases in the system and how much is greater criminal activity).
- It will take a while for a "reconciliation" in Australia. Better awareness and working out of issues are still going on.

This is what I perceived and observed back in 2001--some similarities, but also differences from what I have seen in the U.S. It would be interesting to see what is similar or different from that perception in 2001 today.

Western Australia to Shark Bay

Northern parts of Western Australia had long distances between roadhouses and towns, dry climate and several mining-related towns with large mineral resources.

The largest single gap between water points came just after Broome. It was 286 kilometers from the Roebuck Roadhouse to Sandfire Roadhouse. My guide suggested some potential water points but wasn't certain. As a result, I loaded my Camelbak and my bicycle with sixteen liters of water and set off for what I planned to be a two-day ride. It turns out I had more than enough water as there was a fruit stand at the 120-kilometer mark.

Also, where I camped, other campers offered me water. I even had one caravan driver slow down on the road when he saw me cycling and ask, "Do you have enough water?" However, better safe than sorry.

Sandfire Roadhouse was in the middle of the Great Sandy Desert and was named for colors of the rock and reflections. It was an arid area and vegetation was short and stunted. This meant more wind, both near Sandfire and later along the coast. I passed through just two years after an American cyclist named Robert Bogucki had decided to set off overland from near Sandfire. He abandoned his bicycle just a few kilometers from the main track and continued on foot. Search and rescue operations stopped looking for him after twelve days, assuming nobody could survive in the desert without water for that long. His parents hired trackers, who eventually found him 43 days after he started and 400 kilometers from his starting point. While it seemed a miracle that he survived, there was also controversy about the stupidity of his act as well as search and rescue resources spent looking for him.

A little farther I came to the turnoff for 80-mile Beach. It was a common place for those with caravans to camp and I was even told there were topless sunbathers to be found, though most of them were over age 70. Despite this inducement, it was far enough off my path that I stuck to the main road.

I did take a rest day when I reached the town of Port Hedland to tour the large BHP iron ore facilities. BHP was the second largest iron ore producer in the world. They mined most of the ore at Whaleback Mountain, some 400 kilometers to the south. Nine trains per day arrive at Port Hedland, and not long before, BHP had created the world's largest train—some 7 kilometers long. There was berthing space to load two giant 250,000-ton ships. Most of this iron ore went either to Japan or China and was processed further there. The tour gave good example of the scale of everything, with huge piles of ore, giant train car processing facilities, conveyor belts, dumpers, etc.

I met a cyclist named Stu in the Outback past Port Hedland--with no panniers, tent or other long-haul gear. He was riding a mountain bike with knobby tires, a slightly rusted wheel and a wobble on the back rim. He had not ridden a bicycle in eight months but had made a wager with friends at work in Port Hedland. If he made it to Roeburne, 190 km, he would earn $600 and give it to charity. I slowed down and Stu sped up, and we cycled together for about 20 km.

Two days after Port Hedland, I came to Karratha as they were celebrating FeNaClNG days. This was a celebration of the most important products of the region: iron (Fe), salt (NaCl) and natural gas (NG). There were large gas fields here as well as the first McDonalds restaurant I had seen since Darwin. Karratha, Port Hedland, and Carnarvon were perhaps the largest towns between Broome and the area close to Perth. After this, there would be mostly roadhouses coming next.

A few days later, I came to small town of Coral Bay. The saying is, "If you don't get trapped in Coral Bay, then you won't get trapped anywhere in Australia." I did enjoy the town enough that I took an extra rest day there. What was particularly interesting was a coral reef that stretched several hundred kilometers down the coast. Unlike the Great Barrier Reef, this reef was right off the shore and thus tourists didn't need a boat to go visit it. A company offered an interesting package deal: half hour glass-bottom boat tour, an hour snorkeling from the boat and then use of the snorkel gear for rest of the day. I showed up at 8:30 in the morning and spent most of the day making several trips swimming over the reefs.

At Coral Bay, I also participated in the Australia census. Even visitors to Australia were asked to complete a census form. I'm not sure how I they counted me, but I should be part of Australia's 2001 census.

Carnarvon was another larger town, 9000 residents, but not large enough for a bike shop. This area grows bananas but otherwise is dry and without much vegetation. I happened to also have strong headwinds, so it was a tough ride. Not much later, I crossed the 26th parallel of south latitude, an official dividing line of the northern parts of WA. I decided to turn off here into an area known as Shark Bay. At the tip of shark bay was Monkey Mia, a resort area known dolphins that visited to be fed by tourists. I saw many of them during my visit.

Cracked frame, 9/11
After Monkey Mia, I took a rest day to let a strong storm blow through. It was evening of that rest day that I made an unfortunate discovery: my

bike frame had a large, ominous crack. On a diamond frame bike, chain stays are horizontal bars that go between the bottom of the frame (at the pedals) and the back wheel. My left chain stay was cracked about halfway around the tube. I wasn't quite sure what caused it yet, but I knew if the crack continued, the frame would snap and I would be unable to ride.

I assessed the situation. I still had 280 kilometers until Geraldton, population 25,000, the next large town and largest in WA outside the Perth area. I wrapped the chain stay with duct tape and decided I would ride with the bike while it lasted and then get a ride to Geraldton. After that I would need to look for a repair or more likely a replacement for the frame.

It took three and a half cycling days and, fortunately, the frame held.

I was at the local bike shop at 8:30 a.m. when they opened. They were very helpful in getting an assessment. First the crack had propagated to be 75% of the way around the tube. Next, they diagnosed the likely cause as the Broome bike shop forcing a mountain bike hub width (136mm) into the width of my touring frame (126mm) rather than taking away some spacers. Not only did this stretch the frame open, but it also made the tire and wheel off-center and closer to the left, cracked side. This meant that sand and grit had been thrown against the inside of the chain stay for another 1500 kilometers I rode to Shark Bay. I had not noticed the Broome bike shop forcing the frame open since I was busy taking my original wheel apart to mail home the hub. Unfortunately, I also had not noticed the wheel being off-center.

Geraldton had a bike shop, but not a large collection of bikes. The nearest metropolitan area with many bike shops was Perth, another 300 kilometers down the road. I called around, and Cannondale was just in the midst of changing from one model year to the next and hence they told me there were no Cannondale bike frames in my size in all of Australia and uncertain prospects of when they might next arrive.

I did have two potential bikes/frames back in the U.S.A. One was my custom bike I had delivered to my parents. The second was my second Cannondale bike I had in storage in San Jose. The prices of shipping a bicycle from the U.S.A. to Australia were expensive and almost 2/3 of the cost it would take for me to fly round trip to the U.S.A., pick up a bicycle and return to Australia. It was this latter choice that I chose. I booked a flight on a local carrier, Ansett, to Sydney and then round trip to San Francisco.

I had the bike shop strip down the bike to the frame and save all the components. We boxed it up. I left my camping gear at the bike shop and took a minimal amount of clothes as well as my bike helmet. I boarded the bus to Perth and then flew from there to San Francisco to retrieve my bicycle. It didn't take long to retrieve the bike, but it required five layover days to get my inexpensive fare. As a bonus, I once again had a sturdy 48-spoke tandem wheel with this bike.

Fifteen hours of travel and twenty-one hours of time change and I was back from San Francisco to Perth, this time with my other Cannondale bike. I assembled the bike at the airport, filled the water bottles and set off to ride from the airport up to Geraldton. I had a much lighter load, and in three and a half days, I was back in Geraldton.

The bike shop did a good job of surgery to selectively replace parts from my original touring bike to the replacement bike I had just ridden from Perth. We replaced the bottom bracket, cranks, and front derailleur. I also got the front rack, front wheel, stem, and cyclometer. We replaced all the cables. A short adjustment ride and all was as good as new. In total, it was fifteen days from when I first rolled into Geraldton until I was ready to continue cycling around. It was now September 4th, 2001.

I took a slightly different route back to Perth than I had ridden from the airport. I mostly bypassed the big city and continued to the town of Freemantle. From Freemantle, there are ferries to Rottnest Island. Rottnest is home to about 10,000 quokkas. Quokkas are about the size of a small cat, have a pointy snout like a mouse and hop on hind legs like a wallaby.

From 1838 until 1903 Rottnest Island was also site of a prison for aboriginals. Over 3000 were imprisoned here and over 300 died, mostly from pneumonia and other diseases. I got a chance to ride around the island, see some of its history as well as the quokkas. There was a lighthouse on the island where one could see skyscrapers in Perth.

After a rest day on Rottnest Island, I cycled down to Rockingham, where I met with Andrew and Joanne[9]. Andrew and I had two connections. The first was when I had visited Darwin, a local ship, the HMS Darwin, was visiting and sailors were on parade through the town. I captured a photo of the parade and posted it on my blog. Andrew was one of the marchers.

The second connection was that Andrew was soon retiring from a long career in the Australian Navy. He and Joanne had outfitted recumbent trikes and were planning to start their retirement with a bicycle ride around Australia. Andrew had originally noticed my blog when researching other cyclists and then had noticed his photo on the blog page. We had been in email correspondence for a bit, and hence they invited me for a visit after I came through Perth. It was a fun visit and a chance to learn from each other, myself a bit more about Australia and Andrew and Joanne some of my experiences so far riding.

I left Rockingham on September 10th. The next day was September 11th- when the planes hit the World Trade Center, Pentagon, and rural Pennsylvania. Australia was twelve hours ahead of New York, and I didn't look at news either the evening of September 11th or morning of September 12th. It wasn't until the middle of the day on the 12th when I met some tourists who noticed my American accent,who asked, "Did you hear about the news from New York?"

They filled me in, and later that evening I looked up both local papers and information I could find on the internet. Wow! It was both surprising and shocking. There was some shared angst in Australia, e.g., what similar attacks happened in Sydney or Melbourne, and a good amount of shared empathy. Over the next days I had conversations with many Australians after they heard my accent.

On September 13th, a more local Australian event happened. Ansett Airlines suddenly ceased operations, stranding many tourists. I realized that I was fortunate to have traveled back to retrieve my bicycle at the end of August. If I had been two weeks later, both a post 9/11 grounding

---

[9] Andrew and Joanne's book, https://www.bookdepository.com/Ants-Dust-Flies-My-Coffee-Andrew-Hooker/9781920884949

of international flights and then cancellation of all Ansett flights would have made my travels much more difficult.

Crossing the Nullarbor Plain

Between Norseman, Western Australia and Ceduna, South Australia, is a 1200km stretch known as the Nullarbor Plain. On the main road the area without trees is only approximately 100 kilometers, though farther north there is a larger stretch without trees. There is one town, Eucla, and otherwise a sequence of roadhouses. Tourist literature described the Nullarbor as the world's largest single lump of limestone. The Nullarbor has reputation for being vast and empty, though I found it wasn't that different from other vast and empty places I had already ridden, e.g. from Kununarra to Broome. What I did find was some segments with wind, both tail winds that let me easily ride almost 200 kilometers in a day and headwinds, where I struggled to ride just 100 kilometers.

There was a roadhouse known as Balladonia that was in the general vicinity where the Skylab Space station had crashed back to earth. The roadhouse had taken this theme and put several spaces and Skylab type items on display including this poem –

> Skylab Speaking
>
> Balladonia here I come,
>   far from where I started from...
> Traveling ever speedier
>   to avoid the media
> Far from the curious populations,
>   Journalists and TV stations...
> Somewhere – nowhere to descend
>   At my epic journey's end
> I have picked out an empty space,
>   Where I see no human face...
> Simple scientific me
>   I abhor publicity

Not long after Balladonia came the "90 mile straight," a section of 145 kilometers of straight road, also flat. It was on some of these long, straight flat roads that I found myself stopping and having conversations with familiar faces. Gray nomads whom I had met several months ago in the Top End were now circling around with their caravans on the way around Australia and back to Victoria or New South Wales. As there was mostly one paved road, they happened to come across the same cyclist with whom they had camped. This was an occasion for a stop, a greeting and, in one instance, an invitation to stop through on my way around Sydney.

I crossed the border to South Australia, reset my watch and came across the border village. After this point was an area without trees and, with my unfortunate luck, it happened to have headwinds on this part. There were, however, some spectacular views to the south in an area known as "the bight."

Who brings a bugle on an airplane? At a roadhouse named the Nullarbor Roadhouse, there was an outfit offering "flightseeing" trips over the bight in small single engine aircraft. I signed up for a trip and my fellow passenger, Evan, showed up with his bugle. Fortunately, the pilot had the sense to get the bugle from Evan and put it a safe distance away. Other than narrowly avoiding a bugle incident in the air, it was a dramatic flight and interesting to see the rocky southern cliffs on the south end of Australia.

Three days later, I reached the small town of Ceduna, known for oysters and could now find an "I crossed the Nullarbor" bumper sticker to add to my bicycle. As expected, it was perhaps slightly less remote than the areas further north in Western Australia.

South Australia brought with it agricultural areas with wheat, sheep, and pastures as well as several nice small towns. It was a pleasant week of riding that slowly brought me to the small town of Port Augusta. I had some "extra time" left in my eight-month circumnavigation of Australia and started to think of how best to spend it. I decided I would have enough time to ride up the middle of Australia to Uluru (Ayer's Rock), particularly if I only rode it in one direction. Hence, I stopped in Port Augusta at a travel agency and booked a return ticket three weeks later from Alice Springs back to Port Augusta on the Ghan railroad.

Up to Uluru and Alice

While not on the original plan, I was happy to have a chance to ride back to the Northern Territory to see the Red Center. I had taken a liking to the riding through the Outback and wasn't quite ready to stop yet. Four days of cycling brought me to Coober Pedy, a most interesting town.

The name Coober Pedy comes from the aboriginal for "white man burrowing." It started in 1915 when William Hutchinson found the first opals and then attracted people from around the world to find their fortunes. The opal fields are an area of roughly 80 kilometers by 100 kilometers. For $35 one can stake and register a claim of 50 meters by 100 meters for three months. An individual can only have one claim at a time. There are about 700 active claims by individuals, and when an individual gives up a claim, someone else can work it next.

The opals are found in seams perhaps 20 meters below the ground. Hence, the "first generation" opal miners use a boring machine to drill a one-meter wide hole down to the opal regions. One must be careful walking in the area as there are many of these vertical holes dug everywhere. I saw one report that suggested there were some 200,000 holes in the area.

It can be expensive to dig these holes, so some miners go after existing claims where the holes are already dug. They descend these holes and plant explosives to burrow out in different directions following the seams with opals. Much of this dirt is then brought to the surface, where different machines mechanically sift through the rocks to expose the opals. That excess rock is then left in large dirt piles.

A third generation of opal miners gets claims of these large rock piles and sorts through them one more time to find any opals that might have been overlooked the first time.

Average summer temperatures can be hot. With all this mining technology, nearly half the town lives underground in caves and hollows they have dug from under the rocks. There was also an underground church and several shops underground as well. The local drive-in theater had a sign reminding patrons to remove explosives before coming to the theater.

Overall, it was a rather fascinating area to visit and I enjoyed a rest day in the area before continuing my ride further north.

Several more days of riding brought me to Mount Ebenezer, where there is a turnoff for a two-day ride to Uluru.

Uluru wasn't like other places in the Outback. The average visitor spends 1.6 days in their visit, and over half a million visited the previous year. There were supermarkets, and they were even open in the evening. Prices on accommodation were considerably more expensive, so I ended up getting a room in a shared hostel. Top attractions include viewing sunrise or sunset and hiking in the area. I heard American accents again and noticed more Japanese tourists.

I took a shuttle bus out to a nearby rock formation named Kata Tjuta and did a nice 8-kilometer hike through this rock formation, followed by a shuttle back and a chance to watch the sunset and changing colors over Uluru. The next morning, I was up before sunrise to join the crowds watching for the reverse, as the sun slowly lit up colors on the rock.

Many visitors climb to the top of the rock, following a 1.6-kilometer route to the 348-meter-high summit. The route starts steep, with cables affixed. However, there was a sign posted that aboriginal owners requested that people don't climb. The reasons behind the request are both because the climb goes on top of sacred paths and because a surprisingly high number develop problems like heat exhaustion or even heart attacks. The aboriginal owners are dependent on the income from visitors, so it was politely worded request rather than an explicit closing of the route. The park does close the route when it is rainy, windy, or too hot.

After reading the considerations, I decided to walk around Uluru rather than going on top. It was 9 kilometers and I passed rather interesting holes and other rock formations.

After this I paid a visit to the cultural center, where I found a display of small pile of rocks that had been "returned." A notebook showed the letters that accompanied the returns. One person sent a long letter describing kidney failure, stroke, divorce, and other woes that had come from his "cursed" rock. Others expressed guilt that this was legally and ethically wrong. Parents sent back rocks their kids had taken.

After Uluru, I cycled back via a camp called Curtin Springs. The name was originally Stalin Springs and then changed during the second world war. There was a night and day difference between the glitzy resort area around Uluru and the much more simple outback station. I met a person here who had walked four camels across Australia from east to west. We figured out he had crossed only four paved roads before reaching the coast in Queensland.

I took a tour of the ranch as well as nearby Mount Connor. Mount Connor was a larger outcropping than Uluru, though not at all as well known. The ranch had 3500 head of cattle and could support up to 8000 head. Once per year, cattle were mustered and put on road trains to South Australia. We got stuck in the mud in our Land Rover and took 45 minutes to slowly dig ourselves out. Overall, it was a rather interesting contrast to see right after visiting Uluru.

Alice Springs was another four days riding and a chance to take another rest day or two to see the sights. I signed up for a "take a camel to dinner" excursion, though it was breakfast instead of dinner. We started with a camel ride and then had a nice breakfast. I also took a day tour out to hike through several nearby gorges.

Rather than bicycle back from Alice Springs, I had reservations on the train, known as the Ghan. It was a fifteen and a half hour trip that paralleled our route and was an interesting rewind as a passenger past places I had ridden. I was now back in the land of small towns and agricultural areas and no longer in the Outback.

A few days ride brought me to the larger city of Adelaide, where I visited the Migration Museum that showed Australia's migration history. Early migrants in the 1840's included those from Great Britain, Germany, Poland, and others, including Afghans, Chinese, Italians, Lebanese, and Scandinavians. Unlike other Australian states, South Australia had an idealistic idea of a state of free settlers. Other states were started more by convict settlers from Great Britain and hence some Adelaide people might still occasionally refer to the rest of Australia as "the convict states."

The Museum described the aftermath of the second world war and the large immigration thereafter. Australia settled more European refugees than any other country other than U.S.A. Three quarters were from northern Europe and had their way paid, and one quarter were from southern Europe.

There weren't as many displays about more recent immigration. More recently, refugees had arrived from Vietnam, Cambodia, Iraq, and Afghanistan. If they arrived on Australian soil, they were taken to detention centers in Port Hedland, Curtin (near Broome) and Woomera (rocket range area) and processed for a three-year temporary visa. Overall, immigration was a hot political topic when I visited, as some politicians took positions of being "tough" on those smuggling refugees and there were also plans to take refugees intercepted on the high seas to other Pacific island nations such as Nauru.

After my Adelaide visit it was comfortable cycling along the coast of South Australia and then crossing the border into Victoria. The Melbourne Cup horse race was held the first Tuesday in November and is known as the "race that stops the nation." I came to the Lavers Hill Roadhouse at 3:15 p.m. to find the roadhouse closed and 25 people in the bar eagerly watching the race. It was a nice little stop.

Along this area were dramatic rock formations known as "the twelve apostles." I only counted eight but this is expected. After this riding, a busy but not too difficult ride brought me into the center of Melbourne, where I boarded a ferry to take a side trip to spend a month cycling around Tasmania.

Tasmania

It certainly was not perfect, but I had made a rough comparison of some Australian states with their American equivalents. Queensland compared with Texas for being both large and at times brash. New South Wales was similar to New York in that they were large states and economic powerhouses, but both also had "upstate" areas. I compared Western Australia with parts of California, e.g. Freemantle naval areas with San Diego as well as huge unspoiled natural areas in the north.

In this comparison Tasmania reminded me most of Maine, a state that is small but has a thriving tourist industry. These two were not always as wealthy as other states but had friendly and plain-spoken people. I had visited Tasmania with a bicycle once before in 1999 and looked forward to having four weeks to make a slow circumnavigation of the island.

I took a large ferry, The Spirit of Tasmania, across the straits. I read that the ferry was the 6th largest in the world. Fully loaded it had space for 1323 passengers, 315 cars and 40 semi-trailers. On our trip we had 1050 fellow passengers, including five traveling by bicycle. It was a 14-hour journey, and I had reserved space in a shared cabin. The fare also included a buffet dinner as well as breakfast.

I slept soundly and then waited patiently for 80 minutes after arrival before I could wheel my bicycle off the ship. We went through a quarantine station, and then I was over to the island.

It was Election Day. I had been following along and noticed a few differences with the U.S. elections:

1. Voting was mandatory, so there was 95% turnout.
2. It was a parliamentary system, and hence the Prime Minister will then pick different ministers to run different cabinet departments.
3. Most interestingly, the Senate used a multi-step preferential ballot, where one placed a rank order on the ballot of first choice, second choice, etc. As a result, most parties put out a cheat sheet suggesting an order that would help them most.

As in the rest of Australia, I cycled counter-clockwise. This meant heading towards the western and less developed areas first. I came past historic areas from Australia's convict past. In the early 1800's some 175,000 people were transported to Australia as convicts. Most completed their sentences and went on as free citizens. However, Sarah Island in Tasmania was one place convicts were sent if they re-offended once in Australia. There was museum here that told of their tales. Sarah Island was later closed in favor of Port Arthur, also in Tasmania. I later visited Port Arthur to learn more of the history there.

Queenstown, Tasmania, is the site of an active copper mine I visited when cycling past. The mine employs about 300 people and brings out 2.5 million tons of ore a year. This ore is 1.25% copper. Four of us on tour put on safety gear: helmets, lamps, safety vests and carried an emergency ventilator. We descended into the mine on a 4-wheel drive vehicle for 6.5 kilometers and were 440 meters below the surface when we saw the mine areas.

It was cold riding, even below freezing, as I slowly made my way across the bottom of Tasmania to the capital of Hobart. It was a bit of a nasty and wet day and hence it worked well for me to take a day to see the city. There was still some rain and drizzle as I made my way to Port Arthur the next day. Port Arthur had been one of my favorite places because of the history and scenery.

Port Arthur was a secondary prison established in 1830. Between 1619 and 1875, the British transported a quarter of a million convicts to American Colonies (80,000), New South Wales (80,000), Tasmania (3000), Western Australia (9700), Bermuda (9000) and Gibraltar (9000). Some would be classified as criminals by standards today, but many also had committed lesser crimes, such as picking apples from a tree. When sent to Australia, some were assigned to settlers, some to road parties and some to their skilled trades, such as blacksmiths, sailors, etc. They would serve terms of 7 years, 14 years, or life with a potential "ticket of leave" granting them freedom sooner.

If a convict had further problems in Australia, Port Arthur was one place they might be sent. Reasons for being sent there included absconding from work (22%), stealing (21%), boys too young to be assigned (25%), crimes of violence, plotting mutiny or refusing work (21%), no specific charge (6%) or being drunkards (5%). Port Arthur was a tough prison with physical punishments and even solitary confinements.

The old buildings were standing, and it was interesting to wander through some of the prison grounds. Also, there was a row of crosses memorializing people killed in Australia's worst mass murder, in April 1996.

After Port Arthur I slowly made my way around eastern parts of the island, seeing small penguins near Bicheno, and then back up to catch the ferry back to Melbourne. Overall it was an interesting ride around the island and gave me some extra time to see places I had missed on my prior trip in 1999.

Once I got back to Melbourne, I had one piece of business to conduct: buying tickets for the rest of the trip. My original itinerary had used a ticket broker in San Francisco to buy multi-step tickets. I had already paid my fees but didn't yet have my tickets. After the 9/11 attacks the ticket broker had gone bankrupt. Other customers and I were now in the unfortunate situation of having paid fees but not receiving our tickets. Fortunately, my father was persistent on my behalf to get my money refunded. However, this did mean I needed to remake my travel plans. The original itinerary was now a lot more expensive, so I rebooked plans to spend a few weeks in December/January in New Zealand and then fly to India for the last six weeks of my trip.

Canberra

After Melbourne the home stretch felt near. I had my tickets and three weeks to get to Sydney to finish my trip around Australia. It was first traveling about a week farther along the coast before going inland to Canberra. This coastal area was sometimes wet and often hilly but nothing I had not encountered before.

On my arrival into Canberra, I had now visited all six Australian states and two territories (NT and ACT). Canberra is the capital and a recent one at that. After spending eight months visiting all the other states, it seemed fitting to spend some time exploring the government buildings and museums. By now I had also read my Australian history as well as their Constitution.

Canberra was established as a new national capital after the Australian Federation in 1901. Rather than pick Sydney or Melbourne, a new area was picked. It was thus also a planned city with wide streets and large government buildings and memorials. Some of the areas were very recent, e.g. the new Parliament House was only opened in 1988 and the Supreme Court had been moved to Canberra a few years before.

What I found particularly interesting was doing my own bicycle tour of embassies. Unlike some other capitals where historic buildings are reused for embassies, in Canberra most countries had a chance to build a new building. This gave a chance to countries to insert some of the national character into the embassy building. For example, China built a large pagoda, the Fiji embassy looked like an oversized grass hut and the Polish embassy was a typically Polish brick farm house. I cycled my way past many of the embassies, taking photos of the variations. It was only the U.S. embassy, looking like Mount Vernon, where guards told me photographs were prohibited, e.g. in the aftermath of 9/11, for security reasons.

Finish in Sydney

After Canberra, the finish line was near. I first rode to Goulburn, where I met with fellow around-Australia cyclists Brendan and Wendy, who coincidentally were just finishing their ride as well. They were from the nearby area of Bowral and had a plot of land in the town of Wingello.

We cycled together to their land in Wingello, where Brendan's brother had set up a big "Welcome Home" banner and their families were there in a welcome ceremony. We all camped for one night on this land.

The next morning was the official arrival ride into Bowral. Part way along we were met by a local cycling group, who joined the last few kilometers. Balloons were tied to Brendan's and Wendy's bikes, and we even had a police escort down the main street. The local Lions Club had coordinated festivities, and a small crowd gathered with balloons and speeches. Overall, Brendan and Wendy had cycled 18,300+ kilometers around Australia. At least as impressive was the fact that they had also raised more than $25,000 for the Leukemia Foundation as part of the ride.

Overall it was nice to be able to join in their victory lap and completion of the ride. They were also nice enough to host me for a night in Wingello as well as the following night in Bowral.

The next morning I visited their parents' farm before continuing my ride on towards Sydney. That evening I had another invitation from gray nomads I had camped with in the Nullarbor – to stay with them when I came through. This was conveniently part way between Bowral and Sydney.

The last day of riding into Sydney was only 70 kilometers. For part of this I found myself on the major motorways. After 60 kilometers, I had passed the airport, and while technically I had completed one lap, I still had another 10 kilometers to go to reach the Opera House.

Hooray! After 230 days of cycling around Australia, I had completed my journey. Brendan and Wendy came down by train to join me in my victory celebration. I took the obligatory finish photos, and then we wandered around the Opera House and main harbor. I thanked them and we bade farewell before I found a place to stay for few last days before my flight departed to New Zealand.

Overall, it had been a great ride. The following were few of my impressions I captured from my blog immediately after doing this part of the ride:

Farewell Australia, at least for now... a day to cycle to the airport and fly to New Zealand, so let me write a few overall impressions:

I have found bicycle touring to be a wonderful way to see Australia. While I have only seen a small slice, I have gone from Australia being a "blank map" to filling in many details, e.g. where to find sugar cane, hills, wheat, sheep, crocodiles, emus, coal, copper, lead, zinc, iron, boab trees, coral reefs, diamonds and so much more. Each day added another ~100 km piece of the montage. I found the roads to be better than those in the U.S. and drivers also slightly better on average. This was particularly true in the tropics. During my several months across the north, I had no rain and mostly tailwinds. What more can a cyclist want! Hopefully this web site can assist and help inspire others to go see more of Australia, even if by car or coach.

On arrival, I noticed obvious differences, e.g. the moon is tipped the other way, revolving doors go the other way, weather systems swirl differently around highs and lows, riding is on the left, little flip switches on outlets, international road signs, colored money, mostly British spellings, etc. At least as interesting is how familiar and similar it feels to parts of the U.S. where I have been, particularly the small towns in both countries. Bill

Bryson has compared small town areas in 1950's U.S.A. towns, complete with old radio songs. It felt more recent to me (1980's or 1970's), but I can see some resemblance.

My favorite riding has been through outback areas. There were long distances between towns and roadhouses, but beautiful scenery, wildlife, and a sense of calm. It is here that I most noticed a unique culture of caravans, Britz vans, backpackers, road train truckies, roadhouses, etc. Tourist regions like the Red Center and Top End blend into the Outback with their scenery, tour buses and mixtures of tourists. It is a bit ironic that so many Australians live in urban areas and around the big cities (and from what I read, many don't get to the Outback).

People have been wonderful, helpful, and friendly. It has added to the experience to visit with locals and learn more. At risk of missing many, I would like to make an extra special salute here to Rob and Becky, Rod and Gwen, Vicky and Darryl, Jill and Charles, Brendan and Wendy. Thanks!

Unlike a country such as Canada, Australia very much feels like one country with not so many differences between the states. Sure, there might be squabbles about what rugby is the "real" one or sport rivalries or regions like Tassie/WA feeling left out.... However, one is struck with how similar and people's outlook is towards one Australia across all the states, e.g. preferring uniform laws and treatment. If there is a split in Australia, it is more between big cities and outback "bush" than between the states.

If I had to pick favorites, my favorite capital city would be Darwin, with Adelaide a close second and Canberra up as well. However, they all have their unique and interesting bits. Picking a favorite region to ride would be the Kimberley, though this is hard to pick because much enjoyment has come from seeing variations and combinations.

After a long ride I typically end with an even longer list of places I missed but would really like to come back and see... the Townsville-Cairns-Normanton circuit or up the Murray/Darling rivers are two examples. It may be a while, but I expect to be back to more of Australia....

Thanks to my parents for their support and thanks to my father for all the work he put into the web site. Someone had to be tracking that red line around the map...

2001 – Tales from New Zealand and India

New Zealand cycling

In this section I will include a few overview notes about my four weeks I spent cycling across the North Island of New Zealand. For a more complete description, I will refer readers to my blog of this trip, www.bike2001.com.

I was surprised with the tremendous variety found in the North Island. In very short distances I experienced both tropical-type areas as well as a more temperate apple-growing region. I saw an active volcanic area but also crossed a large city of more than a million people. There was a cultural center in Bay of Islands to learn about the Maori culture and the capital city of Wellington to explore. There was a surprisingly large amount packed into a small area and just a few weeks.

Cyclists will vary in the amount of preparation done for a trip or even the preparation one cyclist does for different trips. Australia and New Zealand were two different extremes in my planning. I had carefully read several books and multiple blogs on Australia. I had mentally recorded lists of attractions, places to visit and side trips I could take. I reviewed what worked and problems others had encountered and worked through my potential responses. While it didn't make sense to plan out a day by day itinerary, I had a wealth of information in advance to work things out as the ride developed.

In contrast, my flight and trip to New Zealand were rescheduled just a few weeks before departure. My tickets were lost after the travel agent went bankrupt and New Zealand seemed to fit right into the gap. However, I had done very little advance planning, reading, or anticipating about New Zealand. I had a rough guide I could follow and other journals to work things out along the way. I had maps and an idea of how I wanted to travel. So, it wasn't completely a seat-of–the-pants exercise, but it was a lot less planned than Australia.

Because I had not fully anticipated New Zealand, I found myself comparing it to Australia and thinking, "This isn't Australia." Perhaps it was going over the holiday season as well, but I noticed a bunch of differences: the roads were narrow, there was a lot of traffic – particularly holiday traffic, and a lot more shorter and steep hills. I had my Australia withdrawal symptoms and couldn't help but think, "This isn't Australia anymore." However, I got myself through that, and particularly the huge variety had me appreciating New Zealand for being New Zealand by the end.

Not far from the town of Hamilton, I found that my drive train was occasionally skipping along. It was annoying enough that I brought the bike to a local bike shop for an investigation. The cassette had worked itself loose, and the mechanic also decided to open the hub and clean everything out. There was a bunch of wear in the hub, and the mechanic ended up greasing everything and putting it all together.

Three days later, my chain was skipping again. I wasn't sure what was happening, but I set off from the town of Tarawera hoping it would diminish. Instead, it became worse, and within a few kilometers the hub started spinning freely both directions. There is not much to do once the pedals no longer drive the wheels, so I got off and started walking while keeping an eye out for a truck or other vehicle that might provide a lift.

After I spent an hour walking up hills and coasting down and reaching the 9 kilometer mark, a small truck stopped. Inside were two New Zealanders from Tonga. They were driving from Auckland to Napier to pick up a load of fruit to sell in the city. It was my luck their truck was empty and they were willing to provide a ride. I was grateful for a 70-kilometer lift and even a stop right at a bike shop.

My hub was a special 48-spoke hub and hence the bike shop had neither a replacement hub nor a separate rim. They could, however, order an entirely new wheel, have it built in Wellington and sent to the shop. It took two days, but without much trouble I had a nice new shiny 36-spoke wheel and hub to continue my journey. The new wheel was perhaps not quite as strong as the original, so I mailed away both my tent and sleeping bag as well as some other gear I wouldn't need in India. Every little bit of weight reduction should help in increasing the reliability.

From Napier it was a few days riding to Wellington, where I finished my ride across the North Island. In total, it was ~1600 kilometers or about 1000 miles ridden with several rest days and shorter days, including several in Napier to replace my wheel.

In the future I would like to visit the South Island of New Zealand and this time do a bit more planning and preparation.

India Cycling

Smells, sounds, sights--India is a land of sensory overload. It starts not long after you leave the plane and continues throughout the trip, so I stopped and took a deep breath and just concentrated on doing simple things one at a time. First, I retrieved my bicycle from the rickety conveyor belt, still in the old terminal building. The box looked OK, and there was no damage. Then I got the rest of my belongings and completed going through customs.

Outside, a throng of people massed at the arrivals hall. I waited and spotted the driver from Hotel Mars, where I had arranged my first night stay, and we got the bike in the van. It was already dark, but a quick ride through streets brought me to the hotel. The porter, Das, helped unload the luggage, brought it to the room and then held his hand out for the expected tip. That and the toilet with the bucket of water were my "Welcome to India" moments for this journey.

In the morning I was up early putting the bike together. After this I took a quick taxi ride into Chennai, where I had arranged for friends to store my laptop and computer gear during my cycle trip. The bike box itself could stay at the hotel. Then it was back to the hotel, and by 10 a.m. I was ready to ride to my first night destination, a resort town of Mamallapuram.

Cycling in India continued with sensory overload as I rode past the airport and the Gandhi statue and then headed out to the coast. At one point I saw workers painting stripes on the road and wondered their purpose as the discipline of staying in lanes was lacking. At another point it started lightly raining and motorcycle riders and I pulled over under the trees to let it pass.

After 25 kilometers, the chaos subsided as I reached the coast and the route became a toll road. I passed a few villages and beach resorts, including some with water slides. Not much farther I reached Mamallapuram and found a reasonable hotel. I walked around town to see the sights, including stone carvers, and in the evening saw a dance performance before retiring early to deal with some jet lag.

On a second day, my route brought me south along the coast. I had fun taking in all the new sights and sounds but also was conscious about standing out. When I was riding, people stopped and looked. Some pointed,, some laughed, some stared. A few made a comment or challenge. Some just slowed down and gave me a good eye over. Where I could, I caught eyes and smiled and often received a smile back. I also stood out less walking as a tourist than on my bicycle with helmet, panniers and all my gear.

After 80 kilometers I passed into the formerly French colony of Pondicherri. It slowly became busier and more chaotic again as I entered the city. I was following the main road south but seemed to miss most of the hotels. Finally, I found a small hotel for Rs 150 ($4). Over time I developed a hotel rating system in which I considered three luxuries: hot water, a Western style toilet, and air conditioning. This hotel had no luxuries. Air conditioning was important not so much because of cooler sleeping, but more because I was very cautious of the mosquitoes and deadly diseases I had read they can bring.

My third day cycling was a longer ride from 6:30 in the morning until I collapsed after carrying my bicycle up two flights of stairs to the hotel in the middle of the afternoon. The heat had been sweltering. I also had not quite figured out what was safe to eat and so had not eaten enough while riding. At least this hotel had all three luxuries. After resting, eating some rice and dosa did seem to revive me.

A fourth day riding brought me to the temple town of Thanjuvar. Along the way, I had my first flat tire. I stopped in what I thought was a secluded spot to fix the tire, though by time I finished, I had an audience of twelve people, including an infant. All stayed at a safe distance but watched this stranger who had landed and was fixing his bicycle. In the afternoon it became warm and I stopped at a shop to buy a drink. During this transaction I noticed at least fifty children had crowded around to watch. At another point I passed road construction, where the road was being smoothed with a 55-gallon drum.

Thanjuvar has a nice Brihadishwara Temple, where I stopped the following morning for a visit. I decided to take a rest day here. By afternoon my GI tract had joined in to let me know it was still getting used to the Indian bacteria. So, I spent a bit more time watching Star TV in between short trips to the bathroom. However, I recuperated after three solid meals and bought some clean water.

After Thanjuvar, a shorter ride brought me to the temple town of Trichy, where I was happy to find a hotel with two luxuries for only Rs 400 ($10). The hotel was a little out of town, so I rode an autorickshaw for the first time. They don't run on the meter, so the first exercise was to negotiate a fare. He asked for Rs 40. I said, "30." He said, "35." This still seemed expensive, so I walked away. He then followed me up with "30," and we were off on a ride to the Rock Temple. It was a different type of ride as we wove between traffic, which seemed scarier from an autorickshaw than a bicycle.

Two days later I had cycled to the larger temple town of Madurai. I somehow bypassed the main parts of town and found myself already 4 kilometers past it. There was a fancy place up on top of the hill. I had to decide whether I should I ride back into town or splurge and stay somewhere fancy for a night. I splurged and rode up to the hotel. It cost me $110 U.S., more than my previous seven nights' accommodations combined, but there was a great view of town and a fancy buffet lunch. After lunch I took an autorickshaw into town to see the temples.

The cab driver brought me to the Sri Meenakshi (Shiva's wife) temple and then told me the temple was closed before bringing me to a handicrafts store. I was not interested in a hard sell of handicrafts, so I decided to walk around town for two hours until the temple opened again. I was accosted surprisingly many times and found myself getting into a defensive mode, "No, I don't need a guide, cab ride, handicrafts, etc. I won't give you money.Stop pestering me!" I could tell this was a town that got many tourists.

Finally, the temple opened again, and I walked through to see the carvings and statues as well as the local shops inside. Some parts were only for Hindus, but there was still a lot to see. Unfortunately, I was in no mood to pay for a guide to tell me more. After visiting the temple, I took an autorickshaw back to the fancy hotel and up the hill, where we had a great view of city lights in the evening.

Two further days from Madurai brought me to the southern tip of India at Kanyakumari. There were many wind turbines along the way, which, unfortunately, also meant lots of wind. This is an important town with a mix of both Western and Indian visitors and enough sights to spend another day looking around. There is an interesting temple, a Gandhi memorial where the sun pokes through a hole just right on his October 2nd birthday, a lighthouse and a small museum, though I also spent some of the warm afternoon hours in an internet café catching up with the world.

After Kanyakumari the road took me farther north along the coast. I had now reached Kerala, my second Indian state. This area has resorts that seem to cater more to Western tourists, and I found myself in Kovalam, one such resort. For the right price a woman will let you take her photo with a fish on her head. Apparently, some fly directly from Europe to this area for a week of "sanitized India," staying in the resort and visiting the beaches.

It was recommended that I visit the backwaters of Kerala by boat. My cycling had brought me farther to Kollam, where I arranged for a day trip ending at Alappuzha. We had a 20-meter boat with upper deck and lower deck and room for ~30 passengers. My bicycle and luggage came along too. From here it was an eight-hour cruise through lakes and smaller canals. Along the way, children yelled out, "Please give me one pen" and similar sayings. One tourist tossed a pen, and it landed in the water. Nobody retrieved it. We stopped for lunch at a nice little restaurant with a dock for the boat. Thali was served from a banana leaf. The afternoon brought another stop at a similar place for tea, and then we finished our ride just after dark in Alappuzha. Overall, it was a nice change from cycling this part of India.

Two days further brought me to Guruvayur. It was a tough ride--not so much the 85-kilometer distance nor the flat terrain, but a tough, bumpy road. I also still was not quite eating enough during the day, settling for biscuits and bananas where I could find them. I arrived in Guruvayur to find I seemed to be the only non-Indian tourist in the area. The town was an important religious site, so there were many Indian pilgrims who had traveled to see the temples, but it was also not on the tourist circuit. It was a night and day difference between Madurai, where I was accosted by many in the touristy town and Guruvayur, where nobody bothered me other than giving me stares and wondering, "What is he doing here?"

The following day brought me as far as I planned to ride up the coast before turning inland. It was an even tougher ride than before, starting with a bumpy road before a set of hills kicked in, including a few that were steep enough for me to walk. In addition, the afternoon brought heat. After 96 kilometers, I stopped to buy some water and accidentally bought soda water instead. Two kilometers later, I felt sharp cramps in my leg. With some difficulty I make it another 12 kilometers to a hotel where I collapsed in my room.

A short while later I went to the restaurant to refuel. I had barely ordered when I felt very sick. I rushed back to my room, where I threw up. I experienced painful cramps all over but particularly in the legs again. I had asked them to bring my food/water via room service and eventually felt just a little better. However, the hypochondriac in me got out my copy of "Healthy Travel in Asia" and started looking up symptoms. Somehow it seems all sorts of nasty things start with nausea, cramps, and tiredness. I started to wonder about alternate transportation and other ways to get me out of the predicament I was in if things didn't get better and I couldn't bicycle from there.

As quickly as the symptoms arose, they also seemed to get better. However, better safe than sorry and I took a rest day in Kozhikode. By afternoon I was feeling better. I met another cyclist, Bill Weir[10], who was also riding through India. I traded some information and worked out a plan to cycle inland via Mysore.

---

[10] Some of Bill Weir's bicycle rides, https://www.crazyguyonabike.com/directory/?user=billweir

It was nice to be on the road again after a rest day. The first 45 kilometers were relatively flat but then a larger hill started. I was not quite sure how long the hill went on and so ended up with a mixture of walking and riding for another 5 kilometers before spotting a passing truck. Somehow my vocabulary for "How much farther is this hill?" was not easily understood. The truck driver was willing to give me a ride. It turned out the hill was only for another 7 kilometers, but I couldn't figure this out, and the driver ended up giving me a ride all the way to Kalpetta, 24 kilometers in total.

Once I was at the top of the hill, the terrain was flatter. Another two days riding brought me to Mysore, with its impressive palace complex. I took another rest day and booked a bus tour to see the temple above the town as well as the Mysore Palace. I also walked through the zoo. The zoo had a reasonable collection of mammals, birds, and other animals in nice park-like settings. I seemed to be one of few non-Indians visiting, and one group of Indians asked me to pose with them for a picture in front of the giraffes.

By the evening our bus trip brought us out to lighted gardens outside town at Brindavan Gardens, a rather impressive spectacle overall.

Ding, ding, where was my bell? Somehow, I noticed a few kilometers after leaving the hotel that my bicycle bell has been pilfered. The bike had been parked underneath the hotel in a locked garage, so I suspected hotel-related personnel. This was one of few places where I wasn't allowed to bring my bicycle into my room, and, unfortunately, I had forgotten to take the bell off the bike. In India, most everything on the road makes some noise and I would miss the bell from here on.

Two more days riding took me to the technology city of Bangalore. On previous trips to India, I had visited Chennai only, where local HP counterparts insisted that I stay in a five-star hotel. Here in Bangalore, the local HP manager offered to let me stay in his home. I didn't want to impose, but he insisted, and we went through another cycle of this before I took him up on his offer. It was a pleasant stay, much more so than at that five-star hotel where I wasn't allowed to open and close my own drapes.

I took a day here to visit the HP offices in Bangalore and meet some engineers I was working with in California. It was a nice combination and pleasant to visit the offices.

After Bangalore I had an important destination in mind, the temple complex at Tirupati. Tirupati supposedly has more religious pilgrims than anywhere else in the world, including Mecca, Rome, or Jerusalem. They come throughout the year, with many more coming at festivals. On average, some 35,000 pilgrims come each day to visit the Sri Venkateswara Temple with well over 100,000 on peak days.

I came to the village at the bottom of the hill and booked a hotel for two nights, with plans to see the temple.

After breakfast on the first day, I took an autorickshaw to the base of the hill, where I figured out the logistics. Admission and viewing of the god is "darshan." There is a general "darshan" for free, but one might have to wait for several days before the queue gets through. One can also pay considerably more for an expedited viewing. I settled on paying Rs 40 for a "special darshan" that gives me a ticket good for admission at 8 p.m., another twelve hours later.

Many pilgrims take the task of walking up to the temple over seven hills and more than ~3600 steps to climb over a nine-kilometer path. I had all day, so I set out on the walk. It was a pleasant route with many vendors along the way.

At the top I reached a giant temple complex at Tirumala with housing for more than 5000 pilgrims and large dining halls. There were many vendors selling everything from food, to travel, to hats to umpteen different plastic items. I stopped in at one of the restaurants for a meal. I was quickly shuttled off to the pay section, where they had nice, filling south-Indian food.

Tonsure is a task taken by many pilgrims. It is a ritual shaving of the head, with hair donated to the gods. It happens in the morning as well as after 4 p.m. I decided to get in line for afternoon tonsure. There was a long snaking set of queues. As I was in the queues, several helpful Indians motioned to me to point out, "Do you realize they will shave your head here?" "Yes," I acknowledged. Eventually, I reached the head of the line, where I was handed a razor blade and a slip that directed me to barber #206 out of a long row of barbers. Due to his quickness and efficiency,, I soon left with a newly shaven head.

By 7:30 p.m., I dropped off my shoes, camera and backpack, which weren't allowed inside the temple and found my way to the special darshan queue. They were allowing the 8 p.m. slot into line, so I followed the maze, which led me to a large holding area, where I joined some 400 others. On the way, I went past a desk where one signs a declaration with name, passport, address, and religion. As a non-Hindu, it also had a simple statement that you have faith in Lord Venkateshwara.

We waited in the holding area until 10 p.m., when they allowed our area to go onto the back of the viewing queue. It took another hour before we reached the inner temple. There were beautiful statues here and lots of gold. The line of people kept up a constant push, and when we reached the sight of the god, there was a brief period to make a wish, while folks grabbed you by the arms and helped pull you past.

After coming past the god, the push of the crowd subsided and things became more relaxed. It was now not far from midnight, and rather than walk down those seven hills, I found a taxi to take me back to my hotel.

From Tirupathi, with a freshly shaven head, I cycled first to the temple town of Kanchipuram and then back to Mammalapuram, where I took another easy rest day. From here I cycled back to Chennai, where I met more HP counterparts and retrieved my computer and belongings. In my visit back to Chennai, I stayed in a much more comfortable hotel than the five-star I was at on the previous trip.

At the hotel was a tour desk, and I saw that Lonely Planet listed a tour that goes past eight different Chennai landmarks. I asked at the desk if they could arrange this tour. Rather than go on the official tour, they suggested having their local taxi driver take me past the same sights. We arranged a fee and scheduled the trip to last five hours, from 2 p.m. to 7 p.m.

The taxi driver took me past the list of places, but for a variety of reasons, we didn't spend much time visiting. One temple was closed. Another church became a "drive-by" visit, as he pointed out the church and quickly drove past. The planetarium was closed on Sunday, and it might have been too late to see the snake park.

The cab driver did try taking me to several expensive handicraft emporiums. I politely visited the first one, but once we got to the second one, I let him know that this was not how I wanted to spend my time. Of my original list of eight destinations, we stopped at three, zoomed past two more, and, for various reasons, couldn't visit the other three.

The cab driver knew that he was not supposed to bring me back to the hotel until 7 p.m., so he decided to bring me to his home. That was where some of the magic of the trip happened. I saw the small 10-foot by 12-foot residence with large water jugs and relatively few possessions. I met his wife and small child. We stopped past the clinic, where his brother worked as a doctor. He asked for email and addresses, and then we also went to visit with neighbors, who were preparing for a small festival. It was a much more genuine visit to see a slice of India than that original list of eight attractions. I didn't stay for the complete festival, since once it came close to 7 p.m., the cab driver realized he could bring me back to the hotel again.

After this there was a ride back to my airport hotel, and my final visit to India ended. While waiting in the Chennai airport, I noted a few of my overall senses of bicycling south India. The following were overall thoughts I captured in my blog:

- While I feel like I have gotten to see a lot more depth than in my last (business) trip, I have only scratched the surface as far as India is concerned. Most of this might never come. For example, while I traveled in regions with four different languages, I wouldn't be able to tell even what language someone was speaking... something rather basic and fundamental. For me all were different, yet for speakers, someone from Kerala might not understand Telegu, etc. I have heard India described more in comparison to Europe, with different languages and cultures and with north different from south. So... take any generalizations I might make with big grain of salt....
- I have seen huge contrasts in most everything. I saw excellent roads and the worst surfaces. I paid 80x more for my most

expensive accommodation vs. the least expensive and 40x for the most expensive meal vs. the least expensive. In India, you can live like a British Raja and stay in the finest places (though be isolated). India is jumping straight from literacy (65% at present) into computer literacy with more Oracle/XML/WAP/VB/etc. posted than elsewhere I have been... but also a third of the people don't read/write a native tongue.

- People I met were extremely helpful and friendly. While they sometimes had a laugh at my expense or posed with me for photos, I never felt threatened ever... just quite out of place at times. Friendliness was particularly apparent out of the most touristy places, where I tended to get a "tourist shell" to ward off a progression of aggressive sales types and hustlers. In the countryside, people were very curious and very helpful.
- Bicycle is an excellent way to travel. It gets one into the countryside and meeting different people. Roads are chaotic but have their own rules. Since there is so much variety in vehicles on the road, it seems as though trucks, buses and other vehicles must watch out and are at least as patient as Western motorists who find a bicycle on "their" roads. There are, of course, enough accidents to keep one slightly wary though...
- There is tremendous culture and history in south India. I got the sense the British period was only a few hundred years--not much compared to ages of temples and former dynasties and empires. Hindu temples are surprisingly open to foreigners who don't necessarily understand (or sometimes respect) their religious significance.
- I felt challenged in different ways than riding elsewhere this year. Much more than elsewhere, I was physically aware of my body and potential for sickness... rather than just mechanical issues.

Overall, I very much enjoyed my travels though India and recommend south India as a destination for bicycle tourists... particularly for those open to a bit of adventure, a bit of culture and a bit of a challenge.

Reflections on a one year trip

One year was an excellent intermission to take this trip, and I was grateful that Hewlett-Packard allowed me the leave and then had an interesting position for me in Colorado on my return. It was an interesting combination of Australia, New Zealand, the U.S., and India, with each different in its own way.

Australia was the main event and what I had spent the most time and energy anticipating. Making one lap gave an overall goal, while also allowing me to stop and explore. Of the 230 total days. I spent 48 of them off the bike seeing different places.

New Zealand, perhaps, I didn't do justice to, since it was the least planned. However, I was impressed with the tremendous variety in such a short distance. A second cross-U.S.A. trip was a good way of easing into the trip and getting back into touring mode.

India was a full sensory overload from start to finish. Placing India at the end didn't give me time to think "My trip is finishing" until right before it did. I pushed things out to the last day, landing back in the U.S.A. on February 28th and then going into work the next morning.

Overall, I felt very blessed to have been able to take this trip as well as grateful that circumstances had allowed me the chance. I also knew that my pattern of working for several years followed by a longer trip worked well. I vowed to myself to do this again with another extended trip, perhaps in another five years. I didn't yet know the destination, but the pattern had been set again.

2007 - Tales from Across Eurasia
URL: http://www.bike2007.com

Plans
Blame it on Russians in fur hats.

At the end of 2004, Vladimir Putin was finishing his first term as Russian president and running for re-election. At the end of February, he made a stop in the eastern city of Khabarovsk to hold a ribbon-cutting ceremony opening a new road from Chita to Khabarovsk. It was now possible to drive all the way across Russia, and their plan was to finish paving the entire road by 2008! A photo of Russians in fur hats bundled up against the February cold accompanied the story.

I am sure the story made its intended splash in Russia. In addition, the news went out across the internet, and this is where I saw the report and started thinking. One road means it is possible to cross all of Asia within one country, with one language and one visa. I started investigating further and looking up journals of others who had made a similar trip.

The Trans-Siberian Railroad first crossed the area in 1916. After that, for many years the area was a sensitive, closed area on the U.S.S.R./Chinese border. Many of the settlements were along the railway line, and there might be an occasional road between two villages or a maintenance road for the railroad. However, there wasn't one single road that connected straight through.

In 1989 Mark Jenkins and six companions first cycled across Russia. Mark wrote his account in a book, Off the Map[11]. It was a great tale I had read many years prior. It was also a tough adventure. In some places without roads, they ended up riding on the railroad tracks. In others they bushwhacked their way between villages.

A more customary route was to follow roads across Russia to Lake Baikal and from there cross via Mongolia and into China, and there were several

---

[11] Off the Map, https://www.amazon.com/Off-Map-Bicycling-Across-Siberia/dp/159486764X

journals of cyclists who took this route. In 1999 Tim Cope and Chris Hatherly described their trip on this route in the book Off the Rails[12].

There were several other journals describing this route as well.

As I later learned from looking at the dates placed in concrete on the bridges, the Russians must have started building some of this road in the late 1990's. By 2001 some Russian friends of ours crossed the route with only a few missing bridges where they needed to ford rivers and only a short section of bushwhacking between villages. Hence, large portions of the route were in place a few years before, but Putin's campaign announcement was the first I learned of this road.

My "mark on the wall" was for another trip in 2007, so this gave me a few years to further prepare for the trip. I enrolled in Russian language classes at nearby Front Range Community College. My brother Bert was potentially interested in joining me for parts of the journey, so we also rode "shakedown" rides in 2005 from Prudhoe Bay, Alaska, to Fairbanks and in 2006 from the Hungary/Ukraine Border to the Volga River in Russia. The Alaska ride was a chance to try gravel road riding in an Arctic environment. The Ukraine/Russia ride was a chance to get experience riding in Russia and, as it turned out, a chance to leave behind a "spare" bicycle with friends in the city of Penza, Russia.

Finding partners for the ride

As the time approached, I considered whether to find others for the ride or do the ride mostly by myself. My previous rides had all been solo, but these had also been in English-speaking countries. The advantages of riding with others were both that there were more people to problem-solve issues and with my still minimal Russian, that there would be someone to speak the language more fluently. The disadvantages were that it wouldn't be 100% my trip anymore and that there would be a little more risk of something going wrong with at least one of the bikes/riders.

In the end I decided to advertise the ride for others and see what happened. I was now a life-member of the Adventure Cycling

---

[12] Off the Rails, http://www.timcopejourneys.com/

organization. One of the benefits of membership was an ability to post an ad in the "companions wanted" section. I wrote a simple ad that said I was traveling from Amsterdam to Vladivostok as well as the rough dates and my age and gender. I also set up a web site that contained links to some previous journals as well as a few other thoughts about the ride.

I received approximately fifteen replies, and my reply would then include a link to the web site with more information. Some were just curious; others were doing a similar trip. However, I received four or five serious responses where we corresponded more. Of these there was one I declined as not being a good fit. This rider seemed nice enough but was getting very concerned about how we might ride separately but still meet up. She started adding a bunch of additional logistical requests. Once the time came, I am sure we would have worked out what was necessary, but I didn't want to nail down too much unnecessarily and jeopardize my ride with commitments to things that later might turn out to be bad ideas.

Another rider was a relative novice, but otherwise enthusiastic. I suggested perhaps we could meet at an upcoming Texas Hell Week event ride and see how things worked. He showed up at Texas Hell Week, but, in the end, didn't get his stuff organized after that.

Towards the end of this period, there was a woman named Mickey who contacted me from Amsterdam. From the start, I could tell she was serious and working through plans and then quickly working out details of visas, immunizations, and other items. We exchanged multiple emails and then also had a phone conversation. It all seemed to fit well, and hence we agreed to ride together. It is always hard to tell, but we also agreed each would have ability to travel by himself or herself if necessary, just in case we discovered it just wouldn't work.

I had taken two semesters of Russian at Front Range Community College and would be in middle of a third semester when the trip started. I decided I would augment this with a three-week Russian language course in St. Petersburg right after entering Russia. Hence, the plan was that Mickey and I would briefly meet the day I landed in Amsterdam, and then I would cycle ahead. She would follow roughly three weeks later, and then we would depart together from St. Petersburg.

Preparations and Texas riding

While I expected the ride across Russia to take approximately six months, I requested a total of ten months of leave. This let me structure the time as follows:

- March, drive to Dallas and do some "shakedown" riding in the U.S. and make sure bike and gear are ready before flying overseas.
- End of March, fly to Amsterdam. Spend a month riding to St, Petersburg and then three weeks of language classes.
- Leave from St. Petersburg on the 12th of May and plan to arrive in Vladivostok by the end of September.
- October through mid-November, I signed up as part of the Tour D'Afrique "Silk Route" expedition. The overall expedition was a ride from Istanbul to Beijing, but I would fly to meet them in western China and then ride to Beijing.
- End of November through the end of the year, fly to Bangkok and ride to Singapore.

At the appropriate time I sent away my passport to do the delicate dance required to receive a Russian visa. This first required a formal invitation letter and then sending the passport with the invitation to receive a visa. The invitation couldn't be too far in advance, so I had to wait before starting the process. Fortunately, there were companies on the internet that could provide invitations and expedite the overall process. My visa went smoothly except the part where I had stated the list of half a dozen cities I might visit. One city was "restricted," and hence I needed to provide additional documentation, including hotel bookings. Rather than let this get too complicated, I decided to drop this city from my formal plans.

I had just enough time once I received my Russian visa to apply for a Chinese visa as well. While my plan was to fly to China in September, I requested the visa period start the six-month time window starting in August. The timing was tight with the Chinese New Year, but I received my visa and passport just a little before my departure for Texas on March 1st. Unfortunately, as I would later discover, I didn't quite check the Chinese visa closely enough. The dates on the visa said "August" and

"February," but they gave me a visa that started immediately (February) and would expire in August.

February 28th was my last day at work, and we had a going away lunch a few days later. I assembled all my gear first in my living room and then packed it into a minivan that I would drive one-way to Dallas. It sure looked like a lot of stuff, though I also planned to take the first several weeks in Texas to sort through what I would really need.

Texas Hell Week

I drove to Dallas, dropped some items like my camping gear with a friend and then dropped the van off at DFW airport. From here it was a four-day bicycle ride down to the town of Fredericksburg. Here I took part in a ride named Texas Hell Week (TXHW). TXHW had been started sixteen years before by Nick Gerlich as an extreme amount of cycling near San Antonio. Nick and his wife, Becky Gerlich, were supreme organizers, and from an initial trip for half a dozen friends, the event had grown to 300 yearly participants. We paid a not very large fee for a map book with the organized rides for each day. Participants reserved their own hotels, and it was a fun event to get out and ride each day with different groups.

For eight days I got in a lot of good unloaded riding in the Texas Hill Country. My brother Bert came down to ride during the week as well. It was warmer than Colorado and except for a day or two of rain, excellent weather. At the end of this week, I turned around and cycled back to Dallas, having gotten in a little over 1000 miles of training. I dropped my bike in for service and otherwise got everything finalized for a flight to Amsterdam to start the main event.

Cycling through Europe to St. Petersburg

Fifty-seven pounds of gear tipped the scales at the DFW airport, and that wasn't including my bicycle. It was similar or perhaps slightly heavier than when I had flown to Sydney five years before.

In Amsterdam I met Mickey for the first time when she met me at Schiphol Airport, and together we took the train into the city and to her flat. It was good to meet in person and discover no awful immune responses. Our plan was for me to depart for St. Petersburg first and do a three-week language class. Mickey would depart later. and we would meet at the end of my class and depart from there.

That evening in Amsterdam I cycled to my Oom (Uncle) Gerard and stayed with him. He had a great flat overlooking the Amsterdam harbor. I decided to consider watching boats in the harbor as a start of one end of Europe/Asia. It would be almost six months later before I would see sea water again.

The Netherlands was a two-day bicycle ride with a stop in Olst visiting my Tante (Aunt) Gea on her farm. The Netherlands was a comfortable place to begin the ride as I was born there, had family there and spoke the language.

The five days it took me to cross Germany were only slightly more difficult. I had good roads, and while I couldn't speak German, I seemed to get by with a mixture of pantomime, Dutch/English, and smiles. Most people knew what I meant, particularly in specific situations like purchasing food or finding lodging.

This became considerably more difficult as I crossed the border into Poland. I had not spent much time preparing for Poland and found myself in a German-speaking part of Poland where my Russian wasn't strong enough, English wasn't very prevalent and I also didn't know much German. Embarrassingly enough, I had not quite looked up the currency used and was initially misled when I saw many prices listed in Euros. It turns out these were advertising prices for the Germans to come across and buy things, but not the actual currency used.

Polish roads also took a bit to get familiar. There were small tiny roads, but these weren't always in the best conditions nor had the best connectivity. The next wider roads seemed to be my preference, and initially, I was happy to find some with a moderate-sized shoulder. However, here I discovered a Polish habit of swerving onto the shoulder to let an oncoming car pass. It all went well, but I needed to be on my toes when riding through Poland.

Kaliningrad border crossing

Without too much trouble I crossed Poland and came to a border crossing into the Russian enclave of Kaliningrad. This little piece of Russia was between Poland and Lithuania and gave me an interesting border crossing.

I left the Polish city of Gronowo and found a spot to exchange my remaining Polish Zloty before riding to the border itself. There were a few cars waiting and so I took my turn in line. A customs official waived me to come up. They asked if I had a visa for Russia. I said, "Yes," and then they looked through the passport before handing it back and saying all looked OK.

I looked for stamps; they noticed and took the passport back and stamped it and waived me to proceed. Hey, that wasn't too difficult, I thought, before remembering all I had done was exit Poland and entry to Russia remained.

I cycled forward to the next set of gates, where a guard told me to wait. He asked the purpose of my visit and I told him it was to "bicycle across Russia to Vladivostok." He went back to the telephone. After a bit, he came up and said, "You can't cross the border on a bicycle."

Now my question was, "Why?"

He again carefully told me I couldn't ride a bicycle across the border.

I was just as insistent, and he told me to wait while he called for his supervisor.

A short bit later, an officer came up in a car. We went through the procedure of his asking me the purpose of my visit, and then he carefully explained that you couldn't cross this border crossing on a bicycle. Only automobiles, buses or their passengers were permitted.

He asked if I understood and I told him, "Yes." However, I then looked rather perplexed and asked, if I couldn't cycle across, then how would I cross the border into Kaliningrad?

The officer explained that I would need to get someone to take me across in a car.

OK, but where would I find such a car?

As the conversation continued, I made it clear that I wasn't challenging their authority, and somehow it turned into a problem solving exercise. Before I knew it, the officer approached a waiting minibus driver and told him that he would take me across the border. It wasn't exactly something the driver wanted to do because of his other passengers, but once he learned I was cycling across Russia and even planned to go through Novosibirsk, his home city, he also became more enthusiastic.

We loaded my bike and gear in the van. They passed me an immigration card. We drove to the real passport control area, where we all got out of the van. They looked through our passports and somehow everyone at this station already seemed to know about me. It wasn't too difficult to drive through here, and then 2 kilometers past the border post, the minibus driver let me out. He wouldn't accept payment but did joke that he wasn't taking me all the way to Novosibirsk.

Another 50 kilometers brought me to middle of the city where I had reserved a hotel for two nights. Kaliningrad was a very Russian-looking city and an interesting place to spend my Easter Sunday walking through town. It also snowed and so was still cold even though it was spring.

From Kaliningrad, I cycled up a narrow spit of land known as the Curonian Spit, a narrow stretch of land and sand dunes approximately 100 km in length. It was cold and there was still snow on the ground. After 80 kilometers I crossed the border into Lithuania with a much easier crossing than before.

Most places in Lithuania were closed for the Easter Monday holiday. I found a café for food, and then shortly later a woman approached who brought her young English-speaking daughter over to help negotiate a room in a small cabin. I was cold, but getting out of the wet weather was a nice relief.

Baltic Republics

The next few weeks brought me through the Baltic Republics. While these were once part of the Soviet Union, the contrast was immediate. For example, the countryside still had an occasional monument to the Russian army as liberators of the area. Most all these, however, had fallen into disuse, with little maintenance or repair. It is in the eye of the beholder whether one is a liberator or an oppressor.

This struck me when I visited Riga, the capital of Latvia. In the middle of town was a large concrete building that housed a museum titled, "History of the Occupation, 1940-1991." Inside I found a fascinating set of displays that carefully chronicled how independent Latvia was forced by Russia in 1940 to accept bases, to make changes to laws and otherwise bend to the more powerful Russian neighbor. In 1941 the Germans attacked Russia and came and occupied Latvia.

The Red Army fought back and recaptured Latvia in 1944. What was fascinating in the museum was that rather than liberation, the recapture was considered just a different stage of oppression. The museum dioramas continued and now showed pictures from the gulag camps and similar Soviet features. This history continued until 1991, when Latvia was finally independent again.

In similar fashion, there was an event in neighboring Estonia that happened close to the time I traveled through. Some Red Army soldiers were buried near the center of Tallinn, the capital of Estonia. The Estonian government had decided to disinter and rebury them in a less prominent location. This led to protests and riots both amongst Russian-speaking populations in Estonia and in Russia itself. One person's liberator is another's oppressor.

As I came through Estonia, I had one day where I struck up a conversation with a fellow cyclist. His name was Indrek, and he described himself as a teacher, philosopher, and bicyclist. We cycled for multiple kilometers as he told me about the area. He asked if I was interested in taking more of a back route. That seemed intriguing, and we took a side road past several little lakes. This slowly brought us to the town of Rakvere, where there was a large castle.

We negotiated our prices, and I got a chance to explore the castle further. Somehow there was also a reporter there who interviewed me for the local paper. By evening they helped me find a local hotel.

The reporter was kind enough to send an English translation of the story which was as follows:

> "Mike Vermeulen (43) arrived yesterday in Rakvere. He is on his way from Amsterdam to Vladivostok. The from origin Dutch biker started in Amsterdam on March 26 and his goal is to finish at the end of September after 13,500 kilometers.
>
> Mike said that until now he had quite a smooth and trouble-free trip. He had some problems at the border of Russia near Kalingrad. With the help of a local microbus driver he was able to get by bike over the Russian border. The Russian border guards didn't believe that one person would have such a crazy plan to travel!
>
> Mike first visited the historical castle in Rakvere. After staying overnight, he continued his journey to Narva. He said: 'I will go to St. Petersburg and plan to study Russian for a good continuation of my travel in Russia.' Answering to the question of Virumaa Teataja 'Are you afraid of Russia' Mike said 'Should I?'
>
> Mike has experience from several bike trips. He has traveled in Hungary and Ukraine last year and five years ago he made a trip all around Australia (8 months and 19,000 kilometers) Why do it? Mike says 'This is my way to relax. By bicycle I will see people and things in another way.' He is manager at a computer company. 'My job enables me to have a long vacation for this trip' says Mike.
>
> Mike pedals 100 km's a day and will lose 20 kg's of weight per 10,000 km's."

It was the day following Rakvere that I discovered my front wheel had a set of cracks appearing. Better safe than sorry so I made a stop in the next town, Narva, to replace my front wheel with a new wheel they had available.

From Narva it was a short ride across the border into Russia. This time it went much more smoothly as I was on a crossing that allowed cyclists and pedestrians to cross. Russia has since changed its visitation policies, but they even helped me fill out the forms. When asked how long I expected to stay, I requested "December." I fully expected to leave the country far before them, but it was easier to have too long a time period in the passport than one that was too short.

Saint Petersburg

I stayed two nights in the border town of Gatchina before cycling into the big city of St. Petersburg on a Sunday morning. Here I was enrolled in three weeks of language classes. As part of the class, I had arranged a "home stay" with a local family. As it turns out, I didn't have many interactions with the home family as it seemed that it was mostly a woman renting an extra bedroom in her home. She also had a daughter, whom I barely saw once or twice. However, it was a nice break from cycling and chance to store away the bicycle and be a student for three weeks.

My routine was now to wake up, eat breakfast and either walk or take the subway to the language school. I then went through my language drills until one or two p.m. in the afternoon. After this I had a chance to walk through Saint Petersburg as well as practice my new Russian phrases on local shopkeepers and other locals. It was a nice break from the bicycling trip.

My stay in Saint Petersburg coincided with two large holiday celebrations. The first was May 1st, the traditional workers' day. The school was closed, and I went out to watch the parade in the city. May 1st has perhaps been less prominent in more recent years, particularly in St. Petersburg. However, this was a chance for the hardline Stalinists to march. The U.S. Consulate had put out some warnings to watch for potential clashes, but the parade itself was heavily guarded and otherwise peaceful.

The larger holiday was the May 9th victory celebration. This was a huge deal, particularly in St. Petersburg, where the city was surrounded for nearly 900 days during World War II and several million people had starved or otherwise perished. It had been 62 years since end of the second world war, and there were still some marchers who, as children, had lived through the war in St. Petersburg. Also along the route was one painted warning that bombs/missiles would hit this side of the street. Flowers memorialized the location.

Many different groups marched, from political groups to one that was protesting a recent reburial of Soviet soldiers in Tallinn, Estonia. There were groups in uniform and others, all with the general theme of victory and praise for the military for freeing the city. I even saw one jeep with a U.S. flag to commemorate the lend-lease program and U.S. assistance.

Otherwise, I spent a nice three weeks in St Petersburg being a student. I took some afternoons to visit museums and one weekend to visit nearby Peterhof gardens and another to see Catherine's Palace nearby. It was a good intermission both to learn Russian as well as experience a more relaxed time in Russia's second largest city.

Leaving St. Petersburg

Mickey cycled up the last few days I was in Saint Petersburg. She stayed in a local hostel as I had a few more nights in my home stay. On May 12th, we were ready to depart.

As we met on the morning of May 12th, Mickey had a horrible toothache. She had fallen on her tooth several weeks before. It was initially ok, but when she was crossing at Narva, it had first acted up. She went to a local dentist in Estonia, and they told her there wasn't much to do other than pull the tooth. That seemed extreme, and the pain was subsiding, so she figured she could tough it out.

Unfortunately, it all acted back up again the night before our departure. We both knew that dental facilities wouldn't get better after St. Petersburg and so we needed to get things taken care of before leaving the city. Without much difficulty we asked around and found a referral to a dentist that could handle the situation. We cycled over, and the dentist took care of the tooth and gave Mickey some pain killers. All this took perhaps the first half day.

Mickey felt a bit embarrassed and perhaps more concerned that on our first day cycling together here she was creating a big problem. I didn't see it that way, and instead viewed it as another part of the adventure and something you just take care of. However, she didn't know me very well yet, and so it seemed awkward that first day.

The other piece of news Mickey had intended to let me know was her age, 62, and history as a cancer survivor. Neither of these was a huge concern for me, but she had been careful not to let the information out for fear that it might make me decide not to cycle together. Neither would have made a difference, but she didn't know that. This information didn't come out until a few weeks later, and by that time it was clear that Mickey was a stronger cyclist than I and rather than my waiting for her, it was more often the other way around.

We left through some rather hectic roads before eventually finding our way to a quieter countryside. Towards the end of the day, we started what I would describe as our "water ritual." A short distance before end of the day we would ask around at a small town or village where we might get water. Sometimes it was a well, sometimes a pump house, sometimes someone would go into their house, but we would then end up with ~10 liters or water we could use for cooking and cleaning.

That first night I also had another surprise. The tent I brought with me turned out to be a one-person tent rather than a two-person tent. This still worked fine, though surprisingly I hadn't set up my new tent before this point and hence didn't discover it until the first night on the road from Saint Petersburg.

Cycling European Russia
As we cycled the next several weeks, we soon settled into patterns and rhythms that worked for the ride.

Mickey was a faster cyclist. This can make it more difficult to spend all your time riding together as the slower cyclist (myself) can feel as though he is holding things up, while the faster cyclist (Mickey) can also find herself waiting more often. Hence, I started leaving earlier in the morning. Mickey would have a little more time to break camp, and then would pass me sometime in the morning. She might wait once or twice at a road intersection or at a café. At the end of the day, we would meet again to find a nearby village and fill up on water before cycling another 5-10 kilometers to find a quiet place to camp.

Wild camping is common in Russia, where motorists also may pull off the road to find a place to camp. While there is private property, one holdover from earlier days is that most land is state-owned and hence outside the villages there are few places with fences.

Over the years my style had developed to staying in a hotel with bed and shower when I find them and otherwise camping in other areas. Also, while I had a stove, I was more inclined to buy "no cook" food or eat in a café along the way. Mickey was more inclined to buy food to cook and more often to find a place to camp.

There were few choices for hotels, and we ended up camping for five nights before reaching the first larger city of Cherepovets, a somewhat smelly steel town. Here we found a small hotel and booked for two nights to give ourselves a rest day and chance to check on the internet, do laundry and complete other chores. That also established a pattern we would follow later of riding 6-10 days between larger cities and hence camping for a week or so before coming into a larger town and taking a rest day.

The roads were rough at times, particularly those that had started out as concrete highways and been allowed to deteriorate. My rear wheel developed a few cracks around the spoke holes. This caused some concern, particularly early in the trip, but in the days following, the cracks didn't seem to get much worse, so I figured I would ride and see what happened.

Near St. Petersburg we had colder nights and even one night camped in an area with lingering snow fields. In the following weeks of May, it slowly became warmer both during the days as well as overnight. There were also occasional thunder showers but no longer rainy days.

Once past Yaroslav we reached the Volga River and found ourselves on a route that roughly followed the river. This area still had many small villages and an occasional church that had fallen into ruins. The routes weren't always well marked, but we would stop and ask for directions. Locals were helpful and friendly to help us find our way and curious about our travels. In one of those towns, I found myself in an interview with local radio reporters. I didn't ever hear the outcome of the interview or talk with someone who heard it.

In another town a local mayor invited us to view the museum and to stay in a town hotel. We politely declined and ended up camping not far out of town that evening.

As we neared the larger city of Niznhy, Novgorod, we decided to bypass the city by crossing the Volga River and cycling on the other side. We had a longer ride planned to Makarjewo, and this was the day we lost each other – only to meet at the end.

I had started riding first, and Mickey came past after I had ridden 10 kilometers on the road. I cycled along and at 20 kilometers missed a turn for what would have been a shortcut. I didn't realize it right away, and it took another 30 kilometers before I adjusted and found my way back to the main road. However, I now wasn't certain which road Mickey had taken and hence whether I was behind or ahead. So, I mostly kept going to our intended destination. Fortunately, once there I saw a familiar bicycle. We compared notes and had surprisingly similar stories. Mickey had also found the route confusing, missed a turn, and waited for a short while before deciding it was better to continue in case I had been on the other road.

There was an old monastery here under restoration. One of the nuns came to invite us in and brought someone from the kitchen who spoke English. She carefully explained that no lodging was available but we were welcome to visit two of the churches. We made some quick looks before camping on the outskirts of town.

The next morning we took the 9 a.m. ferry back across the Volga River and began what would be one of our most difficult days. While the route started out on smaller roads, we soon found ourselves on the M7 Motorway, one of the larger routes across Russia. The road had a lot of trucks and started out OK, but we then came to an area of road construction with traffic diverted into one very rough lane. This was an obnoxious ride, with many of these trucks wanting to pass. I tried alternatives of walking or riding through closed areas, but they weren't much better. Finally, after 25 kilometers we got through this section.

Unfortunately, the road didn't improve after that. The edges of the road had deteriorated, and the roadway had also developed deep ruts. There wasn't anywhere good to ride, and I kept looking in my mirror to decide whether to stay in the ruts or veer off to avoid an oncoming truck. Mickey didn't have a cycling mirror and found it even worse. When we decided to call it quits after only 77 kilometers, the hotel we treated ourselves to had problems, including no running water. Mickey told me that evening I was welcome to ride on this big highway – but if I did, she would find other smaller roads instead.

We got out our maps, and after a short section of M7, we got ourselves on smaller country roads. It was a day and night difference. While the road surfaces weren't necessarily much better, we no longer had to contend with the truck traffic. We also came through several small villages where we were even more of a spectacle than before. In one of these villages, I found several people crowded around Mickey. It turned out that this was the day of the town festival with singing, dancing, and athletic games. We hung around for a short while, had a shish-kabob and then continued our route.

The following day as I was riding along, I saw Mickey's bicycle up against a house but didn't see her. I heard a knock on the window and saw her inside. She had been photographing a woman carrying water with two pails hung around her neck who noticed and invited her in. We had a good conversation, tea, and bread, and out came the photo albums. The woman was originally from Uzbekistan and had immigrated to Russia after the Soviet Union had fallen apart and there wasn't work in Tashkent. She worked as a nurse and had three sons. She enjoyed traveling and had many photos of visits to East Germany as well as the Baltic states. This was no longer possible due to visa reasons. We saw family in different photographs and had a pleasant visit.

After this the road worsened further and we found ourselves on a mud road in the countryside between two towns. Fortunately, a more normal road continued once we reached the town. After camping that evening we had only 40 kilometers and a ferry ride to the larger city of Kazan. In Kazan we found a reasonable hotel and were back in the pattern of a rest day in a larger city.

Lost in the Urals

We left Kazan at 6 a.m., as the weather forecast called for a hot (39C, 102F) day. This had the added advantage that the roads were still quiet. My GI tract had acted up some the previous evening, but some Imodium helped. Before leaving I mentioned to Mickey that I wasn't feeling 100%.

We both left at the same time, and at 10 kilometers I came to an intersection where Mickey was waiting. There was a small village at the 35 kilometer point where I expected to see Mickey. I was surprised not to see her there, since Mickey would often have stopped already either at a gas station or café. As we later pieced out together, Mickey had stopped somewhere earlier, but I had passed by, and neither of us had seen the other.

This put us in an unfortunate situation. I thought I was still behind, and since it was becoming warm, I kept going so as not to keep her waiting too long. When I got hungry, I stopped for a short break at 63 kilometers and then for lunch at 100 kilometers. In the early afternoon when I had cycled 118 kilometers, I stopped for the day and pitched my tent in a location where I could see the road and keep an eye out in case Mickey passed.

Meanwhile, Mickey remembered my comment about not feeling 100% and was more patient than normal in waiting for me. Eventually, when I didn't appear, she thought I might be stopped beside the road sick and turned back to see if she could find me. She cycled all the way back to our hotel from the previous night. By now the city traffic was busier and complicated by a power outage that stopped the electric trams. It took her long enough that she decided to stay back in the hotel that evening and get back on the road the next day.

We could have avoided our dilemma if we had had Russian SIM cards, not necessarily to call, but a simple text message would easily have sorted things out. Unfortunately, we had not taken this extra precaution. The other possibility was an internet contact. I knew the post offices often had a few internet-linked computers and decided to keep an eye out for upcoming post offices.

Mickey didn't show up that evening. I asked several Russians I met along the way if they had seen a cycle tourist with red panniers but those relies turned up negative. Still not sure what had happened, I decided to proceed. I was 40 kilometers from the wide Batka River where a ferry service crossed the river four times per day. I figured that was one last possibility for a meeting point, and otherwise it would be time to stop at the next post office.

Mickey wasn't at the Batka River either. I briefly lost my wallet there but was fortunate to circle back and find where it had fallen on the grass when I stopped. Once on the other side, there were 24 kilometers of unpaved road, including some tough pushing through sand. This made for a shorter ride.

On the following day, the route split, with the main road a longer and more certain path and a shortcut heading more directly east and across gravel roads. By now there were enough splits in the route that I had given up on finding Mickey ahead and instead would try using the internet. Unfortunately, the towns also became sparser and in one of the only post offices I found, all the terminals were in use by teenagers, and I wasn't certain when they might be free. So, I put this behind me and figured it would all sort itself out once I came to more populated areas.

Over the next few days I cycled into an area of small oil wells. One evening after I had done my familiar wild camping off the road, I was startled by three armed guards outside my tent. The tent was bright orange, so I wasn't particularly trying to hide. However, the guards let me know that I was unexpected next to their oil wells. With some halting Russian conversation, I told them of my trip, and they agreed to let me camp overnight and leave the next morning.

The boundaries between oblasts, administrative divisions like "states" or "provinces," often still have a less connected road network than within an oblast. It was in one of those boundaries that my Russian maps showed a faint road that looked like a shorter distance than the normal route. I asked several locals if this road was paved. A truck driver assured me it was a paved route.

At the road intersection I discovered this was incorrect and the road was gravel. Not to worry, my map told me it would be another 26 kilometers to the small village of Altynoe and then 28 kilometers after that. Another 54 kilometers of gravel would be slower but otherwise still fine to ride.

As I was cycling along this gravel road, another truck driver stopped and asked if I had a map. I showed him my map, and he told me it wouldn't make sense to cycle all the way to the village but instead to turn at the preceding village, Ozerki, 7 kilometers earlier, and take a shortcut across. When I asked what this shortcut looked like, he pointed out a nearby rutted path.

At Ozerki there wasn't just one rutted path but what seemed like several, so I stayed on the main road to Altynoe. Altynoe had a small store and a ruin of a church. Otherwise, it had an "end of the road" feel. Despite being on both my maps, two different locals told me the road to the next town didn't exist and suggested I follow local paths roughly north and overland. I now had a dilemma, since I had spent 26 kilometers riding on a gravel road to get to Altynoe, and it would be a shame to ride all the way back again. However, I also couldn't be certain that I would find the route across to the next town.

I found a rough path that went mostly the way the locals suggested and walked another 12 kilometers before setting up my tent for the night. I figured I would walk farther the next morning and hopefully find my way to a highway again. Overall, I gave myself a "budget" of 30 kilometers total before I would declare myself lost and backtrack to Altynoe and then to the main road.

The next morning the path continued and I was even able to cycle short portions. After 13 kilometers I crested a small hill and spotted a small village below. There were cars in the town and their license plates started with "59," so I knew I had crossed into the next oblast even if I wasn't sure of my location. Leaving the town the road became paved, and soon I saw a sign for a town on the main highway. My shortcut had worked!

Two days along this main highway and I reached the large city of Ekaterinburg. Here I found a large hotel not far from center of town and booked for two nights to take a rest day. It had been ten days cycling since we had left Kazan and Mickey and I had missed each other. In the afternoon I found an internet café and sent out an email that essentially said, "not sure how we lost each other, but here are my plans."

My front hub had developed a strange wobble, so I also brought the bike to a bike shop, where they diagnosed it as a ball bearing that had disintegrated. The wheel was one I had bought in Estonia and wasn't the highest quality, but it rode better once the bearing was replaced.

On the morning of my rest day, I was leaving the hotel to walk through town when I spied a familiar bicycle. Mickey had arrived that morning. We compared stories and figured out what had happened. Once she had returned to Kazan, she knew I was ahead but also didn't know my location. She had been cycling slightly longer days to catch up but one of those days made a wrong turn and ended up 60 kilometers off-route before getting a ride back. Locals had been able to tell her I was still ahead once she described me as a large guy with a beard. However, it had been pure happenstance that we had both picked the same hotel in a city of 1.5 million people and that I had wandered past just around the time she arrived and parked her bicycle.

I made reservations for another night in the hotel, and we agreed we would take a bit more care to avoid missing each other in the future.

Mosquitoes and the West Siberian Plain

Shortly before Ekaterinburg I had crossed over from Europe to Asia. In this area the Ural Mountains are mostly lower hills, and I didn't see a sign or other indication. However, at some point I crossed a continental divide where waters now flowed to the Arctic instead of the Atlantic and was now in Asia. In the days leaving Ekaterinburg, the landscape became flatter, and there were fewer trees.

Flatter landscape brought marshy terrain along the roadways and the start of what would be more than a month of the worst mosquito and flying insect regions I have encountered. While I had been to individual places in Alaska and Yukon Territory with many mosquitoes, what made this part of Russia particularly severe was the consistency. With the exception of largest cities, such as Novosibirsk and Omsk, the bugs were there day in and day out. When we stopped along the road, there were many bugs. Stopping too long meant keeping a careful eye looking for the large deer flies that would pause briefly after landing before making a painful sting.

It was worst when we would stop to find a place to camp for the night. This led to a specific approach. First, after stopping, we would don our mosquito nets and raingear to cover up any bare skin. Out would come our tents that we would quickly set up. Once the tents were up and gear stowed, we would dive into our tents, zip up the door and spend some time squishing any bugs that had gotten inside. From that point in the afternoon until we departed the next morning, we would spend the entire time inside our tents behind the bug netting. The next morning we would reverse the process with a quick departure. On some days the bugs were bad enough that we would wait to go to the bathroom until a few kilometers down the road outside the worst bug zones.

The roads in Siberia became somewhat better than we had seen in European Russia. While there were still sections of poor roads, these were less frequent, and we no longer had the worst deteriorated concrete roads. We stayed on the major highways, and these continued to have cafes every 45 kilometers or so where trucks and other traffic would stop. There were also still small villages to get water and some small towns.

We met different people along the road, including those in a set of antique cars on a 100th anniversary ride of the "Peking to Paris" rally. Also we found that people were friendly particularly as we stopped in the smaller villages. They tended to separate some by gender, with the women approaching Mickey and men approaching both of us. There were, unfortunately, a few spots where drunk people in these towns also approached. They thought they were witty but mostly ended up being annoying pests. Fortunately, they were not too difficult to avoid.

The long flat steppes region meant cycling wasn't difficult, particularly in days when we also had a tail wind. We had a few days of rain here but mostly dry and warmer weather. We were in the middle of summer, and a few days were particularly warm. Otherwise, I found this part of Russia to have a lot of similarity from day to day. There were more trees than on the Great Plains in the U.S. or Canada, but, otherwise, a lot of repetition in riding though similar looking landscapes.

The three largest cities we crossed, Omsk, Novosibirsk and Krasnoyarsk, were a contrast to the countryside that surrounded them. Each was a large urban area with a city core surrounded my residential areas and industrial zones. In each we found a hotel close to the city center and took a rest day. In Novosibirsk, it was two rest days. These were big contrasts from our tents in mosquito-infested areas and a chance to get laundry done and take care of other errands.

In Novosibirsk I found a local bike shop and brought my bike in for service. When I mentioned that we were cycling from Amsterdam to Vladivostok, the shop owner told me, "You are not the first." He showed me a wall with photos of several cross-country cyclists in front of the shop. He also showed me a scrapbook with notes and some photos. I counted three from the Netherlands, two from Japan, one from Canada, half a dozen from Germany, one from Austria, one from Switzerland and one or two from Russia. There were some impressive rides among the collection. For example, one of the Japanese had ridden from Magadan to Murmansk during the winter. It was also interesting to read some of the "I came to the shop with broken X" accounts of parts people had had repaired.

As we checked, we also noticed that the axle on my front hub was either bent or broken. This was the same wheel that had already lost a ball bearing and was only so-so in quality when I bought it in Estonia. While the wheel still spun, it was a bit rough, and there was noticeable up and down movement. The shop had a good parts supply, including a higher quality hub, so I had them rebuild a front wheel with a new hub and my existing rim.

Two days after leaving Novosibirsk we took one of the smaller back roads rather than the main highway. We came past an army base and over the next 45 kilometers were cycling alongside Russian army tanks. They were riding on small paths alongside the road and were traveling at approximately the same speed as we were on the road. Folks in the tanks seemed friendly and even responded to waves from us cyclists. Mickey discretely took a photo or two. I was a little more cautious and decided not to take photos.

Not far from town of Kemerovo, two reporters flagged us down, and we gave our third press interview (first one in Estonia and the second a little past St. Petersburg). They tended to ask similar questions as we often got along the road, e.g. Where are you going? How long will it take? How do you like Russia? My Russian was fine for this sort of conversation, and I got chances to practice it most days. Even on occasion the police would ask us these same questions. Before traveling I had read stories and was concerned about bureaucracy and being stopped by the police. While we were stopped at least a dozen times, it was much more for idle curiosity than anything official. On not one of those stops was I ever asked to show any identification or anything official.

As we cycled past, people would occasionally yell out, "Otkuda," meaning "Where are you from?" When asked this way by a stranger, I would respond, "iz Gallandia" or "iz Amsterdam" rather than from the U.S. It wasn't so much that I had concern about revealing U.S. nationality in Russia, as often the U.S. was widely admired or seen positively. However, on occasion people would have strange pre-conceived notions as if we were all rich or lived like people in Hollywood films. Russians seemed to have fewer pre-conceived notions about Dutch people and beyond windmills or wooden shoes, it was more common to bring up names of Dutch football players from the Ajax football team. While I also didn't know the Ajax players, if someone gave me an unknown name, I would ask "Ajax?" and often I was correct.

An answer of "Iz Amsterdam" was technically correct if misleading. I had been born in the Netherlands, and we had started our trip in Amsterdam. Mickey was also Dutch. However, when asked in a more official capacity, such as in our Kemerovo newspaper interview or checking into a hotel, I would more precisely answer that I was a U.S. citizen.

The city of Krasnoyarsk was one of my favorite Russian cities. While many of the cities are similar, with large concrete squares not far from a central railway station, Krasnoyarsk had a smaller feel to it. There was music on some of the streets, and people seemed friendly. I was a bit surprised at how "white" the people seemed in these towns, as now we were no longer as far away from Central Asia or even China. I also seemed to be one of the few people with a beard.

The other thing I noticed was an increased percentage of left-hand drive automobiles. Apparently, many of these had started in Japan and then been imported into Russia.

Not long after Krasnoyarsk we came to a construction zone and the first of what would be longer stretches of gravel roads. We saw our first vehicles with taped up windows to guard against flying rocks. Also, at times there would be one vehicle towing another or a small vehicle up in bed of a larger truck. As we would later discover, we learned that many of these vehicles originated in Japan, where the second-hand car market led to declining prices. Entrepreneurs drove the cars across the gravel roads and resold them in the larger cities, particularly in Siberia.

In the days following Krasnoyarsk, we noticed some subtle changes. The mosquitoes gradually became less severe. The roads more frequently had gravel patches. People more often would ask us "Baikal?" It took some days, but we were slowly approaching Irkutsk and the Lake Baikal area.

Baikal!

It was a great feeling to climb the last hill and look out on the waters of Lake Baikal. We had traveled more than 8800 kilometers since Amsterdam, and Baikal was the one place I had most anticipated. The lake itself is large and contains approximately 20% of the world's fresh water that is not ice. This makes both a large lake and one that is particularly deep.

Our ride from Irkutsk had been the hilliest day cycling since Amsterdam. At one point a local cyclist came past. As we talked, we learned he was a Russian speed skater who was cross training by cycling up these hills. After our conversation he quickly left us and our loaded touring bicycles far behind.

That morning we had left the city of Irkutsk. Irkutsk was a popular tourist destination and had a different feel to it than other large cities we had crossed. Many of these tourists were crossing large parts of Russia by train, and Irkutsk must have been one of the most popular stops to get out and visit. We had spent five nights in Irkutsk in both a hotel and a hostel.

It took us several days to slowly make our way past Lake Baikal. The waters were clear and cold, and we camped close to the shore. Nearby was the Trans-Siberian Railroad, with several trains through the day and night. We crossed multiple rivers that emptied into Baikal.

After several days we came to Ulan-Ude. One claim to fame for Ulan-Ude is that it is the site of the world's largest Lenin head. This area also had more Buryati peoples with more similarity to Mongolian and Chinese. We had also seen more Buddhist monuments with prayer flags tied to the trees on our ride prior to Ulan-Ude.

My brother Bert and sister-in-law Jean also met us in Ulan-Ude. It was like Christmas in July as Bert had brought several supplies. Of most concern was a new rear wheel. My previous wheel had developed ominous cracks around some of the spoke holes. When we replaced the wheel, I looked more carefully, and while none of the holes looked much worse, I did discover a crack was starting to split the sidewall of the rim. Hence, it was fortuitous timing to be able to replace the wheel. It was also nice to get some spare brake pads, new toe straps and other supplies.

Bert had also brought his bicycle, and the plan was for him to join us from Chita, a little way down the road. So, it was also welcome that he brought a two-person tent to replace the one-person tent I had accidentally brought with me.

It took us a week to bicycle to Chita. Along the way we crossed a continental divide and were now in the watershed that drained to the Pacific Ocean. Previously, all waters had drained to the Arctic Ocean.

The night before we arrived in Chita, we had what was our most disconcerting encounter with local people. As had been our normal plan, we stopped at end of the day to fill up on water for cooking and washing. After that we went another 10 kilometers to find a place to camp. Our campsite looked fine and was near some small lakes. What we had not realized was that it was also not far from the next village and a popular place for locals to visit.

Two guys came over when they spotted my orange tent. I was sitting inside the tent with the door open and my panniers off the bike and in front. The conversation started out as they often do with an "Otkuda?"

and my reply that I was from Amsterdam. We then talked about Dutch football and the Ajax team players. However, not much later some of the questions took a more ominous tone. They asked if I was traveling alone. They had not seen Mickey's tent, perhaps forty feet away and dark green. I said no and mentioned that my brother was joining me.

They next asked if I had any money. That seemed like a strange question and I became a bit more guarded and careful. Hence, when their next question was whether I had any matches, my answer was a more immediate "No." They seemed baffled and said, "Not even for tea?" I again said "No."

One of the guys reached over to my pannier as if he wanted to open it. At that point I got up out of my tent and stretched to my full 6-foot 4-inch height. I put my hand on his chest and loudly and firmly said in English, "DON'T TOUCH!" I pushed him back and away from the pannier. I crossed my arms and scowled.

The conversation took a quick turn, and the guy's friend tried to defuse the situation, saying, "Be calm, can't we talk about football?" At this point, I had had enough and wasn't going to risk a misunderstanding, so I decided I would stick to English. I also let my body language clearly indicate the conversation was over.

Fortunately, they got the message, and, after a short bit, they both decided to leave. After that conversation, I thought things through a bit more. I am pretty sure they had both had a bit to drink before arriving, and that didn't help their behavior. I also am not quite sure what to make of some of their more disconcerting questions about money or whether I was traveling by myself – but decided it was also better to be safe than sorry, and, if it happened again, I would take a similar tack.

For all the stories and cautions I had heard about Russia, including about mafia, corruption, bribes, and similar tales – it was also reassuring that this turned out to be the most disconcerting event and in the overall scheme of things wasn't particularly menacing or with a poor outcome.

The upcoming section of road after Chita was one about which we had heard the most tales, including ones of 1700+ kilometers of road construction. Car drivers often traveled in packs for safety. Tales described abandoned cars, sometimes burned, since if they broke down, there would be no way to get them fixed. This supposedly was also an area influenced by Russian crime gangs.

I wasn't certain how many of these tales were true and how many exaggerated in their retelling. However, we would soon find out once we passed Chita.

Chita and the Amur Highway

In the week preceding our arrival into Chita, the landscapes had changed to drier, open valleys that reminded me of the American west—with places like the dry grasslands of Colorado. The terrain was mostly flat, though it seemed the road builders had found some of the available hills and built the roads up and down along the edges of the valleys.

We took a rest day in Chita and prepared for the road ahead. This would be our last larger city before the Amur Highway. We weren't sure how often we might be able to send out updates. Bert had brought a cell phone, and one thing we found worked reasonably well and inexpensively was to send short SMS messages with our GPS coordinates.

The first day and a half was still paved road. On the day we reached gravel, I stopped briefly to celebrate 10,000 kilometers cycled since Amsterdam. There was still construction here, though I also found one of the bridges marked as September 1995, so work on this road had been going on for a while. Despite Putin's 2004 election claim of a fully paved road by 2008, in 2007 there remained ~1500 kilometers of gravel.

What we found was most of this gravel road was wide but in varying condition. Often there were piles of loose gravel graded over a very hard surface underneath. At times this led to conditions of having a road that was simultaneously too hard and too soft. The hard parts were washboard road underneath, and the soft parts were loose gravel.

Most of the vehicles we met were coming from the other direction. These were often small Japanese cars with right side steering wheels being driven in groups of three to nine vehicles. These had temporary "in-transit" stickers instead of license plates for their sale in Siberian cities. They came past raising clouds of dust that took several minutes to settle.

One morning I counted and found approximately 100 vehicles coming the other way in an hour. This meant a lot of time spent in dusty conditions. Occasionally, the road was a softer clay. This sometimes hardened into washboard roads but also was sometimes softer and easier to ride.

At the end of our second day of gravel road cycling, we spotted a hay field with newly harvest hay placed in haystacks. We asked the locals if we might camp. Bert's Russian was better than mine, and we soon learned more of the story.

In days of the Soviet Union, this had been a larger collective farm. When the Soviet Union collapsed and many of the workers left, this local family had gained control (not sure of ownership) of the land and now farmed it. It was a tough and simple life, but they had what they needed in terms of hay, livestock, and basics on their farm.

The next day we were delighted to find 75 kilometers of new freshly paved roads. This was part of the recently completed road construction. This road went past a small village. As I understand things, after completion of the Trans-Siberian Railroad in 1916, the Russian government forcibly settled people into many of these small villages along the railroad route. When it came time to build a road, the road came past many of the villages and hence was typically not far from the railroad. There was one section of approximately 200 kilometers where the railway and and the road took separate routes and there were also no villages, but, for the most part, we were never very far from villages. In my experience the northwest parts of Australia had larger gaps between settlements and services than this sparsely settled part of Siberia. However, in both cases, if one had left the primary roads, one would have been in vast unsettled regions.

The bumps and rattles took a toll on our bikes. Bert discovered several screws missing from his racks. My front rack brackets broke several times, and I had to get inventive on how to attach the rack to the front fork. Problems with my type of front rack had happened to others and not long after my trip, the manufacturer, Surly, redesigned the rack and sent me a new set of brackets.

When we filled up on provisions, I placed food in a bag that I tied on top of my panniers. One morning I awoke to find the bag missing. Apparently, a dog had come by and taken off with my bag. I more carefully guarded my food after that experience. Other than some local dogs, it surprised me how little wildlife we encountered in our travels on this highway. In contrast, in Canada I would have encountered moose or bears along similar roads.

After finding replacement food, we had a day where we decided to deviate from the main highway. There was a service road that ran along the railroad tracks. The road was narrower and had some steeper hills. The surface wasn't much better than the new road, but it had the advantage of far fewer cars to raise the ever-present dust. We did have to ford a river with our bikes as there wasn't a bridge.

A little past that point, we reached a smaller town of Mogocha and made a reservation for two nights and a planned a rest day. Bert departed at this point, and we were back to two cyclists on the road. In total, we had cycled 432 kilometers on gravel roads with a lot more still to come.

After Mogocha turned out to be some of our toughest cycling. We were back to the main road and all the dusty, washboard and loose gravel conditions. In frustration, we tried finding a local path along the railroad tracks again, only to go for a few kilometers before finding the route impassable, with large mud puddles and not much path. Reluctantly, we retreated to the main road.

The following day, near the village of Amazar, Mickey had been sick overnight. She felt bad enough that we cycled into Amazar and considered our options. As best we understood the helpful woman, the passenger train stopped here but the one with baggage cars didn't. Hence, if we had wanted to travel with our bikes, we would need to cycle at least another 100 kilometers to the next town that did have a baggage stop. We instead cycled back to the woods slightly outside Amazar and camped.

The next day it was raining, and Mickey was still sick, so we camped out in the woods as a rest day.

The rain had mostly stopped, and Mickey felt better after a day and half of sickness, so we were back on the road. Mickey was still feeling weak, and we discussed the possibility of taking a train from the town in two days riding.

For once I was cycling ahead, and Mickey was behind. As I came up a larger hill, a large auto transport stopped. Mickey's bike was tied out back, and she was up in the cab. She had flagged down Victor and Valerie and gotten a lift. We tied up my bike, and I got in the cab as well.

Victor and Valerie were in the auto transport business. Every two weeks they would make a round trip from Vladivostok to Krasnoyarsk to pick up a new set of used Japanese cars. Their huge trailer held eight cars but was now empty on the return trip. They were happy to give us a lift and wouldn't accept payment.

We traveled with them until the end of the day, a total of 263 kilometers. This was some of the roughest roads yet with a lot of construction, including several temporary bridges for new spans under construction. It took more than eight hours to travel that 263km; we averaged less than 30km/h (20 miles per hour), so it was slow going and likely would have taken us a week to travel the same distance.

This was the only section of the trip across Eurasia that we didn't bicycle. While it meant not riding every single inch of the route, in hindsight we had also gotten to the point where, with sickness and road conditions, we weren't in a position to enjoy the ride.

Fortunately, as we cycled the next day, we found the road surfaces, while still gravel, had improved from before. Our hitchhiking had gotten us past the worst of the Amur Highway construction. It was also nice to look at the map and realize we were getting to the halfway point of our gravel riding. Unfortunately, the following afternoon we ended with a rainy afternoon. It rained all the next day as well, and so we camped in the woods rather than try to ride on the muddy surfaces.

It was still lightly raining, but we had eaten most of our food, so we set off after our rest day. Some of the road surfaces were what I called "peanut butter roads," soft and creamy in texture. It took some extra care to avoid the worst of the road surfaces. We at least got ourselves to the next village and could replenish our food stocks. Unfortunately, as we were doing this, Mickey had parked her bike and some local hoodlums had stolen her pump. I had an extra pump with me, however, so I could lend her that one.

In the evening prospects of another night camping in a wet tent in the rain were unappealing. We were surprised to find an old abandoned factory. It was a bit of a cave, with the far recesses dark. However, we could clean off some of the concrete surfaces and remove a bunch of the broken glass and camp inside.

The sun came out the morning after our camping in the abandoned factory, and road surfaces quickly became better. Over the following days we started to encounter more sections of pavement as well. Locals and those traveling the road still thought we were a novelty, however, and more often wanted to stop and take our photos. There was a larger town of Svobodny, where we took a rest day. We were ~2/3 of the way along the Amur Highway, and it was nice to get showers and wash dirty clothes.

At the end of one day of cycling, we found the locals surprisingly hostile when we stopped to ask for water. At one house, we knocked on the door, and, when a woman saw us with our bike helmets, promptly turned back and went into the house. It took a little bit to figure what had caused the sudden change in reactions.

We had met a local cycling group from Poland a day or two earlier. They were on a supported ride from Poland all the way across Russia, staying with local churches. They were also using this as an occasion to spread a religious message and had appeared on the local TV station with a story about their trip. As best we could figure, these locals now assumed we were there to evangelize door to door (or perhaps had already encountered this group) and wanted to clearly express that they weren't interested.

Fortunately, the case of mistaken identity was only on that one day, and locals became friendlier again after that point. We also had our own TV interview with local television Station 12 one day after leaving Svobodny.

On the first of September, we came past a turnoff to the small village of Apxapa. The village wasn't on the main road, but we came to a large bridge and decided to get our water there. The bridge was guarded, and when we asked the guards for water, they told us they would fill up our personal bottles with water and we could get washing water from the river. As we walked in to get the water, one of the German shepherd dogs walked along and unexpectedly bit Mickey behind the knee. The guards apologized and got out a first aid kit to bandage the wound. We cycled another 10 kilometers up the hill and camped.

Mickey and I had discussed immunizations as well as rabies shots, but neither of us had decided to get the shots (both because of the expense and because it appeared they were only a partial solution and one would still need to get shots following a bite, though perhaps less urgently). Overnight as Mickey thought more about that dog, she worried more, and in the morning asked that we go back to check up on that dog and make sure it wasn't sickly.

We cycled back to the bridge. The same dog was there. It was on a rope and barking more furiously. It was hard to tell, but it seemed healthy as well. We decided to take it easy and cycled into Apxapa for a rest day anyways, as this was one of the places with a larger gap between services.

A month later, after Mickey had returned to the Netherlands, she went to her doctor, who advised her that it was still prudent to have the rabies shots just in case.

Three days riding from Apxapa, we came to the last of the gravel sections. We could tell because of the stopped Japanese cars, with people busy taping up most of the windshield and forward surfaces to guard against flying gravel bits on the road we had just cycled.

A day of riding farther brought us to Khabarovsk and the endpoint of the 2165-kilometer Amur Highway. It was on a bridge across the Amur River that Putin had made his announcement about the opening of this road as a paved route across Russia. The road had been tougher cycling than we had anticipated, though we didn't encounter any evidence of the tales of bandits or other lawless behaviors. While we would still need another eight days of cycling to Vladivostok, I took an inventory of what had lasted and what had worn out:

- Bicycle: replaced front and rear rims, replaced front hub, one flat tire, replaced one rear tire, four brake pads, two broken toe straps. Front rack broken (twice). Rear rack broken (once). Handlebar tape re-wrapped. New cassette and chain.
- Camping gear: updated one-person "Hubba" tent to a two-person "Hubba-Hubba." Split one tent pole. Alcohol stove didn't work.
- Other gear: shoes almost worn out, lost cycling mirror, lost "bite" valve on my Camelbak, stove valve snapped.

Vladivostok and completion of the ride across Russia

Fall was coming and with it cooler temperatures. We also cycled through a temperate rainforest and had a few wet days on our last week of cycling. A local geologist told us some of the extra rain might have been from remnants of a tropical cyclone. The days were also getting noticeably shorter than those long daylight hours we had had earlier.

It was nice to see Vladivostok appear in the road signs and the kilometers start to decrease. We passed through more populated areas, and there was more traffic on the road. The balance of traffic also shifted from the Amur Highway, where it seemed as if 90% of the vehicles were going the other direction. It was harvest season, and we passed vendors along the road with stands selling produce.

On the last day before arrival, we passed a bay that was part of the Pacific Ocean and started to see sea gulls. We stopped at a small motel not far from the airport as we knew we were close.

The last day into Vladivostok was only 36 kilometers, but it was a busy ride and not for the faint-hearted. Vladivostok is at the end of a natural peninsula connected by two main roads. We seem to have picked the more popular one, and there wasn't much in the way of shoulders. The edge of the shoulder was sometimes rough, and one needed to be constantly on alert for potholes ahead, traffic behind and a constant rush of traffic alongside. There were also a set of hills to climb over.

After 9 kilometers we saw the Vladivostok city limits signs and took the obligatory photos. It was still another 27 kilometers before we were in the main square and downtown Vladivostok. After 12,749 kilometers from Amsterdam, we had finished the ride September 17th on Mickey's birthday. We picked out a restaurant for a celebration and even bought some Russian champagne to celebrate.

The following was the ending summary I posted in my blog a few days later as I had time to reflect on the trip:

> On completion of a trip like this, there are always mixed emotions. It is nice to have completed the trip, particularly a goal such as having crossed two continents on a bicycle. At the same time, you realize that this adventure is over and it is now time to do the next thing. It is also a time to compare how the trip went against what you expected or what you might do differently if done again. It is a time to thank those who helped make the trip possible. Finally, from a trip like this often spawn the first seeds of what you might do on future trips.

> **Thanks:** I realize that I am very fortunate to be able to do a trip like this. There are many people to thank for having made this possible. I am very grateful to my employer, Hewlett-Packard, for granting me a leave of absence from work that made time available. I thank my managers for allowing it in a time of change in the tech industry. Now, I am getting ready to get back to work!

> My tenants watched over the duplex in my absence. Friends in Russia provided logistical support, including storing the "backup bicycle" in Penza. My parents helped in many ways, particularly in keeping this web site in good order, paying the necessary bills, contesting property taxes, and receiving/sending the various backup supplies I had sent to Colorado. All these little things from different people make a trip like this possible. For example, my brother Bert brought a new back wheel to Irkutsk just in time, as the old bike rim was breaking apart.

> There were a lot of little things along the way as well, so I hope I didn't accidentally slight someone by forgetting to mention it here.

> **Reflections and comparisons with expectations:**
> A bicycle ride across Russia had been in my plans for a while. I spent time reading other trip reports and studying the area. At

the same time, one can't anticipate everything, and things don't always turn out as expected. The following is a slightly eclectic list of reflections on different aspects of the trip:

Cycling alone vs. with others On my other big trips, I cycled alone – for this one I placed a "companions wanted" notice on the Adventure Cycling web site and magazine. I am glad I did this and really enjoyed cycling these months across with Mickey. We weren't always matched in speeds but would generally meet up during the day and camp together. In a country where you knew just bits of (Russian) language, it was great to talk with a partner or solve problems together. I was also very fortunate to find a cycling partner with the right combination of humor, patience and problem solving to make this a more enjoyable trip. In response to my "companions wanted" ad, approximately twenty people contacted me. I would point them to the web site and to past journals to describe the trip. Most people I didn't hear from again, and a few I heard from more than twice. Mickey was one of the later to reply but quickly organized things and got set for travels. I also enjoyed the time Bert was cycling with us and the extra logistical help he gave during the start of the particularly tough spots in the gravel road, including the SMS/cell phone solution to almost daily location updates and his better Russian backup contacts and language skills. Too bad he wasn't there for more of the trip.

Weather We were fortunate with weather. Most of the bad weather happened on the "edges," with headwinds, rain or snow on the approach to St. Petersburg or in the last week to Vladivostok (well not snow yet there). In between it is surprising how much good weather we had during the months of May, June, July, and August. Also, it was surprising that if we had winds, they were more likely tailwinds than headwinds.

Insects I expected there to be many insects. However, it still surprised me how consistently we camped with insects *day after day after day*, during the stretch from the Urals to close to Lake Baikal. I had anticipated they might let up occasionally more than they did. As a result, for almost two months the pattern was to duck into the tent as soon as we arrived at camp. A trip like this is not for the claustrophobic.

Other animals I expected to see other animals, such as deer, smaller mammals like weasels and reptiles – either explicitly on the road or as road kill. I was surprised at how few of these we saw on the trip. It was only really in the natural history museums that I saw some of the fauna of the area.

Plants and landscapes There are some long stretches of taiga forests that are very homogeneous in a ride across Russia. I expected some of this (e.g. from people who have taken the train and remarked at days of sameness) and was even accustomed to some of it in previous rides, such as that around Australia. However, there was at least as much homogeneity in plants and landscapes between the Urals and Baikal as I expected. It was after Baikal that I saw some more of the variety, such as the steppes, valleys, flat parts, hills, and others, that I expected.

Gravel road While I knew there would be 1600+ km. of gravel road, it still turned out to be more difficult than I expected. Perhaps my expectations were informally set based on gravel roads in Alaska or Northern Canada. On this gravel road, there were two key differences that made things just a bit more difficult: (1) Traffic – there was a steady stream of imported Japanese cars raising dust when it was dry, splattering mud when it was wet, frequently with drivers who just kept wanting to know where you were from. (2) Surface treatments seemed to be primarily the spreading of coarse rocks and loose gravel. In northern Canada, there would sometimes be oiling of the roads or other treatment that would make things smooth. In contrast, this gravel road continued to be rough. Overall, Putin's expectations of a paved road by 2008 were not met, but each year the road would become easier to cycle[13].

---

[13] The Amur Highway was finally declared paved in September 2010

Hitchhiking On a ride across Eurasia, there is, of course, a strong feeling that one should cycle every single kilometer and that hitchhiking is taboo. Otherwise, what is the point? There is a slippery slope—where one can just as well ride the train for the entire distance. It was with some trepidation that we ended up hitchhiking. On reflection hitching a ride was the right thing to do, particularly for the part we skipped (263km). Other than the ability to say, "We rode every kilometer" and the 4 or 5 days of tough slogging we skipped, we really didn't miss much by hitchhiking. It helped our spirits and progress at a particularly difficult part of the ride, and I would hitchhike again in the same circumstances. As a bonus we got a view of how truck drivers saw the road.

Asphalt roads Russia has some particularly busy asphalt roads. Once we passed the Urals, most were in better condition than I expected. Prior to the Urals, we had some particularly difficult roads (M7 is notorious but there were others) that were narrow, busy and in very poor condition. The trick to watch in the future is both to investigate roads as best you can – but also have enough flexibility to change plans to alternate roads if the ones you are on bad. It is also interesting that once we left the "standard routes" for more secondary roads, we tended to have roads that went through rather than around villages, which led to more interactions with locals and we tended to get more unique experiences, such as cycling with tanks or having tea with railroad workers.

Bureaucracy Prior to cycling Russia I expected occasional hassles with police, including roadblocks, checking of paperwork and similar encounters. Somehow the stereotype of a Russian police state was still in my mind. It simply didn't happen this way. There were occasional road checkpoints on the road. These seem to be oriented towards inter-oblast truck traffic like the "weigh stations" in the U.S. While there were five or six times agents at these blocks would ask me to stop, it was always a very friendly stop with a "Where are you from?" question. I never had to show any documents or otherwise justify where I wanted to go. The one spot we seemed to have occasional bureaucracy was in finding a hotel in the big cities. Each would have their system and rules for things such as registration (with official stamps), and these weren't always the same. It was occasionally a hassle to be able to bring bicycles inside.

Where are you from? By far, this was the most common question. My answer was Holland (Галландия) rather than U.S.A., unless I was showing my passport. The reason was primarily that there seemed to be associations on TV, in media and others with the U.S. (at least as much as Americans might have with "Russia" if a large number of the films on TV depicted a representation of Russia). Most of those perceptions were positive, but it was more likely to have the occasional bad perception of the U.S. than of a country where the most prominent thing mentioned was the Ajax football team.

Russian people, crime, and annoyances My overwhelming perception of Russian people towards us as touring cyclists was, "curious," "cautious," "friendly," and "generous." Curiosity would come with the where are you from questions and the friendly/generous would come from the things offered to us or the general admiration I sensed of someone crossing Russia on a bicycle. On rare occasions people would avoid us or specifically walk away to avoid us. We were sometimes asked if we had encountered "bad people" or ones who might want to hurt us or steal things. This was much less than one would expect from how often the question was asked. Mickey did have some youths steal a bicycle pump. I had something (a dog?) take a food sack. The largest annoyance we had was from public drunkenness. It seemed, particularly on weekends, that we would run across people who had had too much to drink, yet still wanted to befriend (read "annoy," "pester") these foreigners and viewed themselves as friendly rather than boorish. Mostly we worked to avoid these public drunks as best we could. As a woman cyclist, Mickey would also relate that treatment of women was also different, particularly in some cases where I wasn't around. There seem to be some more rigid communication patterns (e.g. women with women and men with men) than in Western Europe or the U.S.A.

Cities vs. Villages Life in the big cities is quite a bit different than in the small villages. Our cycling patterns were also different with tent camping vs. hotels and the presence of many shops vs. just a small shop or two. We developed a pattern of several days of riding to reach the next big city and taking a rest day there to recuperate before repeating the pattern.

I was surprised at how homogeneous these cities were and how life in, say, Novosibirsk might be more similar to that in Ekaterinburg than in villages 100 km from either of these cities. I was also surprised at how little ethnic mix we saw before Ulan-Ude (e.g. small Chinese sections in Irkutsk or Krasnoyarsk). If there is a division in Russia – it seems to be more between big city and small village than between parts of the country we saw.

Mike's Recommendations for Russia Travel

Several of the recommendations are listed among the expectations above. Russia is an intriguing country that I would recommend others visit. A somewhat eclectic list of recommendations for Russia travel, oriented not just at cyclists (I am still adding to this list), include the following:

Go beyond Moscow/St. Petersburg.There is a lot more of Russia out there.

Learn a little Russian language, if only the Cyrillic alphabet.It helps in reading signs.

If traveling by train, make a stop in a smaller city rather than just the largest ones. For example, our stays in Svobodny or Apxapa were quite different from those in the big cities.

Stay long enough to have interactions with locals.

Cyclists, the challenge with a cross-Russia trip will be more mental than physical. It is not particularly tough terrain, though there is a lot of it, and you will need to keep going amidst some of the items listed above.

Closing Thank You

Thanks to those of you who have read along with this journal, including sending occasional words of encouragement or helpful pointers. Getting a sense of Russia while also accomplishing a goal of cycling across Eurasia has been a highlight of this trip. I hope I have inspired some of you to travel or to ride a bicycle, if only for a shorter trip. In any case, be mindful if you see a touring cyclist out there on the road. It could be someone like me.

A few days after completion, Mickey left and went back to the Netherlands. My flight wasn't until the 29th of September and thus I had a dozen days in the city. I found a tourist agency and was able to book a less expensive home stay option with a woman who rented out a room in her apartment. Otherwise, I looked around the city and prepared for my next step of adventure, a seven-week ride across China.

2007 – Tales from China and Thailand

Side trip to Hong Kong

The idea started as an insurance policy. A company named Tour D'Afrique (TDA) was conducting a supported ride across Asia from Istanbul to Beijing. As I made my plans, I realized their completion date was a month or two past my likely completion of riding across Russia. I signed up for the last 1/3 of their trip as a way of hedging my bets. If unforeseen problems arose and I was unable to ride all the way across Russia, then I could ask to join the TDA Silk Route ride. If it turned out that my Russian ride took longer than expected, then I would have some sunk costs but otherwise could skip part of the ride through China.

As it turned out, the time to complete my ride across Russia was what I expected and hence I booked a flight from Vladivostok to Urumqi in western China. I would have almost a week to spend in Urumqi before cycling ~200 kilometers to meet the ride as it came through the Turpan Depression.

On arrival in Beijing I hit a glitch, a big one. It started when I went through Immigration Control and heard, "Your visa is not valid. Please sit over there." I had ordered my Chinese visa at the end of February. On the form I had requested a visa that started in August and was good for six months. They had instead given me a visa that started in February and had expired in August.

I sat on a chair behind Immigration Control while they brought someone over from Vladivostok Airlines to help sort out my options. The airline had some responsibility, since they could have checked my visa more carefully before allowing me to fly. One of the options would be for the airline to take me back to Vladivostok. Another alternative they I presented was for me to buy a ticket to fly to the U.S.A. Neither seemed particularly desirable, but there wasn't an option to sort this out in either Beijing or Urumqi, since you need to be outside the country to apply for a visa.

On further exploration another option appeared. It is also possible to apply for Chinese visas in Hong Kong. I went for this option without knowing exactly what it entailed. Vladivostok Airlines helped me sort out the flight alternatives, since it was also easier for them. I bought a new plane ticket and made hotel reservations. Once my arrangements were complete, Immigration gave me a conditional stamp in my passport that let me into the rest of the airport needed to catch my flight to Hong Kong.

I arrived in Hong Kong on Saturday of a long holiday weekend. This gave me two days to assess the situation before the Foreign Ministry office opened. There were many small travel agencies that could submit a visa for processing. These seemed to be only for 30 days, and I needed a 60-day visa. However, I could print out the visa forms in my hotel with a 60-day request and get the required pieces, such as a visa photo.

On Tuesday morning I was at the Foreign Ministry an hour before they opened and number twelve in a line that grew steadily. As my number was called, I presented my documents to a woman behind glass. I had attached some documents that included my rationale for the ride, including that I was traveling with TDA and had already paid for the trip. She took the visa application and documents and disappeared--not a good sign. She came back and informed me that to bicycle in China I would need an invitation letter from the Tourism Office in China. There was no place in Hong Kong to get such a letter; it would need to come from Beijing.

I asked if I could get a visa if I wasn't cycling. Yes, but only for 30 days. I went back from the Foreign Ministry and assessed my options. Since I could only get a 30-day visa in Hong Kong, I went to one of the visa offices and had them complete an application. This time I was careful not to mention anything about bicycling. The visa office submitted my application, and 24 hours later, I had my visa!

After a few days as a tourist visiting Hong Kong, I was back to the airport and flew on to Urumqi. It was a six hour flight and otherwise uneventful. I arrived at night and found a taxi that took my bicycle box and me to a hotel.

The next morning I assembled the bike. I got most things assembled correctly but had problems with the derailleur. The bike shop had unscrewed it from the frame and taped it out of harm's way. First, I couldn't get it screwed in. Once I had that done, I noticed that I had the cable and chain wrong. Rather than unscrew things again, I broke the chain and put it back. When putting the wheel back in, I noticed the chain was still incorrect and so broke it again. My chain tool suddenly broke. I went to the reception desk and asked for bicycle repair shops. They didn't know of repair shops but mentioned repair people just a block or two over.

I found a repair person. Rather than break the chain, he undid the derailleur cable and took out the pullies. It was all fixed in a matter of minutes for 2Y (25 cents). Once I was back on the road, however, I noticed something wrong. I could only use my three highest gears. The derailleur adjustment must have been off. With some fiddling, I could get a few more gears. However, more disturbing was that the chain link was partly open. I did the best I could to close things up with needle-nosed pliers to squeeze the chain together again. It was a step I would need to repeat multiple times over the next 200 kilometers, but it eventually got me to Turpan.

The city was big and congested. The Chinese lettering made finding my route more difficult. However, I quickly learned the characters for Turpan and found myself on the toll road, where it was smoother riding. After a bit, I came to a toll booth, where they looked at me funny but let me pass. Unfortunately, somewhat later police passed and requested I ride on a side road instead of the freeway. I had to get past one closed bridge but could find my way.

After 135 kilometers, I camped a little way from the highway and not far from another toll booth. The following morning, I rode the remainder of the distance into Turpan. The schedule was for TDA riders to arrive the following day, but as I wandered around town, I met a rider who had skipped ahead and was taking an extra rest day.

Deserts of Western China

The riders and staff came in the following day after a long 150-kilometer ride with headwinds. There were twenty-two Canadians, four British, two Dutch, half a dozen Americans, one Kiwi and a few other nationalities.

I got my bike tags as well as a "red box" that would go into the truck with my gear. Phil, the mechanic, could sort out both my derailleur and chain and get things working again. I bought an inexpensive Chinese sleeping bag to use as a second blanket as fall nights were starting to get colder. Our first week there the temperature was typically -3C (mid-twenties Fahrenheit) and fall was just starting.

The following seven nights to Dunhuang set the pattern for the ride. Each day we cycled between 100 and 150 kilometers, spending four nights camping in the desert mixed with three nights in hotels. I no longer needed to worry about finding places to stay, or finding food and water or cooking. Instead, the pattern was to pack up my tent and gear, get breakfast, check the white board and ride. At the midpoint in the route, a TDA truck stopped with lunch items. At end of the ride, we would have a riders' meeting and then dinner. It was cold in the evening and would get dark quickly, so it was into the tent for an early night sleep.

As cyclists, we departed at slightly different times and mostly made our way in small groups or individually. The route description was posted on a white board. In this part of China, the description was usually simple because there were few alternate roads. If there was a more complex turn, then staff would have placed red "flagging tape" on nearby trees that we looked for. I was perhaps slightly slower than average but still found it reasonable riding.

I found it interesting to join a trip in progress, because the group dynamics had already formed, including cliques, patterns, and norms. People seemed to separate some based-on language, nationality, and age as well as riding speeds. Riding speeds made most sense to me since people of similar speeds could spend much of their times together, but having Americans associate more with other Americans and not mix as much with Canadians seemed strange to me.

Parts of the ride were difficult in terms of weather as well as rough roads. A few riders had enough of camping in the cold and riding through the desert. This also surprised me a bit since both were factors they should have been able to figure out prior to the trip. A set of riders had gotten into a pattern of skipping ahead a few days to the next town and waiting for the rest of the group to arrive. However, most of the group, including me, were serious about riding each day on what was still a challenging trip. There were even three who had the exalted EFI status of having cycled every f* inch.

Three days of cycling brought us to our first town, Hami, an otherwise dry and dusty town. As in Russia, these towns were a sharp contrast to the surrounding areas with shops, people, traffic and noise. In contrast to Russia, the surrounding areas were predominantly arid desert regions. Hami was also the spot where some of the younger riders found fireworks. During the following night or two, we would hear the pop, pop bangs of fireworks.

Four days of riding from Hami brought us to Dunhuang and a rest day. As we approached the city, we passed irrigated areas with cotton farms, and we saw trucks heaped high with cotton. Dunhuang was a chance to see an impressive Magoa cave complex with elaborate paintings and sculptures inside. What impressed me was these were old (older than Mesa Verde in Colorado) but still well-preserved.

From Dunhuang we followed a route named the Hexi Corridor to the city of Lanzhou. This was a historic trading route that was part of the Silk Roads between Central Asia and the more populated areas of China. There were more towns than before in this area, and we also had more riding on newly paved freeways. Some of the signs on the freeways had both Chinese and English descriptions, and I found some of the translations amusing, e.g. "do not chuck jetsam." As we reached the town of Jiayuguan, we came to the end of the Great Wall. The Great Wall is not just a single wall, but in Jiayuguan was an old fort that marked the edge of the historic Chinese empire. This area is known as "the mouth" of the Hexi Corridor, and soon thereafter we would travel through "the throat." More of the throat was irrigated, and hence we also saw more crops, such as sugar beets, cotton, corn, cabbage, and onions. We stopped for a rest day in Jiayuguan and got a chance to explore the fort further.

Overall, I was impressed with the helpfulness and friendliness of the Chinese people I met. I sometimes saw them staring at me (both as a foreigner as well as being tall). I would smile and invariably get a smile back. In Jiayuguan my cell phone was no longer working and gave messages of "network blocked," perhaps because the SIM card was regional. I found a store near the bus station with cell phone symbols and showed them the phone. They couldn't read the prompts, and I couldn't read the symbols. However, through charades, examples and mixing and matching of SIM cards, they understood mine no longer worked. We tried two different SIM cards before getting one that worked. We figured out the payment amounts and after a "bye" in Chinese and English, I left with smiles all around.

We came through another larger town of Wuwei and areas that were higher in elevation. A day after Wuwei we climbed up and over a pass that was 2900 meters high. By our lunch stop at 80 kilometers, we were at 2200 meters elevation, and it was lightly snowing. I had, fortunately, bought some warmer gloves in Wuwei, but it was still below freezing, with a stiff north wind. About half the group decided they had had enough and caught the van from lunch, but I, as well as others, continued up and over the pass. I ended up walking with another rider the last 2 kilometers before the pass.

The descent was at least as tricky as the climb, since the road was potentially icy. Since we were no longer climbing, it was also cold. My derailleur cable froze, so I only had a single-speed bike. It was a slow and steady descent, but I made it the 37 kilometers from the top of the pass to our hotel in the town of Tienzhu. I started shivering before I could change into dry clothes, but a hot shower helped things. I compared notes with other riders, and very cold riding and single-speed bikes were a common theme.

The following day was 149-kilometer ride into the larger city of Lanzhou. It was a big contrast in several ways. First, the temperature had warmed up to a balmy 8C. There was a lot more cultivated land and then the last 45 kilometers were mostly on a busy expressway. Fortunately, we also got a reasonable shoulder, and close to the city some areas had a frontage road.

It was Sunday, and on Monday morning my first task was to find the visa office of the Public Safety Bureau (PSB). I was the first customer through the doors when they opened at 8:30 a.m. and I filled out an application to renew my 30-day visa for another 30 days.

"When would I get my visa?" they asked when I was leaving, and I told them I wanted to leave later today or at the earliest the next morning. They told me it would take three days to renew the visa. Unfortunately, this meant the visa would be ready on Wednesday, and the TDA ride would be two days farther down the road. After my experience in Beijing, I decided not to bring up the topic of bicycling and figured I would place my bicycle on the TDA support vehicles and catch up by bus.

Later in the morning I was talking with one of the TDA staff and learned that he had also applied for a visa renewal and had been told his visa would be ready the next morning. I went back to the visa office and pleaded with them to see if they could also expedite my visa since we were on the same trip. While they could make no promises (and I didn't want to be too pushy), they did tell me they would try to complete my visa renewal by 9 a.m. the morning.

Riding to Beijing

The following morning I put my bike on the TDA truck and joined the staff member in going to the PSB. My visa renewal was complete! The other riders had already left, but I was able to catch a taxi to the TDA vehicle and ride this until lunch. I missed a morning with some pretty climbing, but at lunch I could retrieve my bicycle and ride the rest of the day.

This area had many terraces where the flat regions were used to grow crops. We camped that evening, but it would be our last night camping, as the weather had become cold enough that the remaining nights were in hotels. We were also traveling through more populated areas of China, where there were now small towns with hotels.

Near the town of Pingliang, we climbed up to 2400 meters elevation before reaching a 2.3-kilometer-long tunnel. These tunnels are dark and narrow and hence there is a need to take extra care. TDA had set up our lunch stop just before the tunnel. Once enough riders had collected, the plan was for a group ride through the tunnel escorted by TDA vehicles and flashing lights. There would be a second ride with the rest of the riders. This created an incentive to ride quickly and make the cutoff rather than having to wait for the last rider. I left early and didn't stop much and, fortunately, was there among the first group. I also still had a flashing blinking light that came in handy in our tunnel ride. The tunnel surface was rough and one had to watch for patches of ice, but it was otherwise a good ride.

Some strains were starting to show in the group. As we collected together at the hotel at end of the day waiting for others to arrive and hotel arrangements, some fireworks went off. These fireworks had been going off occasionally the past several weeks, including one morning at 4 a.m., interrupting riders' sleep.

One of the riders had had enough. He spotted the culprit walking away from where the blasts occurred. He asked if a broom was needed to sweep up the mess and followed this with some colorful language. "Don't disrespect me!" was the response. Unfortunately, things escalated from here, with abusive language and threats to the point where the larger rider ended up pushing the smaller rider down and onto the ground. Dukes were raised, and the rest of us jumped in to constrain the riders from getting into a full fistfight. Otherwise, efforts were made to calm the frayed tempers.

One of the TDA staff also witnessed the incident, and that evening we learned that the rider who had pushed his fellow rider was asked to leave the tour. By raising his verbal abuse to physical violence, he had violated his rider agreement. It was a tough call to make, but I appreciated TDA for enforcing their rules. There were some, particularly those in this rider's clique, who questioned why both riders were not expelled. The combatant who remained was fortunate, particularly that we had constrained him from attacking back. He might have thought so as well, as he was noticeably more careful about his language and behavior after this.

Expelling a rider means that he no longer takes part in the tour services, such as having his gear carried or hotels arranged. However, in this case it didn't mean this rider left China or went home. Instead, as we discovered, over the next two weeks he continued to "shadow" the original group, and we kept seeing him in towns where we stopped. There was some suspicion that some of his friends were stowing some of his gear on the TDA trucks, but otherwise he was carrying a larger backpack. This made for a somewhat strange situation, as we kept getting reminders of the fireworks incident over the next weeks when we kept seeing him showing up.

A few more days of cycling brought us close to Xian. The day before we cycled into Xian, our faces were black from coal dust but still had smiles. The road was backed up, with a line of trucks stretching for more than 30 kilometers. We could ride past these stopped trucks, but the TDA vehicles had traveled an alternate route. The truck engines were off, as they had been there for a while. As we climbed the hill, we came to a tunnel near the top. This time there wasn't a convoy, so several of us banded together and put on our available lights and cycled through the tunnel. After this there was a second tunnel before we came to what appeared to be one of the causes of congestion, some road works that had closed the lanes to stop all truck traffic. Fortunately, not much past this we came onto an expressway, and traffic was much smoother.

We waited for the TDA trucks to arrive. Our faces and bodies were black because this was a coal region and a lot of the coal dust from the road had been raised by our tires. Fortunately, we had only one more day of riding before a double rest day in Xian.

Xian was a great city to explore. One of the staff had taught English in China. He had taken a sightseeing bus trip with his parents that he recommended and volunteered to coordinate the same trip. More than 30 of us took this trip to see the Terracotta Warriors. Wow! We also had a nice lunch and a tea tasting as well as a stop at a handicrafts area.

From Xian, it was only 12 more days riding to Beijing, including a rest day and conversations invariably turned to "What are you doing next?" We saw our first road signs showing distances to Beijing. The areas we cycled through were now more populated, and we still had some more dirty coal mining areas to cross. It was otherwise not particularly difficult but also not particularly exciting cycling. What also surprised me some was that a few riders had become tired enough of the trip that they were taking the vehicles most of the time, even on easy riding days.

I was surprised when we crossed some very large cities I had never heard of before the trip. For example, the city of Shijiazhuang has 2.1 million people. Apparently, there are quite a few of these 1+ million-person cities in this part of China. Also, fortunately these cities weren't as difficult to cross as a similar-sized city would be in the U.S. While there were plenty of cars and trucks and some of these truck drivers were somewhat aggressive, there were still enough other bicycles on the road as well as bicycle routes that the cycling felt reasonably safe.

Once we got close to Beijing, we learned that our large baggage truck wasn't permitted into the city. Hence, we had to repack from our red boxes into bags that were shuttled into the city and the hotel. TDA took a few other logistical steps to make sure everyone made it safely into this large city. The cycling instructions were more complex, and TDA staff were at four critical turns to make sure nobody went the wrong direction. We also were given an assembly point 92 kilometers into the ride and asked to be there by 1 p.m. It was an easy ride and from there we cycled as a group into Tiananmen Square for the obligatory end-of-the-ride photos and then found our hotel.

Overall, I enjoyed my 4016 kilometers of cycling with TDA through China. It was an interesting contrast between mostly cycling with one person, Mickey, to being part of a group of forty riders and staff. Some things were easier, including the logistical support of having gear carried and being in a group with cooks and a bike mechanic. At the same time, the routes, and distances themselves became more fixed.

It was now the 18th of November, and I had a little less than a week in Beijing and around six weeks before I would return to work.

Thailand cycling

The plan for the last part of my trip was to bicycle from Bangkok to Singapore. After almost two months of cycling in a larger group, it would be nice to cycle by myself again in this last trip. Unfortunately, as it turned out, bike troubles meant that I only rode to southern Thailand before cutting the trip short and taking a train to Kuala Lumpur and then flying back to Colorado.

The flight from Beijing was uneventful, and after the cold November temperatures of Beijing, it was nice to be in a more tropical Bangkok. I had caught some sort of bug the last days in Beijing and despite using Imodium, my GI tract wouldn't quite seem to settle down. After looking on the internet and visiting a pharmacy, I found some Cipro, and this seemed to fix the problem.

I had a day of looking around Bangkok. The Thai King's birthday was coming up on December 5^{th,} and there were already large images of the monarch displayed and surrounded by some yellow flowers. I spotted one of these images across from the U.S. embassy and stopped to take a photograph. What I had not realized was that the embassy complex was on both sides of the streets. Guards came over and pulled me into their office. I wasn't supposed to be taking photos of the embassy. I explained that I was taking photos of the king (hopefully allowed). I offered to delete the photos. They held me for a short while longer and eventually figured out there wasn't much they could do in detaining me and let me go.

Roads leaving Bangkok were busy and chaotic with cars, trucks, and scooters. I found the cycling somewhat easier than in China, as it seemed the drivers weren't as aggressive. It was still occasionally slow as it was election season and I encountered marchers with banners proclaiming their candidates. Otherwise, the roads, including some of the larger roads, were flat and had enough shoulders. In the afternoons, I found some of the larger towns with beach resorts. The prices in these hotels were surprisingly inexpensive.

Over the next week I slowly made my way down the coast and through larger towns of Surat Thani. There were travel warnings for the southernmost provinces. While Westerners or tourists weren't a target, there was some violence associated with an insurgency, and one needed to be cautious to avoid the crossfire.

After I passed Surat Thani, I had a day where my bicycle stopped working. The chain had occasionally skipped. As I crossed up a small hill, the chain stopped grabbing going forward and spun freely both directions. It was the same problem as I had had in New Zealand six years before--my rear hub had failed.

There wasn't much to do other than get a ride to a larger town and sort out the situation. Soon enough a pickup stopped by. I didn't speak Thai, but we were able to communicate enough that they offered me ride another 12 kilometers to a "fixer." The fixer was a roadside business that mostly repaired motorcycles, and it was apparent quickly that there wasn't much they could do to repair a broken bike hub.

We waited a short while, and a shared taxi vehicle came past. It was a small pickup truck with rows of seats on both sides. We could put my disabled bicycle on top, and I hopped in for a ride to the next town.

Once in the town it was time to assess the situation. I had approximately three weeks left in my overall trip. There wouldn't be any place to fix or replace the hub/rear wheel here, and one most likely would need to travel back to Bangkok to get a replacement wheel. If I had had more time left in my travels, this is what I would have done and continued from Bangkok.

Instead, I decided to make a more mellow ending to my trip. I booked into my hotel for a few nights. After this I planned a train trip to the Malaysian capital of Kuala Lumpur, where I would spend another week before flying home. It was a nice and enjoyable end to what had been a ten-month trip split between Texas, Europe, Russia, China and now Thailand.

2013 - Tales from Across Africa
URL: http://www.bike2013.com

Plans

I signed up for my ride across Africa more than five years before I went. It was November 2007 and I had just completed the Silk Route ride with Tour D'Afrique (TDA). My pattern had been to do some long ride every five years or so, and it had just seemed to make sense to sign up for the signature ride with TDA. After I sent my signup, I got a query "Are you sure this is for 2013 and not 2010?" "Yes," I confirmed.

While my previous four long trips had been self-supported rides, I made a conscious choice to cross Africa in a supported group. The reason was primarily logistics: ten countries and multiple languages made this more daunting than mostly traveling across a single large country. I also had had a chance to see how TDA's organization and tours operated when I rode the last part of the Silk Route ride across China.

I now had five years to anticipate and slowly prepare for the ride. Most of those preparations didn't happen until the last year, and TDA sent out a helpful set of emails gaving tips on different areas such as packing lists, bike selection, vaccinations, etc. In addition, I carefully followed multiple blogs during the 2011 and 2012 rides and made notes of what riders reported. Some of my areas of preparation included the following:

- Picking a bicycle and other equipment
- Bike school and wheel building classes
- Getting things set up at work

The ride had rougher roads and more off-road riding than I had done on previous trips. While my Trek 520 touring bicycle had done fine on the gravel roads across Russia, I thought I would be more comfortable on a bike that could fit wider tires. TDA suggested several bicycle types, including cross bikes and mountain bikes. The former were likely faster and often a choice of riders interested in making the ride using the race option (though I found later that there were riders such as Freek that were quite fast on their mountain bikes, so often the rider made at least as much difference as the bike).

I didn't have a mountain bike but did a supported ride in Thailand and Cambodia in 2010 that used Trek mountain bikes and found those worked reasonably well. Hence, I bought a mid-range Trek 4500 model and rode it in Portland and then later took it with me to India when I spent six weeks on business in Bangalore in summer of 2011. I left that bicycle in Bangalore and ended up buying a newer model Trek 4500 mountain bike in 2012 and updated some components for the ride.

As a heavier than average rider, one of the key components has always been my need for a sturdy set of wheels. Portland, Oregon, where I was now living, is a bike community with multiple bike-related businesses, including a wheel builder, Jude, and her Sugar Wheel Works company. I signed up for a wheel building class in 2012, which had the advantage of both learning how to build wheels and of ending up with a set of hand-built wheels at the end of the class. I took the class to build sturdy touring wheels, though I also had Jude double-check and make the final adjustments. This also let me order extra parts, including enough to build an entire rear wheel: hub, spokes, and rim.

In addition to the wheel building class, Portland also has a bike school whose classes include a basic one-week home mechanic course. I had taken the class once before in Ashland, Oregon, prior to my 2001 ride around Australia. A refresher was helpful, particularly because in the basic class, you work on the bike you bring to class. So, I took my class and had a nice exercise of taking major systems apart and putting them together again.

When I signed up for the TDA Africa ride at finish of my 2007 ride with TDA across China, I was working for Hewlett-Packard in Fort Collins, Colorado. In the summer of 2009, I changed employers and ended up taking a job with Advanced Micro Devices (AMD) in their small Portland, Oregon office. I waited until 2011 before letting my boss know of my cycling plans, and we agreed to otherwise keep it quiet. With the exception of one business dinner where my boss had some wine and told people I was planning a cycling trip across South America, it worked well. Once the time came closer, I turned my informal plans into a more formal leave of absence (LOA) request. I was grateful that AMD granted my LOA request, though as always there was no job guarantee when I returned.

There were, however, other changes also afoot at work. In March 2012, AMD announced that our Portland office would close and primary compiler work was transferring to the San Francisco Bay area. AMD offered me a transfer to California. I first helped employees in my group through the surprise/shock but then also talked with my boss about the possibility of my transfer being to our Austin, Texas, office instead. My boss agreed, and in summer of 2012, I emptied my condominium and placed it on the market. I moved my belongings mostly to an apartment in Austin but also moved some to storage. The Portland office itself would close at end of 2012, and I wanted to help in cleanly wrapping things up, but also realized it would be better to do this from Austin.

A further change happened in October 2012 when AMD had a sequence of layoffs and downsizing. I ended up leading a small team in a smaller but more focused server group. While it was two months before I would depart for a six-month LOA, I did what I could to get the new team up and going as well as prepared for a handoff during my absence. It was a lot of change in a short amount of time, though it all ended up working reasonably well.

In the last months before departure, I stopped by a travel clinic to get recommended vaccinations. After our experience in Russia, I got a rabies vaccination this time as well as yellow fever, malaria pills, etc. I also applied for the necessary visas from Ethiopia and Sudan. The Ethiopian visa came back without problem, but the Sudanese visa took so long that I asked the visa expediter company for my passport back since I was running out of time. I would need to try for this visa in Egypt.

As Christmas 2012 rolled around, I emptied out my apartment to place everything in storage and drove up to Colorado to celebrate New Year 2013 before my flight to Egypt and the start of the ride.

Egypt
At the airport my bike box tipped the scales at 60 pounds. Inside wasn't only my bicycle but also four extra tires and an extra rim. Two duffel bags each weighing 43 pounds brought my total weight to over 140 pounds.

TDA had a baggage weight limit of 100 pounds, and it was going to be close.

Five years after registering for the ride, it was nice to finally arrive in Egypt. My brother Bert met me at the airport, and we took a van to a leafy neighborhood where Bert had a temporary place as part of a house exchange for his Colorado property. It gave me an easy place to land as I adjusted to time differences, got a SIM card, and prepared for the ride.

TDA is sometimes described as "not only a ride, but also a social experiment." Part of the fun is traveling with others who had also come for the adventure. TDA had given us the demographics, and we had shared on social media, but it was a few days later that we first met. The demographics of the fifty full-tour riders included the following:

- 33 men and 17 women
- 15 countries: Canada (10), Britain (7), U.S.A. (4), Germany (4), Netherlands (4), Australia (4), New Zealand (4), Switzerland (3), Ireland (3), Italy (2), Denmark (1), Brazil (1), Norway (1), South Africa (1).
- Age demographics: teens (1), 20s (15), 30s (8), 40s (10), 50s (10), 60s (5) and 70s (1).

As I looked around, I thought that this was a serious group of people. While I was above average in the amount of touring I had done, I expected to be below average on overall fitness and speed on the road.

We held our first rider meetings, where the staff introduced themselves and explained overall logistics. Since the first ride across Africa ten years prior, TDA had conducted a stage race as part of the ride. Not every kilometer was part of the race, but many of the days one could click in at the start and end of the day with records kept of the fastest for each day, section, and overall ride. There were some who had come to race, and I was impressed by their overall fitness and speed, as they usually arrived in camp hours before I did.

Those who weren't racing were "expedition riders." I was definitely in the latter group. However, one could still get a race token and check in/out on race segments. This meant your statistics would appear on the web site and hence there would be an informal record of riding for others to see.

That seemed reasonable, so I also decided to get a token. As it turned out, I was part of the official race until the last day and ended up as the slowest male rider. I was never a threat to any other rider for placing on any of the days I cycled.

We placed our baggage outside for inspection. While nothing went on a scale, mine passed muster.

Our first day on the road started with a breakfast buffet at 5 a.m., and later we assembled for a "convoy" ride to the Great Pyramids. The riders rode together as a group, with vehicles guiding us from both front and the rear. Here some short speeches were given, and a group photo as well as individual photos were taken. There were 57 riders in total. Most were full tour riders, but a few joined only for a section.

Our first 40 kilometers were in the bike convoy, and after the pyramids we cycled through city traffic to the "Ring Road," a major highway across Cairo. We had both police escorts and local cyclists to help us along the way. These local cyclists even went as far as to cycle ahead to on-ramps and briefly stop traffic to prevent it from entering across our convoy. Overall it was an interesting experience on what otherwise would have been a hectic ride across a huge urban area.

Our convoy disbanded at a gas station at the 40-kilometer mark, and from here we cycled individually along a major highway to our first night desert camp. I arrived not long before sunset but with enough time to set up the tent and get dinner.

Our second day was a "mando" day. This meant it was mandatory for the racers to ride to win. What it meant for the rest of us was that mando days were typically the most difficult days of riding and the distance of 166 kilometers, often with headwinds, predicted a tough ride.

Winds were calm as we cycled the first 17 kilometers to the Red Sea. From here we were fortunate, as we had tailwinds rather than the more typical headwinds! It went quickly as we passed "Santa Claus," "Cancun" and other local resorts where Cairo residents could escape to the sea. After this we crossed more open desert before camping in the lee of a large wall as part of a desert complex.

Two further days of riding with still favorable winds brought us to a small resort town of Safaga. By now we were developing a rhythm as a group. Sunrise was shortly before 7 a.m. Half an hour earlier there was a wakeup toot on the horn, but this group really didn't need a reminder. Some had started perhaps an hour or so earlier to pack using head lamps and otherwise get ready. We would get gear packed up and cycle clothes on and set up our bike ready to ride. A good breakfast of porridge, granola, banana, and tea, followed by a last check of the white board for directions, and we were off.

At a midway point TDA would have a lunch stop with pita bread and various types of spread along with a chance to top up on water. I would mostly ride by myself but would also see others through the day.

When we arrived in camp, the first step was to click in to record my time on the race. After this I would find my bag and a good place to pitch my tent. Soup was often on and was good enough to tide us over. Around 5 p.m. or so, we would have a rider meeting, where we would review highlights as well as the upcoming day's ride. After that, dinner was served. It would get dark early and cool in the desert, so it was an early night into the tent for some reading, checking the cell phone for internet connection and otherwise relaxing and early to bed to be ready for another day.

From Safaga it was a day and half cycling back from the Red Sea to the Nile River valley. Our cycling along the Red Sea was on sparsely traveled roads. We had police escort vehicles, who would trail behind and give heads up as we passed through several police checkpoints. While Egypt had particularly been in the news since the Arab Spring uprisings two years before, we were never in any situation in which I felt unsafe. What we did observe was that tourist areas, such as the pyramids or Luxor, seemed deserted and remaining vendors were aggressively going after remaining business. It was a bit sad.

The Nile River valley was more populated than the area around the Red Sea, and we traveled through many small villages and more agricultural areas, including sugar cane. When we stopped for lunch, we now had an audience. Perhaps it was a bit like the circus coming to town complete with performers in brightly colored outfits and strange bikes. Meanwhile we would watch the locals with carts and donkeys who, in turn, were watching us.

After lunch TDA staff suggested we travel together in groups, not because of a particularly dangerous situation but because as the circus came past, some kids might throw rocks or sugar cane as they had the previous year. I traveled with a larger, slow group of about twenty riders, which made us even more of a spectacle to watch. We got some shouts, but there wasn't much concern about the kids we passed.

When we reached Luxor, I discovered that, unfortunately, my rear rim had developed a split. Just six days into the ride and I already had a serious mechanical problem. We had a rest day coming up, and one of the mechanics was gracious enough to offer to rebuild my wheel with the new rim, but I then lost some insurance, given that I had lost my spare rim so early. I put a request out to see if a later sectional rider might be able to bring a replacement rim as well as a query to the wheel builder to understand the situation. As it would later turn out, Velocity replaced the rim under warranty and Ben, a sectional rider, would later bring a replacement rim to Nairobi. Certainly, I was appreciative of both.

A day to see the temples in Luxor and then two further days of cycling along the Nile River brought us to Aswan. In between we stayed in the small town of Idfu on the edge of their soccer field. Several mosques were nearby, and we had competing calls to prayer at 5 a.m.

Aswan was a larger city and close to the endpoint of our riding in Egypt. In 2013 the roads between Aswan and Wadi Haifa, Sudan, weren't yet open to regular traffic and hence our method of travel would be to take the ferry on Lake Nassar.

Overall, I had spent a little over two weeks in Egypt and traveled a little less than 1000 kilometers. The riding wasn't yet as difficult as it would later become further south, and we had solid days of riding on mostly reasonable roads. I found the Egyptian people generally friendly and curious and the tourist vendors at times aggressive. Both Egyptian police and local security carefully chaperoned our group, and we were fortunate not to have any real issues. It also meant that by the time we reached a security roadblock, they would wave us through.

Sudan

It was a hurry up and wait day.

Our first hurry was cycling over the Aswan Dam accompanied by police escorts. After this we arrived at the ferry docks and got to wait. We waited as different officials tussled with each other as they figured out to handle the group and all our bicycles. One official told us to line the bikes on one side so they could count them, while another official was herding us through a narrow gate for a count. One mentioned us to go through the entryway, and the other pointed us in the other direction. They sorted out this situation quickly enough, however, and now was the time to hurry and board with our bikes.

Now it was time to wait as every sort of person and every sort of household good was loaded up on the boat, sometimes stacked high up on the deck. We had cabins below with two bunks for three people with the idea that many would want to camp out up on deck. That worked well until those who had camped up front on the boat were told to clear away and other places on the deck were no longer available. We waited as it took five hours to completely board the boat.

Sanitation levels weren't high, but I risked it as they served a meal. Otherwise, I had a restful sleep in my top bunk. The following morning, we awakened to see the Abu Simbel ruins on the starboard side. Not much later we were in Sudan. It still took until noon before the ship docked and another five hours before we were completely through customs and disembarkation checks. These included the following:

- Waiting until others got off (quick)
- Being told to congregate in the dining area before it turned out this was too cramped, so we needed to show up ten at a time.
- Receiving two forms to carefully complete and having them checked by immigration and receiving a yellow receipt.
- Finding the person with a stapler to attach a photo to the forms.
- Leaving after showing a disembarkation permit.
- Helping load the trucks and then cycling a kilometer to the customs area.
- Retrieving my bag and having customs place stickers on the bags.

- Having customs check the stickers on the bags and placing a sticker on the bike.
- Riding off to camp

Prior to this I had been fortunate to get my Sudanese visa arranged in Cairo. This had taken two days. The first took two and a half hours of standing in lines, filling out forms and carefully following the process. I then arrived at the office the next day only to discover that it appeared to be some sort of holiday with the office closed. However, fortunately the guards located my passport with the completed visa.

Once in camp we got our first look at the TDA trucks. Rather than drive the big trucks into Egypt, TDA had rented smaller trucks, and we had placed our luggage a duffel bag. We now had a locker. The large truck had some 45 lockers and only two entrances, so only a few people at a time could access their locker. Hence, it was important not only that everything fit into your locker but also that you could quickly locate things and pack and unpack. I had brought four smaller cycling panniers, which worked well since I could take the panniers out and wait until I was outside the truck before rummaging to find the precise things I needed. Over time people became better at packing and unpacking, though there always seemed to be a little congestion when everyone wanted to pack and leave at the same time.

Sudan felt different from Egypt. Our first three days were spent riding across the desert to the small town of Dongola. The riding was mostly flat, and we had tailwinds, but distances were long and afternoons started getting hot. One afternoon my cycle computer recorded 40C (104F) before I decided to stop looking at it. The informal plan became to "beat the heat." Riders were up in the wee hours of the morning with head lamps on to get packed and gear stowed in order to leave as early as possible. We were asked not to ride before sunrise, but breakfast times were advanced to allow an early start.

Our route roughly went parallel to the Nile River and after reaching camp on both afternoons, I could get to the river and get a soak. The water wasn't the cleanest and getting to the banks was a muddy mess, but it was cool and that was what mattered.

First along the river and then later throughout the day there were hundreds of small flies. Apparently, the worst infestations happen right about time the dates are flowering, and we were close to peak season. Apparently, they had not been there the previous season. Local entrepreneurs were ready to sell small head nets against the flies.

On the day we rode to Dongola, TDA had organized the ride as a team time trial. I joined with a group of several others in forming "team slow." Our goal was to have fun rather than win the race, though we did want to finish the time trial itself. We stayed together and had a nice ride.

In Dongola we camped at the zoo. The animals had long departed, but there was flat and grassy ground as well as a garden hose to fill a tub of water and wash clothes. We had a rest day and chance to check a local internet café. Here it surprised me to find accessing the Google Analytics web site resulted in a blocked message: "A connection has been established between your IP address and a country sanctioned by the U.S. government."

The sanctions dated back multiple years to actions of the Khartoum government, including hosting Osama bin Laden. Western countries still also had some strongly worked cautions in their travel advisories, and apparently credit cards drawn on U.S. or European banks wouldn't work in Sudan. While we didn't have much interaction with the government of Sudan other than visas and customs, I found the local Sudanese people we met to be friendly, curious, and helpful. They weren't as pushy aggressive as people had been in Egypt but, instead, were more reserved.

We arrived on a Friday, the holy day and Dongola felt very much like a religious town and was quiet. Our rest day was on Saturday, and more of the town appeared open, though at midday rows of prayer mats were placed on the streets.

After Dongola our next day riding was to Dead Camel Camp, named because of the camel skeletons found along the way as well as one at camp. What I found at least as interesting was a small abandoned mosque a short distance from our campsite. We were fortunate in that our tailwinds continued and flies became less numerous.

Sandstorm! The wind increased the following afternoon. By the time I reached camp, it was blowing quickly and raising a big sandstorm. Riders grouped together to help set up our tents since with just a single person, he or she might otherwise blow away. Even with the tents, the sand seemed to get in everywhere. I was careful not to use my camera, as I had already had one camera start to misbehave after sand in Egypt. The zippers of my tent never quite worked the same after that night camping in the sandstorm.

The following morning, I carefully plotted things out in my tent. I first put everything in my panniers. Was the rainfly so light it would blow away? To be safe, I brought the rainfly and other items to the truck. Now with some large rocks and careful staging, I could get the tent packed away—a big accomplishment, since the tent did seem to weigh more with some remaining sand inside.

There were still only a few hundred meters of visibility. TDA cancelled the official race for the day. Fortunately, the wind gradually subsided, and sand clouds lessened to point where the sun came out enough to see our shadows again.

The following day we cycled into the big city of Khartoum. We could tell we were nearing a larger city as the thorny plants started to sometimes have plastic bags and other debris attached. In the morning we had an individual time trial where each rider could see how quickly he or she would cover a 40-kilometer distance. I came in 26th of the 29 total competitors, so not particularly fast. However, it was fast enough that a lot of riding was done early and after lunch we gathered together for a convoy ride into the big city.

For our Khartoum rest day, I decided to get a hotel instead of staying at the camp along the Nile. It was great to sleep in a real bed and particularly to have a nice shower. Our camp was in the downtown business district not far from the confluence of the White Nile and Blue Nile. This made it easy to walk around through the markets. I found Khartoum to be a curious mix of new and modern as well as older areas. At one point, someone called attention to my bare knees. I was wearing basic travel shorts and wasn't sure if they thought it was the crazy foreigner (there were few other tourists) or perhaps the knees themselves, but I did become more conscious that the locals weren't wearing shorts.

Khartoum marked the end of the first of eight sections. We had completed ~2000 kilometers and the riding had not been very difficult. This was about to change, as the next section would become both warmer and, once we crossed into Ethiopia, hillier.

It was busy leaving Khartoum, but soon we were back in the countryside where two longer days riding brought us to Sennar. In contrast to desert areas further north, this area seemed to have more agricultural and irrigated areas. This also meant we needed to be more careful with our bikes, as the previous year two had been stolen from one of the campsites.

Sennar put out the red carpet for us cyclists. The local town dignitary came and gave us an official welcome. The local karate and gymnastics clubs came and gave us exhibitions. Each rider received a cola drink, peanuts, and a banana. We received brochures about tourist highlights of Sennar Province. I talked with local officials, and they clearly wanted to get the word out about their area.

In the afternoon riders changed out their tires since there would be a lot more off-road cycling ahead.

We had 7 kilometers of pavement before we started with off-road cycling for rest of the day. The informal theme was "follow the abandoned railroad." At times the track was easy to find but, on other occasions, the road might go through a wet, marshy area and then one would need to find alternate ways around the muck. This backfired for me prior to the lunch stop, when I discovered myself across a wide irrigation canal from the lunch truck. I backtracked a kilometer and a half and was then back on route and on to lunch.

As I got to camp, I inspected my tires and pulled out a long thorn. This was one of two flat tires I would have during the overall ride. This ended up being lower than average, though there were a few riders that did the entire ride without a single flat. On the other hand, this first day from Sennar there were also cyclists who ended up with up to a dozen flat tires just in that one day. It was some trial and error as cyclists discovered tires that weren't only wide enough for the rough roads but also tough enough to cope with the many thorns found along the way.

The second day cycling from Sennar turned out to be even tougher than the first. What made it particularly difficult was the large number of corrugations on the road. The road itself seems to have started as informal paths across open fields. Once the dirt dried, it had cracked and those cracks then became corrugations. I wasn't quite sure how to approach these continual bumps but ended up cycling rather slowly, pound, pound, pound. It wasn't much quicker than walking, but, with a stop every so often, I slowly progressed. Others tried variations of standing or trying to cycle faster across the bumps, but it was difficult no matter how we tackled them. It was five in the afternoon by time I arrived at camp after my toughest day so far.

The third day from Sennar turned out to be even tougher than the second. It was also the day I ended up losing my EFI (every f* inch) status due to heat exhaustion. The previous night I didn't quite have an appetite for a second helping at dinner. We started out with corrugated roads again, though they were slightly better than the day before. The morning steadily heated up, however, and by time I reached the lunch truck, it was warmer than any of the days before.

I wasn't feeling 100% at lunch and could eat only one sandwich. I contemplated taking the truck and mentioned it to one or two others. However, a bit of an extended break in the shade and a bit of watermelon, and I felt good enough to ride again. Furthermore, TDA had anticipated the difficulty and placed an extra "refresco" stop another 20 kilometers down the road. The plan was to break the trip into small bits and first ride to the next stop and refresh again.

It was hot cycling to the refresco, and the road was at least as bad as before. My cycle computer recorded temperatures as high as 47C (117F), including a few ten-kilometer sections over 43C (110F). It was hot overall, and I again took a longer pause to cool down and consider my options. It was another 18 kilometers to the next coke stop and 22 kilometers until camp. I decided to go for it. This turned out to be a mistake.

At first the cycling went OK. I had drunk at least ten liters of water that day and had another five liters with me. However, the corrugations were still bad, and I had an energy deficit from not eating as much at lunch. After 10 kilometers I got off the bike and started to walk past some of the corrugations. I alternated walking and cycling some after that. At 15 kilometers, I knew I needed to get on the next truck that came past.

Fortunately, a TDA vehicle came along quickly after that. We dumped water over my head, and I drank a cold bottle of water, but I was still feeling nauseous. As we drove to pick up other riders, the bumps in the road didn't help. I opened the door and threw up. I stayed in the shade once we met other riders before getting to camp.

At camp I tried to drink, but it wouldn't stay down. I ended up in the heat exhaustion ward as the medics started an IV solution to help replace my fluids. There were about six of us total. Other riders had been very helpful in setting up my tent and saving some dinner as well as getting out my gear. For that I was very grateful.

Heat exhaustion gave me enough of a scare that I decided to play it safe. I had not eaten much and the following morning wasn't feeling 100%. I couldn't tell if I was feeling sick, feeling hungry or something else. I had put on my cycling gear, but then I decided to ride the truck that day and ended up with two half days after that. As I heard from other riders, the day I rode the truck was at least as hot as before, though now on paved roads. That day brought us to a town just across the border in Ethiopia.

Ethiopia

It was surprising how many things changed at the border between Sudan and Ethiopia. We left an Islamic state for one where Christians were a majority of the population and Muslims were a large minority. An implication was that alcohol was now more easily available, and some riders looked forward to having a beer after the ride.

Ethiopia seemed significantly more densely populated. We saw it in the numerous villages along the way and when we stopped in seemingly empty places only to find several onlookers who had come over. One of those times I came onto a fellow cyclist from New Zealand, who had a flat tire. Approximately 30 kids watched and poked and prodded to observe the operation. Two other cyclists and I came over to put ourselves and bicycles between the tire fix and the crowds to push them back a little.

Starting with the first evening at our camps as well as lunch stops, TDA placed a small red rope on stakes around the camp. Some locals were enlisted to help police the perimeters and keep the curious outside. It was a curious division, with our circus of mostly Western cyclists and our high-tech gear inside and curious onlookers politely but carefully watching our moves from the outside. One of the images I retain from that first evening was a set of riders sitting on chairs watching a DVD player movie of the Lion King. Just behind the player is the red line and a handful of curious kids watching not the screen, but the cyclists.

Ethiopia also introduced us to the toilet tents. In the deserts of Sudan and Egypt, it had been easy enough to have a few shovels and ask cyclists to go some ways from camp and carefully bury all their waste. In the towns of Egypt, there were either small community toilets, often disgusting but still usable, or we might be close to a hotel where there were also toilets. Neither of those alternatives were particularly practical in Ethiopia. Hence, a deep hole was dug, and a green tent not much larger than a phone booth was placed around it. This was still sometimes disgusting but the best alternative available.

Ethiopia brought us to much more hilly terrain. The first two days cycling took us to Gondar with 900 meters and 2500 meters of total climbing respectively. I was still cautious from heat exhaustion and cycled only the first half of each of these days. While it was still hot, the climbing also brought us to higher elevations and slightly cooler temperatures. Later in Ethiopia we would reach the highest elevation for the trip at slightly over 3000 meters as well as an overnight that was just a few degrees Celsius above freezing.

As we cycled up to Gondar, we passed remains of a burned-up and broken-down double-trailer tanker truck. It blocked an entire lane and had been there for three years but otherwise left to rust. It was on a 16-kilometer climb. The grades weren't particularly steep (~5-6%), but they required shifting into a lower gear and making a steady pace up the hill. It felt like a real accomplishment to reach the top of that hill and look back on the winding road below.

In Gondar, we took two rest days. This allowed one day for errands and rest and a second for sightseeing. I brought my bike to the "bike clinic," as I had discovered the front lockout that kept the suspension fork from bouncing had failed. It turned out to be a stripped screw. We tightened what we could and I sent email to the shop that had sold the bike. Some weeks down the road, a replacement end cap was couriered to me with an incoming rider.

In the middle of town was the Royal Enclosure and inside it six castles that dated back to the 1600's and 1700's. These were mostly in ruins but still interesting to walk through, as were nearby ornate churches.

We had two not-so-difficult days of cycling after Gondar before reaching another rest day at the small town of Bahir Dar. Very little of the route was flat, but even with rolling hills, it wasn't difficult riding. I observed what seemed to be effects of foreign assistance – sometimes helpful and sometimes seemingly out of place. There were signs describing assistance projects along the way. We also observed foosball tables and pool tables placed in some of the villages.

One curious thing I observed were crosswalks painted on the road in some of the villages. There were people and cows wandering all over the roads, not just at the crosswalks – so it seemed somewhat pointless, and I wondered if this had come from a Western aid project that wanted to help curb traffic fatalities.

As we cycled past, some of the children would yell out "Money, money" or "Birr birr" or "You you you" or "Pen" in addition to their normal curious queries such as "Where are you go?" There were enough of these queries that riders started getting inventive in their responses. One Canadian rider would answer "China" on the location question. I figured some of these children had barely traveled to the capital of Addis Abada, so notions of a ride across Africa would be completely strange, but it was at least part of the ritual.

What was more difficult were the numerous children who would throw rocks. Ethiopia has a rapidly growing population, with more than 40% under the age of 15. The parents would work in the fields, and children were only in school in mornings or afternoons. This meant a lot of unsupervised children along the roads, often in groups. When I could catch an eye of an adult in a town, this often helped in restraining behaviors. However, throwing small rocks also seemed to be part of the culture when tending animals. We also saw it as those we hired to police our thin red line would sometimes throw rocks at potential trespassers.

We had read about the rock-throwing children from previous trips and tried various approaches. I tried initially to engage them in conversation, e.g. saying "Hello" or something else to start an engagement. I tried watching and glaring. As a larger cyclist, I tried just riding confidently, letting my size be an extra menace. These worked to varying degrees, though I still didn't escape having rocks thrown at me. It did seem that later riders as well as smaller riders or women received more attacks.

Some cyclists were more aggressive in their response. They would pretend they had a rock and ride towards the perpetrators as if they were going to throw that rock. At least two cyclists reported tales of being so frustrated that they hopped off the bicycles and chased the offending children back into their village. One cyclist almost took a door off the hinges to confront a child as well as his mother.

I am not sure there is any ideal response. The sad thing was that not all children were rock throwers, but we also became more defensive and suspicious in our view of local children because it happened often enough. Also sad were one or two cases of injury from thrown rocks.

After Bahir Dar we had five days of cycling to the capital of Addis Abada, including one day where we descended to cross the Nile River and then climbed back some 1200 meters up the other side. I am cautious in cycling and hence found the descent at least as challenging as the climb. I knew I would be slow and hence took the truck the first half of the ride, so I could make the descent at my own pace.

At the bottom, once we crossed the bridge, we started a 20-kilometer climb out of the canyon. TDA had organized this as a time trial with a cyclist departing every two minutes and racing to see who could complete the climb the quickest. It was a mando day and required for racers.

The fastest racer made it to the top in an hour and twenty-two minutes. My riding in the truck meant I was the first to depart and I could cheer these other cyclists as they came past. Almost all the other cyclists passed me, as it took a little less than five hours for me to reach the top. I wasn't quite the last one to camp because some had started a lot later. Otherwise, it was a nice climb that was hot at the bottom and became cooler as we climbed and could stop in a few villages and get a drink.

On the day we cycled into Addis, we had a long ride to a point that overlooked the city for a final descent. TDA asked riders to arrive by 3 p.m. for a final convoy into the big city. I figured the only thing less pleasant than descending into a big city would be descending in a big group into a big city and opted to ride in one of the trucks. This turned out to be a mistake, as the descent didn't turn out as bad as feared. More significantly, as the truck was making its final approach into camp, one of the staff was on top of the truck pushing hanging electric wires out of the way and over bikes on top. He stepped on a skylight window, which came hurtling down – and onto me as I was peering through that skylight from below. I escaped serious injury, but the window glanced off and chipped a tooth. I ended up visiting a dentist to get this fixed along, accompanied by a different rider who had coincidentally been injured in her lip and tooth by a rock thrown earlier that day.

Addis marked the end of the second section of the ride. These sections were becoming more difficult. While most cyclists had completed the first section to Khartoum with EFI (every f* inch), a number, including me, had lost that status on this section. Illness seems to have taken a toll, as there was a bit of sickness that spread amongst the group. There were also some difficult days and a mix of mechanical and related issues. The cycling wasn't going to become easier with the next section to Nairobi rated as "5" on a 1 to 5 scale for difficulty.

From Addis to our last town in Ethiopia, Yabello, was another five days of cycling. Somewhere in here my thermarest air mattress sprang a leak. It was a common issue as we had camped amongst areas with many thorns. Those who brought compact folding cots seemed to fare better than those with inflatable mattresses, though it was also possible to patch the mattresses. As it was, I would wake up in middle of the night, roll over and blow up the mattress again.

I would describe the parts of the route south of Addis as a "mission district." We saw more churches as well as signs that indicated Western Christian churches had come to partner with these churches as part of a mission. However, we also passed through Islamic areas, and I crossed one town where I saw women in full bourka.

As we neared the border town of Yabello, the roads became rougher and the area less populated. The day we cycled into Yabello itself was a mando day and a particularly tough day cycling. Some others and I ended up in the truck for the ending of the ride and could cheer on those worn out riders making their way into camp. We had a rest day here and there wasn't much more at our hotel camp than a worn hotel with a small restaurant. It was still a welcome rest as we anticipated the cycling into Kenya.

Kenya

It was now time for our third border crossing and another change in environment. Crossing into Kenya the differences didn't seem as abrupt, however, as differences were primarily between northern, mostly desert, areas of northern Kenya and the wetter and relatively more prosperous south. In all of Kenya we were now free of annoying rock-throwing children and would instead see them walking on their way to school, dressed in uniforms and carrying books.

Our first day from Yabello was mostly in Ethiopia and was followed by a day of cycling northern deserts to Sololo. In Kenya, we crossed paths with a train of camels before crossing into a small village. The Kenyans seemed shyer than Ethiopians but would still yell out, "How are you?" I tried replying, "I am fine. How are you?" This was met with another "How are you?" response at least as often as anything else. I can't complain too much, however, as they seemed to know more English than I knew Swahili. We did try learning a few words, including greetings and numbers, in Kenya as well as in other countries we crossed.

It was slow cycling on corrugated roads during our ride to Sololo. I got my second flat tire of the trip. A short while later I passed a TDA truck that was stopped, as the welds holding a small trailer hitched behind had failed. The staff was figuring out how to get it repaired again.

In Sololo we were updated with plans for the next few days. Kenya was holding a much anticipated national election in two days. The aftermath of the previous election in December 2007 led to disputes, and the subsequent violence led to hundreds of deaths as well as the displacement of half a million people. Election unrest continued through March 2008 when that year's TDA ride had skipped the entire country. Eventually diplomats from the UN and elsewhere brokered a solution that included power-sharing as well as an end to the unrest.

Nobody knew what this year's election would bring. The common wisdom was that Kenya, which had the largest economy in east Africa, including a large tourist industry, couldn't afford a repeat of the previous violence. A new Constitution was in place, and reforms had been made by a new election commission to prevent a repeat of violence. For example, to avoid fears of a single national election where a president and his party would get all the spoils of victory and the losing parties receive nothing, greater power-sharing was set up with governors of local states as well as with a Senate. On a more technical level, a new electronic voting system was established to allow returns to be reported as they were tallied rather than waiting until weeks later and revealing results in a large surprise.

Despite all reforms Western travel advisories from the U.S., U.K. and Canada all urged some caution on unnecessary travels. TDA consulted with local officials, including our accompanying security officers, as well as with the home office. TDA determined that we wouldn't travel on Election Day itself as well as a day or two following. This would give us time to observe how the election occurred as well as the immediate aftermath. Furthermore, the northern desert parts of Kenya were a potentially more difficult place to stay than areas further south with more people but also a larger network of roads that, in worst cases, could bring us more quickly across the border and into Tanzania.

The town of Nanyuki, another 500 kilometers farther south, was an ideal place to bring the group as we waited out the election. It was a military town with both a British Army base and a Kenyan Air Force base. It was in a more populated part of Kenya with a better road network. There was a large hotel that could accommodate our group.

We made plans for a two-day bus ride. Sixty bikes were carefully placed wherever room was found: stacked on top of the vehicles, in the aisle of our large truck, etc. An extra-large bus was used for the riders and an accompanying armed security officer. Plans included a first day bus ride to the town of Marsabit, followed by a longer bus ride to Nanyuki. Marsabit was originally a planned stop and rest day. In a TDA ride a few years before (2010), however, bandits had robbed a few cyclists and thus the plans for subsequent years had included a bus trip across the worst, although considerably shorter, parts. – though considerably shorter.

On our bus trip we observed that the two days cycling it would have otherwise taken to get to Marsabit would have been particularly difficult days. The road surfaces were badly rutted. We passed a notoriously difficult section of lava rock road that some riders on previous tours had found at least as difficult as corrugations in Sudan. In addition, the sun was hot and desert otherwise relentless. We passed a few small towns, but it was mostly dry and dusty desert.

On our arrival in Marsabit, we saw the town alive with noisy election-eve rallies. Each side had its prominent color: one group with orange, one mostly red and a third mostly yellow. Through all this came our big bus filled with Western tourists. Some cyclists leaned out the windows to take photos before being reminded that this wasn't the wisest behavior.

Once past Marsabit the landscapes changed dramatically. While the first 120 kilometers were still on rough unpaved roads, we soon came to much smoother paved roads. In addition to better roads, the landscape became lusher and more developed. Soon we saw both corn and wheat fields. Shops seemed more prosperous. We saw more people, but, in proportion, election posters seemed less prominent.

The following day was Election Day in Nanyuki. Voting was at a large park block in town. Along one side was a row of tents marked alphabetically by "stream" and then a first name. I understood stream to be like a last name.

In front of these tents were half a dozen lines with people patiently waiting their turn. Unlike the political rallies, I didn't see much in the way of bright campaign colors. News reports told us of an 86% turnout of registered voters going to 33,000 polling stations with 100,000 police to stand guard. Overall, however, Nanyuki seemed very quiet and orderly.

Once people voted, their index fingers were marked. I talked with one man who showed me his finger and asked if I had voted. I told him I wasn't Kenyan and hence it wouldn't make sense for outsiders like me to vote. He laughed and observed I probably would have been an Odinga (opposite of his favorite party).

As the returns came in, tribal affiliation seemed to be a big part of how people voted. In some states, more than 90% of the voters picked either one candidate or the other. Some people interviewed said, "I am not voting just based on tribe, but we know X and he just happens to be our tribe."

The Election Commission had up to seven days to declare a victor. Initial returns seemed to going smoothly, as tallies were steadily updated, and with the exception of some isolated violence along the coast, all appeared calm. A short while later some further cracks appeared as the color-coded ballots seemed to have a higher, ~5% tally of spoiled votes and the electronic tally system suffered foibles of having non-technical people required to send in results via complex methods. However, it still mostly appeared calm.

We hung around our hotel, and, as it appeared we would spend several days to await the outcomes, also made further plans. We ended up holding an "equator party" one evening, as Nanyuki itself was right next to the equator. Several of us went on a longer hike up the slopes of nearby Mount Kenya, and a few riders made an even longer guided hike to the 5200-meter (17,000 ft.) summit.

Fortunately, after a four-day pause, we were ready to get on the road again. After a brief stop for the requisite equator photographs, we cycled on nicely paved roads. Traffic was busier. We passed areas of tea, bananas, and tropical fruits. We even saw small stands selling fruit. The area appeared more prosperous. People along the way were still reserved, though less than the tribal Masali in Northern Kenya.

The following day turned out to be another bus ride, this time to Nairobi. We had planned for a half day of riding before election results were announced. When results came early in the morning, this turned into a full day of riding the bus. Under rules of the Kenyan election, a runoff would occur only if no candidate received 50% of the initial vote. The announced results were 50.07% for the winning candidate or some 8000 votes over the threshold. As it turned out, there wasn't much violence on hearing the results, though we had been careful just in case.

In Nairobi we came to a huge "overlander" camp, where vehicles were serviced and tourists could arrive for their trips. Our TDA trip now included 20 new sectional cyclists, as the next parts were more popular than the difficult areas north of the equator. It was fun to meet new people, though difficult to remember all the names.

After a rest day in Nairobi, we had two longer days cycling to Arusha, Tanzania. Despite the longer riding, the roads were good. On arrival into camp there was a deluge of rain. Slower riders like me could wait and set up our tents after the worst rain had stopped.

The following morning we arrived at the border with Tanzania, where we filled out a yellow form to exit Kenya and a blue form to enter Tanzania. We exchanged Kenyan shillings for Tanzanian shillings, taking care to avoid being swindled in the exchange. After this there were some gentle climbs and a descent into Arusha for a few rest days. Between Nanyuki, Nairobi and now Arushu, it seemed like we had been resting a lot, but this latest stop was to allow riders to take a safari trip in nearby areas.

Tanzania
Safari time!

Arusha is a common jumping off point for safari trips to nearby Serengeti and Ngorongoro and other parks. This was close to our halfway point, and TDA scheduled three rest days to enable riders who wanted to take a safari. We grouped together to look for safaris, both because it is more fun to go with others and because there were discounts for multiple people.

Ours was a camping safari with two nights in tents. We saw many animals, including elephants, giraffes, zebra, lions, rhinoceros, hyena, ostrich, wildebeest, water buffalo and impala. However, what stood out for me most was one morning in camp when an elephant came over and visited a nearby water tank for a drink. On return the elephant slowly came through the area with parked vehicles. The contrast between elephant and vehicles was very apparent. What was also fun was seeing the long convoy of twenty or so elephants walking in the distance with large bulls up front and smaller elephants in the middle.

After Arusha, we had several days of cycling on paved roads before a longer off-road section. The first night we camped near the village of Magugu. Once again we had a lot of interest from locals observing our camp. Unfortunately, we also had some theft. Overnight someone stole one of the two toilet tents. We thought that it was a pretty bizarre thing to do. Also stolen were a bag or two that a staff member had placed just outside her tent but underneath the rainfly and thus out of view. We reported the thefts with local authorities, and others lent spare clothes (I didn't have much in women's small size).

A few days later we also had two bicycles stolen overnight. This time reporting the theft to the locals and relying on their assistance did result in recovery of these bikes a few days later. Still it was a distressing situation for the riders affected.

Another misfortune struck one of the riders when a bee flew into his shirt. He wasn't traveling fast, but in the subsequent attempt to rid himself of the insect, he fell off his bicycle in a way that created a serious and painful injury, breaking his pelvis. The only saving grace was that we weren't so far from assistance, and they were able to evacuate him. However, his tour was over.

We had a few of these sorts of injuries during the ride. It surprised me that they were as frequent as they were, since this had not happened as often in my self-supported riding. However, the combination of cycling in close groups as well as pushing ourselves over rough and varied terrain resulted in an occasional crash. I think there were at least two broken collar bones during the complete tour in addition to some dislocations and other injuries.

We now had 65 riders in the group. Areas we cycled continued to be lush with sunflowers, corn and other crops grown along the way. This was a wetter area than the deserts before, and the rainy season was starting. We had showers on several days. We were headed for five days of off-road riding where clay/dirt/gravel roads and rains now meant mud. Some days it was a brief shower or two, but one morning it really poured and riders and bicycles were completely covered in red splatters of mud. Some enterprising teens set up to wash bicycles for 1000 shillings (sixty U.S. cents), and many riders took them up on the offer.

On another day we crossed an area where they had graded soft loose dirt on top of the road just before the rains. This turned into a thick pasty mud that got everywhere on our bikes. Those with fenders had it worst as those completely stopped up, but even bikes with derailleurs, internal hubs and brakes also got stuck. Adding to the challenge were stuck vehicles. A large truck had slid sideways and not far from that a bus was also stuck. As cyclists we could walk or slide past the worst muck, but the TDA vehicles also had to get past the stuck vehicles as well. Reports were that it took the large TDA truck a few hours to get past the worst section. Overall, the reports also continued to praise the skill of our truck drivers in carefully navigating these obstacles.

Earlier in Tanzania I had gotten a small cut on the back of my right calf, most likely from repeated strikes from a pedal. It wasn't particularly serious, and I kept it open to heal. Once we came to the off-road section and the mud, I placed a bandage over it to keep the worst of the dirt out. As I would later discover in Malawi, that was a mistake.

The off-road section was a fun few days of muddy riding past some small villages. Each day we seemed to have what I called our welcoming committee of villagers who seemed to spend hours carefully observing the circus that had landed in their midst.

Our last day into Mbeya was a mando day, and hence we could expect it to be extra difficult. The plan was for over 2000 meters of climb and 1500 meters of descent spread across 111 kilometers. I was always more excited by climbing than by steep descents, so I decided to take the truck in for the final descents into Mbeya. Prior to that, the climbing as well as the views from the top gave a "top of the world" feel with great views.

We followed our descent to a relaxing rest day in Mbeya and chance to get laundry done, dry our tents, air out sleeping bags and otherwise anticipate the riding to come in Malawi.

Malawi

Malawi would turn out to be a country for sickness, though I didn't know it yet the first day we cycled across the border. Our first day cycling we were back onto pavement and after a climb out of the Mbeya valley, we made a long descent down towards Lake Malawi. As we descended, the air became more humid and the landscape even more lush. Near the bottom was a sign, "The End of the Dangerous Zone," which seemed amusing as we had not been cognizant of entering this zone.

I exchanged money without problem at the border. However, perhaps half a dozen riders ran into scams. A common way this happened is someone would approach on the street offering a good rate. They would take your cash and dash off to get some in exchange. You would then be told that, unfortunately, they wouldn't be able to make the trade. Your cash would be handed back, but once you counted you would discover that the $50 you had handed them was now $20 or that the bills had been exchanged for counterfeit.

After the border the road became flat, hot, and humid. Kids were unrulier again and asking for money. Overall, it seemed to be a poorer area than Kenya or Tanzania. We also came past areas where people were drying corn and another flaky white crop.

Our first full day in Malawi continued along the lake. There were a few hills and a slight headwind but otherwise not too difficult a ride into our first rest day at Chitimba. Meanwhile, however, the cut on the back of my leg was starting to look worse, so I took the bandages off and tried to let it heal in the open air again – only putting bandages back if it rained or was muddy.

We had a bunch of rain overnight before we left Chitimba as well as the next morning climbing away from the lake. With the rain came many waterfalls, both small and large. Despite this section being another time trial, I took the climb particularly easy to stop for photos and to help another rider fix a flat. The day ended up being a long ride of 136 kilometers, and I felt tired when I finally arrived at camp after 4:30 p.m.

The next day had another 2000 meters of climb. I decided to take it easier and took the truck from lunch into camp. We camped not far from a school, where there was a Peace Corps volunteer from Seattle who had lived and taught in this village for the past two years. We could see many children running in packs through the area though the adults were still back in their homes.

The following morning, I felt OK getting up and put on my cycling clothes. Unfortunately, after getting things packed, my breakfast came back up, and I felt sick. I took the truck to camp and found a hotel room. By afternoon the sickness in my GI tract felt better, but my right leg was starting to swell up.

The swelling was worse the second day, so I took the truck into Lilongwe and our planned rest days. I had promised another rider that I would save her a hotel room at camp and found that that was the last hotel room. I still wasn't 100% up to sleeping in my tent and so set off to walk to find another hotel nearby. By now, walking on my leg was increasingly painful, and it was clear that infection had set in. I couldn't stand without pain, and my right leg appeared twice as big as my left.

I was fortunate that some of the other riders had also picked the same hotel for our rest day as I had. Silvia was a surgeon by training, and her medical perspective as well as increased pain finally beat some sense into my head about the stupidity of trying to suffer through this infection. One of the TDA medics came by in the afternoon, and then we went past some medical clinics in town to find a better and different antibiotic than I had been using. We elevated the leg. The following day was a rest day, and, by the end of that day, it seemed as though my leg was getting just slightly better.

However, it also became apparent that I would ride in the truck until the leg was well enough for me to ride. I felt fortunate to at least stay with the group as another rider with an infection in Ethiopia had ended in the hospital before returning to the ride. Without the right precaution, an infection like this could easily end the trip.

Zambia

I missed the first two days of cycling in Zambia. It was tougher than I expected, not physically tough--that was left for the riders--but mentally tough. I couldn't help but share in the excitement as other riders prepared for the cycling day or finished after a difficult but satisfying ride. I was on the dinner truck, so this meant we would be the last to leave after camp was picked up and then among the first to arrive as camp was set up. I did some helping where I could, e.g. packing up chairs but otherwise felt a bit useless and in the way. While I had ridden the truck a few times for a half day when things were difficult, I had come on the trip to ride my bike, and it was difficult to skip an entire day, let alone more than one in a row.

On the second morning it still hurt when I stood up, but I got my cycling clothes on with anticipation of perhaps trying to ride a little. I went over and talked with the medic, who looked at the still swollen leg and recommended that I really wait a day longer. It was tough, but I realized she was right and went back and decided to ride the truck for a second day, though not until after a brief cry in my tent.

On the third morning I decided to finally give it a cautious try even though my leg was still swollen. It was a long day, 172 kilometers planned with 80 kilometers expected until lunch. Rather than going all the way to lunch, my plan was to get out early and ride as far as I could until the dinner truck came past. I organized my gear, was first in queue for breakfast and set off as soon as I could.

It was nice to be riding again after my infection, including the days prior to Lilongwe. I had a good two hours of cycling before the truck passed. I was still feeling strong but wasn't trying to overachieve on the distance and got on the truck. While I still had a way to go and was going to be careful, it felt great to be back in the saddle again. I ended up taking the following two days as half days as well before eventually declaring victory over the infection.

On our second day in Zambia the group found itself in the middle of riots in the small town of Katete. It was an unexpected and dramatic event. The Zambia Daily Mail provided the following description:

"About 288 people have been arrested in Katete following riots over alleged delays in arresting suspects who gang-raped and strangled a grade 12 schoolgirl last week.

Police reinforcements were deployed in the district to calm residents who torched shops belonging to a businessman of Indian origin whom they accused of being linked to the murder.

Acting President Edgar Lungu, who is also Home Affairs minister, confirmed the disturbances in an interview yesterday.

The rape and murder of Naomi Zulu, who was a student at Katete Day Secondary School, sparked an outrage in a normally 'serene' district.

Eastern Province commissioner of Police Grace Chipalila confirmed the arrests.

The rioters, armed with stones, fought with riot police for over three hours until more officers from Chipata arrived around 11:00 hours in the morning.

Business ground to a halt in the district with Government offices closing prematurely for fear of the rioters venting their anger on civil servants.

The mob hurled stones at law enforcement officers and one policeman was injured and hospitalized.

The rioters burnt two shops, including Kayson's Wholesalers owned by a businessman of Asian origin, and Mr. Paris, which belongs to Alex Banda."

I was riding in the dinner truck, and we found the group stopped at the 80-kilometer point. The fastest racers had already arrived, and other riders were slowly arriving as well. All were asked to stop and wait. We saw the police reinforcements mentioned in the article come past in jeeps and carrying rifles. We saw an ambulance pass as well.

A short while later, the all clear was sounded, and we were told it was ok to continue. Our dinner truck filled up to eight cyclists as prospects of cycling through the riots and then riding another 100 kilometers was more daunting given the delay.

The other cyclists formed together in convoy mode. Up front was a truck with Zambian soldiers. Following this was the entire group of cyclists and after that the TDA vehicles. Slowly we traveled past the worst trouble spots. At one point we heard a few gun shots behind the group, though we weren't sure of their origin or target and they didn't otherwise affect our group. At another point one of the suspects who was on the ground, guarded, took a chance and jumped up and ran through the cyclists.

After a few kilometers of cycling through Katate, the coast was clear, the Zambian police pulled aside and cyclists were again allowed to proceed at their own pace.

Overall Zambia was a more prosperous country than Malawi. We also came through an area with more lodges and camps where we would stay. These might have a few rooms for rent and a larger area for the trucks and tents. At the Luangwa River bridge, there was even an opportunity for an organized trip on the water. I mostly still took things easy and elevated my leg as much as I could to help it heal. The capital city of Lusaka also felt more prosperous, including a fancy mall.

After Lusaka, we had three longer days of cycling to reach Victoria Falls. These were through a savannah area and not particularly difficult, though my leg was feeling it on the third day, so I took a half day ride that day.

Once we reached Livingston we had the second bicycle donation ceremony of the trip. A small portion of our entry fees will fund one bicycle for each full tour rider. In addition, some additional donations are also accepted. This meant that in Zambia TDA contributed a total of fifty bicycles to the chosen cause, a local school district. This school was loaning them to children to make it easier to travel to/from school and improve attendance. The ceremony was interesting to watch, as it also included a presentation from the local kids and talks from local dignitaries.

Victoria Falls was a planned two-rest-day stop. It is a touristy hot spot with exotic events, including bungee jumps, ultra-light aircraft, helicopters, and boat cruises in which some of the riders also participated. My list was simpler: I wanted to continue to heal and rest and I wanted to travel 10 kilometers to see the falls.

I was impressed. While the falls are not particularly tall, they are massive and the claim is that they produce the largest "sheet" of falling water in the world when measured as width times height. They are approximately twice as high as Niagara Falls and one and a half times as wide. I took the paths along the falls where there was a constant mist/rain, at times quite heavy and a good test of my rain jacket. I could also see the bridge in the distance with bungee jumpers.

Victoria Falls is at the border between Zambia and Zimbabwe. It is also very close to the only point in Africa where four countries meet at one spot: Zambia, Zimbabwe, Botswana, and Namibia. We would cross this area on our way to Botswana to continue our ride.

Botswana

Ethiopia was the hilliest country and Botswana the flattest. Long distances and, except for some road construction, nice paved roads meant long distances and good riding. TDA had named this section the Elephant Highway, and we saw them several times. On our first full day riding, we were accompanied by an elephant man, Darryl, who was accompanying us in a safari vehicle. He saw several elephants when he went off-road, but I didn't see any until a few days later. Apparently, Botswana has ~160,000 to ~180,000 elephants, which is about ~60,000 too many. A charging elephant can be dangerous, so we were advised to give them wide berth if possible. Most I saw were either farther away or clustered under trees to avoid midday heat.

Zambia had been more prosperous than countries earlier, and Botswana continued that pattern. We made roadside camps a few times and stayed next to lodges. In addition to camp areas, these might have a bar/restaurant. Otherwise, it was four longer but not extremely exciting days riding to Maun.

I did see my first touring cyclists we encountered on the trip, two French cyclists with all their gear. They had started in the Democratic Republic of the Congo, cycled to Arusha and after that mostly along the same route we had taken. Africa from the equator southwards seemed easier for self-supported cyclists than our travels further north and hence made more sense for a self-supported ride.

Maun was a nice small town and the site of our next rest stop. Some riders took flights over the nearby Okavango delta or canoe trips. After doing laundry, it was time for me to get some equipment repaired. My drive train was occasionally skipping. The TDA mechanics opened the hub mechanism and told me the spring was broken. I had brought a spare hub, and they were able to swap internal mechanisms. My camera had jammed, third broken camera on the trip, and I was able to find a replacement. I bought new batteries for my headlamp. Otherwise, I took it easy in anticipation of five upcoming cycling days that would total more than 800 kilometers.

The first of these five days was 160 kilometers but would have been easier if not for a head wind. We had a bush camp off the main road but were also told this might be one of our last, as Namibia would have more private property and with that more fences. A group our size would need to camp in more official camping lodges.

The following day we saw our first road signs indicating South Africa. It was a long day riding but broken up with a team trial with a twist. Once again we formed in groups of four or five. However, instead of seeing which group was fastest, the goal was to establish a target time and see what group could ride and most closely match their time. For this to work it also meant that no cycle computers, watches, or other gear could be used. We were again with "team slow" and set a target of two hours eleven minutes and three seconds for a 40-kilometer distance. We came within five minutes of our target. That was good enough for fourth place, and other teams were all within three to seven minutes of the target. I was surprised at how close all the teams were.

Unfortunately, just prior to the time trial I made the surprising discovery that my rear rim had split. I had had this problem once before in Egypt and was happy that Ben, a sectional rider, had couriered a new rim to Arusha. However, rather than risk having my wheel break on me, I took the truck after the time trial. I also ended up missing the following day, 207 kilometers to the border with Namibia. It was the longest ride of the trip, and I felt unfortunate to miss it. I was grateful, however, when one of the mechanics rebuilt the wheel using my spare rim, as it meant I would be back on the bike in Namibia and South Africa.

Namibia

Our first night in Namibia we held a TDA version of "burning man.". The organizers built a large wooden man made of wood. Each person could write a note of bad thoughts or things they wanted to get rid of and have burned along with the man. Mine simply said, "Broken rims."

Our route across Namibia took us away from the main roads and mostly along gravel roads through the deserts. Of the three largest sections of off-road cycling (Sudan, Tanzania, and Namibia), it was the one I enjoyed the most. The roads had occasional sandy patches but were otherwise great cycling. What I enjoyed most were the sweeping desert vistas and changing scenery. These reminded me of the wide sagebrush valleys in Nevada and Utah.

The first two days riding brought us to Windhoek, the capital of Namibia. Windhoek had a surprisingly modern feel, with malls and shops that felt more like those in the U.S. than areas we had previously traveled through Africa. I had lost my fleece in the deserts of Egypt, and a modern mall in Namibia was the first time I could find a replacement in my size.

Once past Windhoek we cycled past a landfill followed by a troop of baboons running across the road carrying landfall loot. Soon thereafter the pavement ended, and we climbed steeply up to Kupferberg Pass. The views were stunning from the top and for the rest of the day. Around each bend and over each hill, there always seemed to be something different to see.

The following day, as we made our way up Spreetschoogte Pass, we rode past signs warning of steep grades and forbidding trucks or caravans. The TDA trucks took the alternate route as we climbed up to the top. The descent was one of the steepest for the entire trip. Rather than gravel we were fortunate the road surface was brick paving stones. Still, I walked downhill for a short while on the steepest bits. The end of this day brought us to Solitaire camp, with a delightful German bakery.

The Naked Mile is a TDA tradition. On what is supposed to be a very remote part of the gravel roads to Sesriem, some cyclists will ride for a mile or more in the buff. In the 2012 tour the year before ours, one rider set a record cycling the entire day without clothes. Our Brazilian cyclists matched the record by cycling an entire day in the buff.

As the riders left in their normal groups and pelotons, they sorted by gender more than normal. The female cyclists allowed the male peloton to go ahead. With the exception of one of the excellent photographers on our trip, commissioned to get a few tasteful photos, the other males were banished. I was slower than either peloton and arrived at lunch after both groups had departed. I waited until I was a discrete distance from the lunch truck, stripped, and cycled the next 3 kilometers before getting clothed again. Task completed.

Sesreim is next to the Sossusvlei region, which has giant sand dunes. On our rest day, I went on a day tour organized by a nearby hotel. We left early in the morning, made a hike around the dunes before breakfast and made a midday return. Some of the major dunes were numbered others had names. Dune 45, Big Daddy and Big Mama, were most common dunes for hikes. Big Daddy is 325 meters high (~1000 feet) but was an easy climb. In the steepest bits, one might slide backwards a bit, but within 45 minutes we were at the top. On the way down I alternated between running, walking, and sliding on my bottom. It was fun even though we ended up with sand everywhere. We enjoyed a fancy picnic breakfast, and then we were back in camp before it became warm.

It was my 50th birthday, and Sossusvlei was a great place to celebrate.

The following day, however, turned out to be one of the tougher days riding. The road had some soft sandy spots, and one could see swerving cycle tracks in the sand as riders had tried, often in vain, to find a better and harder route. As we cycled, the wind slowly picked up. At first it was a cross-wind, but after 20 kilometers it became a strong headwind. It got warm, and I started to ration my water after 50 kilometers.

Fortunately, one of the vehicles came back and helped us refill water, and, after five and half hours, I made it to lunch. I wasn't the only late cyclist. As I calculated the remaining distance to camp and hours of daylight left, I realized I would likely arrive after dark and decided to take the truck from lunch. I wasn't the only one; the truck was completely full, including one rider who opted to ride on the roof.

As we got close to camp, one rider in the truck was starting to feel the heat, and we paused to get him cooled down. With such a full truck, I asked the driver how close we were to camp and he said, "3 kilometers," I could walk that, so volunteered to walk to make a bit more room. It turned out that we were 12 kilometers out instead of 3, though I got a ride on the last bits from one of our other vehicles.

Also, fortunately the following day we had mostly pavement and an easier ride. This was followed by three slightly tougher days riding until we reached Felixe Unite. We had reached the far southern border of Namibia and across the river could see South Africa, the last country for the trip. We were in our end-game mode now, as there would be only six more days of cycling to reach Cape Town.

South Africa

Border crossings seem to have become easier and less expensive as we went along, and our crossing from Namibia was quick and free. Our first three days cycling through the desert on mostly paved roads brought us to Strandfontein on the ocean. There was a heavy fog as we came in. It was the first time we had seen the ocean since departing the Red Sea at the start of the trip.

The following day was our last official day of timed racing. I had been near the bottom of the race timings for a while, particularly since some others had decided to stop being official racers. I had not really worried about racing or my time, but instead used it more like a time card to punch in and punch out so someone could see, "Yes, he is still alive and riding." It had served its purpose.

The riding was straightforward and, after the race ended, even a bit more relaxed. We took some of the back roads along the coast, including a private road that went along the railway. There was some question of whether we would be allowed on the official R27 highway, as there was some permit that was now required. The local officials insisted it was for the safety and protection of cyclists, though once they stopped being bureaucratic and we were eventually allowed to pass, this highway had the widest shoulders of any highway we had been on in South Africa.

Those shoulders were occasionally used for passing traffic, but sight lines were good, and it was smooth cycling.

It was exciting to now see multiple road signs indicating distances to Cape Town, with those distances slowly decreasing. In a group as large as ours, with a lot of type A personalities, there had been talk of the "end of the trip" and questions such as "What are you doing next?" probably since the last third of the ride, but this had become much more real as we were riding through our tenth country. It became exciting as we even saw the mesa above Cape Town as we cycled into our last night at a campground.

This evening was an awards ceremony. The staff had worked out a sequence of goofy awards and were careful to give one to each paid rider. It gave us a chance to reflect on some of the quirky parts of the trip and was also interesting to see how one might come across to others. I received one for an expression I often asked, "Are we having fun yet?" and for being cheerful.

As we came to our last day riding, I couldn't help but reflect on four months: sandstorms in Sudan, riots in Zambia, two broken rims, one infected leg, one broken hub, two broken tent zippers, heat exhaustion, stones in Ethiopia, an election in Kenya, mud in Tanzania, hustlers in Egypt and a naked mile in the deserts of Namibia. It had been an eventful if intense trip but was now ending.

We cycled 61 kilometers before grouping together for our final convoy ride into the city. Our assembly point was on the beach with Table Mesa and was also a point for champagne and a set of end photographs. There were many reasons to celebrate and special mention went to both the race winners/places as well as those who finished EFI. Approximately a third of the group were EFI, and I believe is much more a reflection of the determination and grit of my fellow riders than any sense of ease of this task. I know from my own rim troubles, infection and heat exhaustion that it is easy to get circumstances to stop EFI, and most of these earning this accolade had put in extra heroic efforts, working through sickness combined with some long days. Also on more than one occasion, cyclists ended up on a borrowed bike after their own had some quirk or break. My hat's off to these riders and the general spirit/determination they and several other almost EFI riders showed.

The final 30 kilometers into Cape Town was simply a fun ride that became progressively more interesting as we entered the urban area. On the final approach we ended up using otherwise dedicated bus lanes and had police stopping traffic as we came into the heart of the city. Finally, we came to the waterfront district and were onto a small path and underneath a finish banner. Our ride was officially complete, but we had a more formal completion ceremony followed by a dinner that evening.

After TDA I would spent four days as a tourist before flying back. The following is a more complete list of lessons learned I posted in my blog as I reflected on the trip:

- Africa has lots of thorns. While my Schwalbe Marathon Plus tires had only two flats on the entire trip,this was lower than average. Bring good tires, particularly for off-road, with good thorn protection (e.g. some riders had more than 10 flats on the first off-road day). What I did find was that my thermarest developed a leak after camping on thorns on day #30. People who brought a small foldable cot seemed to avoid this.

- Africa has sand. I went through three basic point-n-shoot cameras that each got jammed due to sand. Next time I would bring a more dust-proof camera and be a little more careful taking photos of sand storms. My tent zippers also failed through the trip, probably due to sand as well.

- Africa does not have much in way of "real" bicycle shops prior to Namibia—or at least we didn't find them. Sectional riders joining later helped by bringing extra parts (e.g. for me a spare rim to Nairobi). Riders that sent parts via DHL or other courier services sometimes were charged very high fees for parts.

- Electronics. I and other riders had our share of electronic toys, including laptop, kindle, cell phone and GPS odometers.

- Solar chargers, such as Goal Zero, worked well at keeping small pieces charged. With so many phones and other toys, outlets were frequently at a premium when we did encounter them.

- Wi-Fi was sporadic, and 60 riders can quickly clog up simple systems we encountered (particularly if some riders skype or video skype). SIM cards and cell phones worked at least as well in some situations. See also web updating below.

- Weather. Africa surprised me in that most days were within reasonable temperate ranges. It got particularly hot (>40C) in the desert of Sudan and next time more re-hydration salts are in order. It also got to ~3-4C once in Ethiopia and at end of the trip in Namibia/South Africa. I ended up buying more warm weather gear in Windhoek, which was very helpful at the end of the trip. Rains we had were mostly all warm rains in areas such as Tanzania. Otherwise there was a surprising amount of time with daytime highs between 25C-35C and overnight lows ~10C-~25C, generally reasonable for cycling.

- Budget.One of the TDA mailings suggests approximately $100 per week as spending money with perhaps some more if you plan extra accommodations or excursions. The following three bullets cover my findings regarding expenses.

- Most on the road days are inexpensive. Coke stops are a dollar here or there and there just are not many places to spend money during most riding days. Instead it is more rest days and cities where expenses are higher.

- Visa fees in the first countries (Egypt, Sudan, Ethiopia, Kenya, Tanzania, Malawi,) come in cash and can be $50-$100 here and there, an expense I had not factored into the equation.

- Kenya onwards seem to have ATMs in border towns or soon thereafter. Some folks had issues with their home banks freezing accounts or more difficulty with Mastercard-linked accounts, but with some patience this works. There also are much more limited places north of the equator to use credit cards such as visa cards (even in hotels). This got easier as we went further south.

- Web page updating. t I received feedback that my web site was among those most kept up to date. I did that with a combination approach including (a) bought a local SIM card in each country.

Used a cell phone and WordPress for Android to provide a short two or three sentence update most cycling days (b) brought a laptop to edit photos and included more complete text when I could, e.g. on rest days (c) organized the site in advance with photos/categories/links so structure/navigation was all set up.

- Favorites. A common but strange question since part of what makes a trip like this interesting is the variety in cycling from one place to the next. However, if I were to list countries in order of my most to least favorites, it would be as follows:

  1. Namibia – beautiful off-road cycling through the desert

  2. Tanzania – off-road cycling through smaller villages on clay/mud/sand/gravel road, challenging but beautiful. Taking a safari was a nice change of pace.

  3. Ethiopia – intense and challenging in its own way. Different than countries either before or after.

  4. Sudan – friendly people, hard to get to. Initial route bypassed most towns on excellent roads and later route went through countryside but on awful off-road. Too bad there wasn't a mix of the two

  5. Botswana – longest riding, flat stretches of road, but chances to see elephants and good weather

  6. Zambia – Victoria Falls, good roads and slightly rolling hills

  7. South Africa – excitement of finishing the trip and some off-road cycling. However, highway riding was longer stretches without many places to stop.

  8. Kenya – wish we had been able to ride more, good riding but elections this year meant we couldn't do as much

  9. Malawi – Infected/swollen leg, caused me to miss some riding

  10. Egypt – Nice desert riding and excitement of starting the trip, but enjoyed other areas more. Assertive people selling things

Epilogue

I had six weeks immediately after the TDA ride before I was back to work, and I used this time to bicycle from Portland to Fort Collins. It gave me a chance to unwind from an intense vacation cycling as well as make visits to two places I had previously lived. Furthermore, I had some items in storage in Fort Collins and rented a U-Haul to bring these with me to Texas.

I brought my two broken rims to Sugar Wheel works. Through Jude's efforts Velocity had already replaced both rims under warranty. I also picked up an Extrawheel Trailer to carry my panniers on this self-supported ride.

The ride to Colorado was uneventful. It was the end of May and after a surprisingly wet ride down the Oregon coast, I turned east not long after seeing the "Welcome to California" sign. One of those days I had more than two inches of rain and made it a short-day ride into Brookings.

Once I left the coast and went inland towards the deserts, it became much drier. I made a diagonal path via Gerlach (home of nearby Burning Man festival) to U.S. 50, the start of "the loneliest road" across Nevada. I had cycled this route once before in 2002, but it was interesting to see it again after I had compared Namibia to Nevada. This time Nevada still felt more like Nevada, though it was nice to reflect on Namibia.

I made a rest day in Delta, Utah, and used it as an opportunity to cycle to the ruins of nearby Topaz internment camp. Approximately 110,000 Japanese Americans had been interned in a series of camps, and more than 8000 had ended up in Topaz. Many of these had come from the San Francisco Bay area, and this camp in the high desert at 4500 ft. elevation would have been a sharp contrast. All the buildings were now gone, but the site still contained small signs indicating where the schools, living barracks, hospital, fire station and churches had been found. There were small plaques here, including some about Japanese Americans who served in the U.S. military, a few of whom had been killed. Some came from these camps or had had families in the camps. It was otherwise a sobering but interesting experience.

After Topaz I cycled towards the Salt Lake City area and then towards Price. Even in mid-June the temperatures were getting considerably warmer, so I modified my plans to visit Moab and instead came via U.S. 40 and northern Colorado instead. Along the way I stopped in Vernal, Utah, where it was nice to visit with a TDA rider with whom we had just finished cycling to Cape Town.

From here I spent a few days in Colorado riding up and over Rabbit Ears Pass and Cameron Pass and then made a long descent down the Poudre Canyon. We had had our official finish in Cape Town, but I could celebrate a second time in reaching my storage locker in Fort Collins. I had not quite had enough cycling yet, so I swapped bikes for one from storage and took that bicycle on an organized Bicycle Tour of Colorado ride for another week before returning to work. It had been a great trip, but now it was time to put my efforts at work dreaming and scheming of another big ride to come in four or five years, this time across South America.

2016 - Tales from across North America
URL: http://www.bike2016.com

Plans

There was a gleam in his eye as the porter spotted me coming out of the minibus with my luggage: two bicycles, a large duffel bag and a smaller bag. His eagerness to help by jumping in front of his competitors betrayed his guess that assisting a Western tourist with as much luggage as I had would lead to a quick and lucrative tip.

Our first delay came as we came to the doors of the terminal building. It was August 15th, 2014, Indian Independence Day, and there was extra security checking at the Bangalore Airport.

"You can't bring a bicycle into the terminal."

"I am flying Lufthansa, and they allow flying with an unboxed bicycle."

We waited while a second security officer went to confirm with Lufthansa and admitted us to the building. They did suggest that perhaps I should have the bicycles wrapped. So, we went to the station where folks wrap suitcases in plastic.

I asked the rate and was told an amount that was double the amount for a suitcase, and this was for each bicycle. It still seemed reasonable to me, however, and I asked them to proceed. As it turned out it was more than double the effort, as suitcases are typically mounted in a fixture that spins and quickly leads to a plastic enclosed suitcase. It took more effort, but the staff was still eager and enthusiastic about wrapping such a bicycle by hand. Perhaps only the porter was frustrated by this second delay.

Without much trouble we got to the Lufthansa counter and waited in line. At the first opportunity the porter asked for his payment and then disappeared to find his next customer, undoubtedly wishing for a quicker turnaround.

Flying back from Bangalore with two bicycles was one of the first explicit steps I took in preparation for my ride across the Americas. My visit included work at AMD's Bangalore offices and a cycle trip from Leh to Srinagar in the Indian states of Jammu and Kashmir. The bicycle I used to ride in the Himalaya was my mountain bike I had used to cycle across Africa. The second bicycle was one I had brought to India for riding around Bangalore during my visits to the AMD offices. I was bringing this bike back partially to retrofit it for my upcoming long expedition and partially because I wasn't certain if or when I might next visit AMD's India offices.

On my previous long rides, I had typically commissioned a new bicycle somewhat before many of the rides: a Cannondale 1000 to ride across the U.S.A. in 1992, a custom bike to ride around Australia in 2001, a Trek 520 to ride across Russia in 2007 and a Trek mountain bike to ride across Africa in 2013. As I prepared for my upcoming trip, I decided to have four of my existing bikes fixed up instead: two Trek 520s touring bikes and two Trek 4500 mountain bikes. I designated one mountain bike and one touring bike as "primary" and one of each type as "alternate". This would let me ride some sections on a touring bike and others on a mountain bike, and, if worst came to worst and a bike was damaged or stolen, then I would have a backup.

I made several upgrades to my "ride around Bangalore" bicycle: stronger wheels, a Brooks leather saddle, and extra grips on my handlebars to provide more hand positions as well as a renewal of the drive train. The wheels cost more than the bike itself, and the bike shop wondered why I was putting a lot of money into a not very expensive mountain bike, so I explained my trip as well as my emphasis on durability over most everything else.

My personality is a type that likes to make lists and check things off as accomplishments. Hence, I pretty much figured I would bicycle across South America even before my Africa trip was complete. This way I would have taken trips across all six continents that I could ride across (Antarctica, the 7th continent, is beyond my abilities). The idea of cycling six continents was reinforced when I learned in December 2011 that AMD would shut down our Portland, Oregon, office and shift compiler work to the San Francisco Bay area. As a manager on the Portland site, I was given an early notice before it would be announced to the team in March 2012. This would also let me better help the team through the announcement and beyond.

With the office closure, a fork in the road was approaching where I would need to decide between one of several alternatives: (a) move to California to follow my job and stay with the company (b) take my planned trip across Africa in 2013, followed immediately by a ride across South America as well (c) create a hybrid option of making my trip across Africa, working with AMD for several years and then cycling across South America. In the time before the office closure became public, I more seriously explored these alternatives.

I traveled to the Bay Area in February 2012, looked at real estate and apartment prices, and figured out how easy it would be to live there without purchasing an automobile. I also more seriously read several blogs and books to see how others had cycled across South America. As I did this exploration, an overall plan and several goals started to fall into place:

- I wanted to stay with the company and help the company and employees through closure of the site. Our team had accomplished a bunch, and it was important these efforts weren't lost.
- I was going ahead with my planned 2013 ride across Africa.
- I wanted to ride across South America, but ideally not right away. Instead, I would follow my Africa trip with another three to five years of work. I had lived in the San Francisco Bay area before, between my 1997 Canada trip and 2001 Australia trip, and knew I could live there again – but I might also explore if I could work instead from another location, such as our Austin, Texas, offices.

The rest of 2012 became a lot more focused on changes at work, including the Portland site closure and then final preparations for my trip across Africa. However, I had also added a future trip across South America to my goals. What I had not completely figured out was exactly when I might make that trip and what else might be included in addition to cycling South America.

The timing and duration of my trip started to fall into place after I returned from Africa and about three years before my next trip. I initially bought web domains for "bike2016.com," "bike2017.com" and "bike2018.com" to hedge my bets on the likely year. While I had already crossed North America twice, I got more excited thinking of a longer Prudhoe Bay to Tierra del Fuego ride rather than just cycling South America. This meant leaving in the Alaskan summer and finishing in the Argentinian summer to avoid weather extremes at higher latitudes. While record holders have cycled this distance in six months, an eighteen-month trip was more realistic.

Tour d'Afrique (TDA Global Cycling) had reorganized their ride across South America to go end-to-end from Cartagena, Colombia, to Ushuaia, Argentina, with the first of these rides scheduled for 2015 and then every two years after that. I preferred to do my own solo self-supported ride, but it was also interesting to me to have TDA South American Epic as a backup plan. If I had bad experiences cycling through Central America by myself, this would let me switch to TDA's ride for South America. This meant starting my overall trip on an even-numbered year--either 2016, 2018, 2020, etc.[14]

At the time I first planned my trip, 2016 seemed to line up well with upcoming work projects and otherwise seemed like reasonable timing, so that became my mark on the wall. It was too early to announce things publicly, but I had set up the bike2016.com with a cryptic countdown clock that counted down to summer solstice in 2016. This countdown had started a little over 1000 days prior to the expected start to my trip.

After I had established rough parameters for my trip, I submitted an entry to the "companions wanted" section of the Adventure Cycling web site. It read,

> "Solstice to Solstice. Plan is to celebrate summer solstice 2016 in Deadhorse, Alaska, and spend 18 months cycling south to reach Ushuaia, Argentina, during summer solstice. Experienced 53-year-old male cycle tourist looking for adventurers to join in all or part of the ride."

While traveling in a group wasn't a requirement for my trip, cycling with Mickey across Russia had worked well in 2007, so I would see what happened.

---

[14] In 2017 the next TDA South America ride was moved to 2020.

I received approximately fifty emails. Some of these were mostly inquiries or contacts from others planning a similar trip. A few expressed interest in parts of the journey, particularly those in Latin America. It was still a while before the trip, so I responded to the emails and provided a pointer to my blog for more information. As it turned out, another cyclist, Dhruv, from India was planning a similar trip, and we agreed to meet in Deadhorse to start together and see how things went. Otherwise, I had many conversations but no specific partners coming from this posting.

I signed up for another wheel building class from Sugar Wheel Works in Portland. While I had taken the class once before, wheel building seems to be skill that improves with practice. A bonus is that you finish the class with a customized set of wheels for your situation. I built the strongest rear wheel I could, a 48-spoke, three cross lacing, using a Phil Woods hub.

By early 2016 I had updated and retrofitted four bicycles in preparation for the journey in addition to outlining a rough route through the U.S.A. and Canada. My plan was to start with roads I had traveled before: the Dalton Highway from Prudhoe Bay, followed by the Alaska Highway down through Canada. Through the U.S.A. I picked out the Great Divide Mountain Bike Route (GDMBR), a mostly off-road adventure along the Rocky Mountains. I wasn't certain how much of the GDMBR I would cycle on the trails vs. on nearby roads but decided to use a mountain bike for this section after using my touring bike to start in Prudhoe Bay.

My sister-in-law and oldest brother have a motel near Glacier National Park. My two older brothers, Rob and Bert, both helped by bringing my mountain bike to the motel in Montana, where I would then be able to switch bikes.

The last few months before departure were busy as I prepared for the trip while preparing my townhouse for rental. It also turned out to be a busy and exciting time at work. As a manager for software and analysis teams, the preparation and arrival of new silicon is a fun time at AMD, a microprocessor company. When I had planned out my trip a few years before, it had looked as though my timing would work well, but as dates neared, it was going to be an awkward time. I thought about delaying my trip by a year but realized this wouldn't let me have TDA as my alternate plan – and waiting two more years was a long time, during which a lot could happen.

In the last few months, I went through everything I owned and divided it into one of three piles:

1. The first pile was everything I would need on my trip, by nature limited to avoid carrying too much.
2. The second pile was to either give away or throw away. I made multiple trips to nearby Goodwill and donated bike parts to Austin's Yellow Bike project.
3. The third pile was to store. I rented a storage locker in Austin and filled it with multiple trips.

Otherwise, I completely emptied my townhouse and worked with a property management company to have it rented during my trip. Some extra income would help during my trip, but at least as important was having someone live on the property and keep an eye on it.

My last day of work was June 10th. For the first time since graduating from college, I would be without an employer. Each of my previous long trips used either vacation or leaves of absence. I had worked for two employers: Hewlett-Packard and AMD and had the AMD job lined up before leaving HP. I was both excited and a little nervous, but the adventure would soon begin. After finishing work there would be a few days to finish packing up my townhouse, drive to Colorado and then depart for Prudhoe Bay.

Alaska

Why wouldn't that drawstring open? My hands were cold as I shivered a bit. The outhouse shielded the worst of the wind, but, unfortunately, the door was welded shut as this would have let me go inside. At least the worst of the snow had stopped. After several attempts I resorted to getting my knife out of my bag and cutting the string. I got the tent out of the bag, set it up and soon thereafter things were looking up.

I set up my stove, boiled some water and fixed a freeze-dried meal. Not all of it stayed down, but hopefully I'd replenish energy from a cold first day cycling from Prudhoe Bay. Overnight the temperature dropped into the

20's, but in the morning the sun was out, and the area was beautiful with freshly fallen snow.

I had flown into Deadhorse airport on June 20th and cycled over to the Aurora Hotel. The hotel was a large pre-fabricated building with a parking lot that had electric plugs for car heaters. One put on shoe covers to avoid spreading the salt placed on roads outside. The cost was high but included meals in a well-stocked cafeteria.

As I walked over to the Prudhoe Bay General store, a motorist in a pickup stopped and told me to be careful because there was a grizzly bear walking over behind the nearby buildings. I didn't see the bear. There was a post office at the General Store, where I went to pick up a package. I had sent myself an iso-butane canister as "General Delivery," ordering it via Amazon. My multi-fuel stove burned both gasoline and iso-butane, but I preferred the cleaner burning iso-butane. The person at the post office told me Prudhoe Bay wasn't a General Delivery location, but fortunately they still had the package.

Dhruv and I had agreed to start cycling the Dalton Highway together. Weather forecasts called for a quick storm to pass through and clear by afternoon. Hence, we agreed on a plan to check the weather at 7 a.m. and, if it looked reasonable, then depart at 10 a.m. Even if it was still snowing, we expected it to improve by early afternoon. There were 24 hours of daylight with the sun above the horizon until July, but we still preferred daytime hours as temperatures were slightly warmer.

At 10 a.m. on June 21st, we met and took the obligatory starting photographs. There was a cold wind blowing, and it was snowing lightly. We expected this to end in a few hours. We were on a flat gravel road but cycled slowly. Dhruv cycled even more slowly than I, and I waited for him after a kilometer and then after another kilometer. It was cold to keep stopping and waiting, so I decided I would ride fifteen kilometers to the first road construction and wait there.

When I reached the construction zone, there was a flagger stopping all traffic, as we needed to wait for a pilot vehicle to return. I asked if I could cycle, and the flagger told me that "unless you want to wait until we leave at 6 p.m., you need to put your bicycle in the truck." I waited a little more, perhaps twenty minutes total. Dhruv still hadn't arrived, but I got my bike in the vehicle and crossed the first zone. There was another eight kilometers of cycling before reaching a second construction zone, where I repeated the procedure: wait, put my bike in the truck, ride in the truck and then return to my bike.

It remained cold as the snow continued to fall. It was a light wind, fortunately a tailwind, and the snow started to stick to my panniers. However, I rode at a steady pace and kept warm through the afternoon. As I neared my destination, the last chance overlook, the road climbed. I saw two tents beside the road and called out, but nobody answered. The next day I met the two Swedish cyclists that were camping in the tents. A little farther and I'd ridden 98 kilometers and reached the Last Chance overlook. After putting up my tent and fixing dinner, I waited for Dhruv for a while and eventually got to sleep. Dhruv never arrived that first day, and I learned later that he camped at the same spot as the Swedish cyclists.

My second day cycling started cold but with a beautiful white world of freshly fallen snow. The road had a few more hills. There was a short section of asphalt, but most of the day I spent riding on gravel. Fortunately, there was good drainage and there were few muddy areas. I slowly followed a river as it climbed slightly. Along the way I saw workers burying plastic tubing as well as an occasional large cooler-size box. It was a new fiber-optic cable to Prudhoe Bay under construction. There were no stores or other services in this section. After 78 kilometers I saw a good place to stop on a slightly higher, but well-drained little hill. A short while later two other touring cyclists arrived. It was the Swedish cyclists I had passed the day before.

Two more days of cycling brought me to Coldfoot. In the morning of the fourth day, I rode up and over Atigun Pass at 1460 meters (4800 feet) of elevation. The last few kilometers were steep, and I walked my bike. Just as I reached the top, a large semi-trailer truck pulled up. The driver offered me a bottle of water and a candy bar. Thanks!

The descent from Atigun Pass was also steep--my cycle computer told me 12%. I walked a short stretch downhill as I am cautious descending steep grades with a fully laden bicycle. Once I reached the river valley below, I saw the first spruce trees. It was a different world from the treeless tundra north of the pass. I cycled my longest day yet, 136 kilometers, but the road surface was good and mostly downhill.

Coldfoot is a small settlement that reminds me of an Australian roadhouse. There is a small restaurant that caters to truck drivers as well as tourists traveling the road. There is an expensive hotel and a small grassy area for tents. I decided to camp and spend a rest day in Coldfoot. The pair of Swedish cyclists arrived the next day to camp farther down the road. Three Swiss cyclists also rode through Coldfoot on the next morning. Dhruv arrived the afternoon of the next day and we compared notes. He would take a rest day the following day, so we planned to keep in touch.

My first day cycling from Coldfoot, I reached the Arctic Circle. There was a sign here for obligatory photos. While I was there, I saw other tourists, including a few on motorcycles, as well as a small minibus taking tourists from Fairbanks to the Arctic Circle and back. I was glad I had cycled through the tundra on the northern slope, as it was quite different from the area around the Arctic Circle. The riding had more hills than on previous days, and a few kilometers past the Arctic Circle, I camped at Fish Creek. Overnight I heard light ticking against the tent. I'm not sure if it was mosquitoes or rain.

Overcast skies at 4 a.m.-- I learned that the noise on the tent was a light rain. I got up, boiled some water, reheated my dehydrated eggs and ate breakfast. While it was only 4:45 a.m., I was wide awake, and since it was full daylight, I got on the road early. The road climbed sharply up a region known as Beaver Slide, and I walked up the steepest parts.

Fortunately, the road was paved once I reached the top and remained paved for a while farther. I passed the Swedish cyclists, who were just breaking camp. I told them about upcoming services along the road, including a restaurant at the Yukon River. With the combination of running low on food and a miserable night in the rain, they were relieved to be getting closer to points of civilization. We climbed to the top of Gobbler's Knob. They climbed the hill faster than I did but waited at the top, and we saw the view together.

A short while later I saw three tents along the road. This turned out to be the Swiss cyclists again.

Unfortunately, not much past Gobbler's Knob, the road became gravel again, including some parts with soft sticky mud. The next 17 kilometers alternated between soft pasty sections and harder gravel sections that were easier to cycle. The rain had mostly stopped, so I passed my "bailout" camp and pressed on, hoping for better roads. As I passed mile marker 75, it happened. The adhesive paste mud had jammed my chain and before I knew it, the torque had busted the derailleur cage and snapped off the derailleur mounting. It was broken--now what to do? There was still too much paste to shorten the chain to make a single-speed bicycle, so I started walking. I periodically stopped to look for passing pickups. Several passed, but none stopped. I guess that the pipeline service pickups specifically weren't allowed to assist.

After five kilometers I passed the Swedish cyclists. They have internal Rohloff hubs, but the paste had also jammed up their bicycles. They'd decided to hitchhike but stayed in one place rather than using my walking approach.

I walked some more. Pleasant and sympathetic folks came past, including ones that offered me a coke. Finally, after 11 kilometers of walking, a nice German-speaking couple stopped. They had a small camper and were willing to give me a ride to the Yukon River restaurant. We very carefully knocked as much mud off the bike as we could before we put it into the camper. I very much appreciated their help. At the Yukon River, I talked with the kind driver of a small Arctic Circle tour bus, and he gave me a ride to Fairbanks (220 kilometers). I stashed my bike at the Yukon River so I could retrieve it later.

It was a long day by the time I reached Fairbanks. The tour bus driver dropped me off at a motel not far from a bicycle shop and not far from a car rental that specialized in gravel vehicles.

The next morning I rented a car. The car rental cost more than average, but I knew I was legal to drive back on the Dalton Highway. At the Yukon River I met the Swiss cyclists when I retrieved my bicycle. They had slept in until noon and thus cycled on the highway after the mud had dried up. In hindsight, if I hadn't departed at 4:45, I would have avoided it as well.

After retrieving my bike I dropped it off at Beaver Sports. They told me their service queue was backlogged and it would take eight days before they could get to fixing the bike. I paid extra and cut my wait time to three days. After that I went in search of a care package I had mailed myself. I no longer had eight days of food to carry or as many warm clothes. In return I retrieved a laptop computer and a bear canister.

Once I had my bike fixed, I had a choice. Should I rent a car to drive back to the Yukon River and start back where I left off, or should I just continue from Fairbanks? A purist would want to bicycle every single inch, though that possibility wasn't possible after the first day construction zone. I decided that I wasn't so much of a purist and didn't look forward to riding gravel highways near the Yukon River again. Therefore, I restarted from Fairbanks.

It was five days of cycling from Fairbanks to the Canadian border. The roads were good and the weather cool but otherwise mostly dry. This was a route I had cycled 19 years before on the start of my cross-Canada ride in 1997. I still remembered parts, though several of the old lodges I stayed at in 1997 were no longer in service. The buildings still stood but now looked run down.

The first two days I cycled the Richardson Highway and stopped at a campground that boasted of hot showers. The couple that ran the place had a familiar story that I would hear many times again. They had first visited Alaska as tourists and come across a run down business. They fell in love with the place and bought it during their trip. Over the next few years investments and improvements had steadily improved their business. However, they were getting older, and it was a harsh life, with a short but very intense tourist season through the summer and a longer, darker winter. For the right price it was now for sale, though they didn't advertise openly along the highway for fear of scaring off customers.

At Delta Junction I stopped for photographs for the official start of the Alaska Highway. Folks at the museum told me about a drive-in restaurant nearby. The gas station next door had a drive-through liquor window, and

I assumed this was the place. There wasn't much to eat, but I bought a few things. Shortly thereafter I found the real drive-in just a little farther down the road.

The day after leaving Delta Junction, I reached Dot Lake in early afternoon. Dot Lake has a picturesque church, where I stopped to get photographs. Sunday afternoon church services had just started, so I stopped to join. The group kept singing hymns, and I later realized that the pastor was away tending an emergency, but they proceeded with services anyway. Once he arrived he delivered a short sermon. I asked if I could camp nearby, and he told me this was no problem. The pastor explained that he had come from the lower-48 and that this community was a mix of first-nations peoples and others like himself coming from elsewhere but falling in love with Alaska.

The following day I replaced my rear tire after having a sidewall cut. I had two spare tires with me and hence still had one in reserve. I reached Tok on the 4th of July and walked through town to find the local celebrations. After Tok it was two straightforward days of cycling to reach the Canadian border and the small town of Beaver Creek.

Canada

There is a boundary marker on the Alaska/Yukon border, a nice place to stop and get obligatory photographs before cycling another 27 kilometers to the Canadian border station outside Beaver Creek. The border guard asked me about my trip, trying to ascertain if I had enough funds. I could see relief on her face when I mentioned renting out my residence. She thumbed through the passport, briefly noting the Sudanese passport stamp. I asked for a Canada stamp on my passport.

Beaver Creek was small border town with a few motels and restaurants and an ATM to get Canadian currency. I took my first rest day since Fairbanks here and did laundry. Local TV cable in northern British Columbia is interesting, as they invariably include local news from a station in the United States. I could thus tune into the news and see how the traffic was doing in Seattle.

After Beaver Creek the road came through areas of permafrost as well as road construction. Some of these areas had also been under construction

19 years before when I cycled across Canada. Apparently, the permafrost makes for an unstable road surface that repeatedly settles and breaks anew. Road construction workers told me some had repeatedly fixed the same road over 30 years.

It took me two days of cycling from Beaver Creek to Kluane Lake, with a stop at a French bakery in between. The bakery was a stop not just for pastries but also for an overnight in their cabin. The couple who owned the place were originally from France, had come to the Yukon and built this bakery. Like many other businesses, there was a discrete "for sale" posting inside. After the bakery it was another day riding to reach shores of Kluane Lake. The settlement of Burwash Landing has an interesting museum that I visited but no motel. The next motel is in Destruction Bay, another 16 kilometers along the lake. There was a headwind, and so I watched my odometer and counted down 16...15...14...13... as I got closer. During the rest of my travels, I sometimes referred to "a burwash" as a 16 kilometer distance, e.g. "I know I am close now since it is only a burwash away."

It was cold and wet cycling along the lake but, fortunately, better by end of the next day when I arrived in Haines Junction. This was a familiar area not just from my 1997 cross-Canada trip but also from a subsequent ride I made in 2000 from Haines, Alaska, to Skagway. I kept my eyes out for bears as I had seen them on the previous rides. Fortunately, I didn't spot any this time. My campsite at Stoney Creek was surprisingly popular, with several vehicles stopping by during the afternoon. I later learned that this is where locals refilled water.

Whitehorse, population 25,000, was the largest town I crossed since leaving Fairbanks. It had a Walmart, a Tim Hortons, and two bike shops. It was also where I took my next rest day. I stopped in at a local travel office and bought a ticket for a tour of the narrow-gauge railroad into nearby Skagway. This tour started with a bus ride to nearby Carcross settlement. At Carcross we viewed totem poles before driving to nearby Fraiser to board the train. The train crossed the U.S. border before climbing to the top of the pass. It was a scenic ride downhill and into Skagway. Skagway itself was a very touristy and very expensive place. I was, however, able to buy a new Schwalbe folding bike tire for my bicycle. At the end of the day, we boarded the bus again for a ride back to Whitehorse. I had another five days of cycling to Watson Lake. I stopped at Nugget City Lodge, 22 kilometers before Watson Lake at the intersection of the Alaska Highway and the Cassiar Highway. During those five days I met several other cyclists, including a Korean couple who had started in Argentina three years before and were close to finishing their journey. When I met many of these cyclists, we would pull off the road and have a short conversation about road conditions. After that I'd ask for a photo and hence had a nice collection of shots that showed different gears and bike setups.

While I stopped 22 kilometers before Watson Lake, I took a rest day at Nugget City and made a day ride into Watson Lake to get groceries and stop at tourist spots. Since 1997, the signpost forest had grown and now had over 80,000 signs from throughout the world. The mocked-up P39 Russian plane was no longer there.

In 1997, after Watson Lake I had continued along the Alaska Highway. In the ensuring years, they had almost completely paved the Cassiar Highway and hence it was an interesting alternative. I mapped out a plan to ride the 720 kilometers of the Cassiar in approximately eight days. While the road was paved, the shoulders were narrower than those on the Alaska Highway, and there were more short little hills.

I saw more wildlife along this route than along the Alaska Highway, including several bears. One morning I was riding along and saw a bear munching clover on the left side of the highway. I paused, took a photograph and made some noise so the bear would notice me. The bear looked up briefly, decided I wasn't a threat and continued grazing. I very carefully cycled past.

Along the Cassiar Highway I met several other touring cyclists. The timing was right for cyclists leaving Alaska to head south as well as for cyclists to make it to Alaska before fall. One group I encountered was texas4000.org, a cycling organization based in Austin, Texas. The group was primarily college-aged students, with the teams providing their own leadership. I say teams, since there were three separate teams taking different routes, all starting in Austin and converging in Anchorage.

In addition to cycle tourists, I also had conversations with other tourists as well as locals in the area. In Mezdian Junction I stayed in the campground but also noticed a work camp nearby. The camp had pre-fabricated trailers for lodging as well as a small cafeteria. It catered to those working at a nearby mine as well as others working in the area. I had dinner at this cafeteria and was seated at a table with several truck drivers. The truck drivers drove log trucks on the Cassiar, and hence we had encountered each other on the road. I found it an interesting conversation to compare notes. In general truck drivers were skilled and careful drivers, though the road also twisted and turned. They explained their apprehension at encountering us cycle tourists unexpectedly in the middle of the lane after they had come around a corner.

I had one day of miserable rain on the Cassiar. Temperatures started near 7C (45F) and never quite warmed up. It never rained very hard, but it continued throughout the day. I was happy to find a dry place inside at the end of that ride.

Along the Cassiar Highway I noticed that my drive chain would occasionally skip forward. I wasn't quite sure what was causing it to skip-- perhaps the chain, the bottom bracket or something else? I decided that I would stop for service at the next bike shop in Smithers, approximately 120 kilometers on the Yellowhead Highway after finishing the Cassiar.

Kitwanga was last village before the end of the Cassiar. The Yellowhead was a busier road but also mostly had shoulders in this section. I looked forward to reaching Smithers both for a rest day and a chance to have my bicycle checked. The chain continued to skip forward, particularly when I was only lightly pedaling and hence not fully engaged. This day I had a light tailwind, and hence this happened more often than normal.

I was approximately 17 kilometers from Smithers when the chain not only skipped forward, but now also spun freely. Normally, a bike hub spins freely in only one direction, allowing one to coast. It was a short hill and I could no longer ride. Since I was only 17 kilometers from my destination and there was plenty of daylight, I started walking.

I had barely gone 100 meters when a pickup truck came past, slowed down and then drove a little ways past before turning around. The driver had seen me and decided it wasn't normal to have a touring cyclist walking a bike. He very kindly offered to bring me to the McBike shop in Smithers. We arrived shortly before the shop closed.

I assessed my options. This was a special 48-spoke Phil Woods hub designed to be extra strong. The shop didn't have a 36-spoke touring hub, let alone a 48-spoke hub. There was another shop in town that had a 36-spoke hub, and McBike had a 36-spoke rim – so my backup plan was to have them build a new strong wheel. My primary plan was calling the Phil Woods service department.

Once I called Phil Woods they offered to ship an internal hub mechanism to the bike shop. This was for no charge, though I did pay extra for expedited shipping. Even with expedited shipping the combination of a three-day holiday weekend and crossing the U.S./Canada border meant I needed to wait a week before the hub arrived and I could get back on the road again.

If one has to break down, Smithers is a lovely place to do so. Smithers is still a small town but is the largest settlement between Prince Rupert and Prince George. Smithers has a small downtown with shops and restaurants. It is also in the middle of a stunningly beautiful area. On day two I rented a mountain bike from McBike and cycled in the area. I also cycled past the parents of Jared, one of my fellow TDA cyclists in 2013. I would meet Jared later, as he was working in neighboring town some 150 kilometers farther.

Once the new hub mechanism arrived, McBike opened the hub mechanism. The Phil Woods is constructed with small pawls that are pressed down in own direction and pop up in the other. A small spring lets them pop up. Apparently, the internal hub was fouled up with a black substance and no longer popped back up. Replacing the mechanism was a big hammer approach to fixing this issue, though perhaps just taking apart the hub and applying new lube would have worked as well. In hindsight I wondered if the same problem had occurred on previous trips in both Thailand and New Zealand--also with Phil Woods hubs.

After a week in Smithers, my bike was ready, and I continued cycling the Yellowhead Highway. Four days cycling brought me to Prince George, the largest town yet. This road was busier, and some sections didn't have good shoulders. When I was in the small town of Vanderhoof, police closed the main road a few hours after I arrived. I saw a sickening sign of a downed motorcycle with side bags. Police were sorting out what turned out to be a fatality of a motorcyclist caused by the collision of the motorcycle and the truck. While not a motorcyclist I was extra careful in that area.

After Prince George the Yellowhead Highway became scenic. I cycled one day to Purden Lake, a resort area with a small campground. I met my brother Bert here. Bert had driven up from Colorado and brought with him my mountain bike, which he had retrieved from my sister-in-law, Natalie, and brother, Rob, at their motel in Montana. Originally, our plans were to cycle across Jasper and Banff parks together, but my delay in Smithers meant that we rode together earlier. We cycled from there to Tete Juane Junction at the start of a very scenic mountain area.

I switched to my mountain bike to let me experiment with the Great Divide Mountain Bike Route that would start in Banff. My mountain bike had only a back rack, but I also had a one-wheel trailer for additional gear. Unfortunately, I discovered that this new trailer was without a hitch to attach it to the bicycle. I wasn't sure if I had forgotten to order it, or if the company had forgotten to send one, but, in any case, it meant I wouldn't be able to use the trailer. This also meant that I needed to reduce my baggage so I could only carry what fit in two panniers. In hindsight, however, that was a good limitation that helped me later.

The ride from Tete Jaune Junction to Jasper and then down the Icefields Parkway was one of the most scenic parts of my ride. The ride was also surprisingly popular both for normal tourists in the campgrounds and also for cyclists I would see along the way. I could no longer stop and greet each touring cyclist I met with a short conversation. I also needed to make my reservations in advance. The campgrounds were often full, but I found several hostels where I could stay. Having fixed reservations also meant that my itinerary of how far to ride each day was fixed. Overall, however, I particularly enjoyed scenery on this part of the ride.

Banff marked the end of what I considered the first phase of my ride. It was mid-August, almost two months and 4000 kilometers from my start in

Prudhoe Bay. After starting with 24 hours of daylight, the days were noticeably shorter and I had a sense that fall was just around the corner. With the exception of my rear hub and a water filter, my equipment worked well. In the next section I would experiment with some off-road cycling.

In Banff, I met up with Trish and Wayne, two other cyclists with whom I had cycled on the 2013 TDA ride across Africa. Otherwise I enjoyed a relaxing rest day before setting off on the Great Divide Mountain Bike Route.

Starting the Great Divide Mountain Bike Route (GDMBR)
Bike packing or bike touring?

The sport of bike packing had gained popularity since I first started touring. A typical bikepacker uses a mountain bike to ride trails or gravel roads off the beaten track. Bikepacking gear often gets carried differently – rather than panniers that stick out and can catch on narrow single-track trails, bikepacking gear is design to be suspended from a seat post or the handlebars. One still needs a tent, clothing, and bike repair items, but many bikepackers also try to go lightweight if possible.

Adventure Cycling first created their Great Divide Mountain Bike Route (GDMBR) in 1997, and this is one of the more popular routes for bikepackers. It first went from the U.S./Canada border to the U.S./Mexico border and later extended north to Banff. It gained popularity after an annual race, the Tour Divide, started in 2008. The fastest racers complete the entire route in a little over two weeks.

Both the GDMBR and some off-route cycling intrigued me. I also thought it might be a good introduction for rougher roads in Latin America and a chance to try some equipment. While I didn't have a very lightweight backpacker setup, I did have a hybrid of both panniers and a few bikepacker bags.

On August 20th I started on the GDMBR just outside Banff. It was near freezing but warmed up through the day. I started by myself, but a little while later, Trish and Wayne joined me as well on their mountain bikes. I found the riding to be a little tougher and had to stop a few times to put my panniers back on the racks after my heels kicked them off. After a few iterations I used an extra shoelace to tie them together onto the rack. It was still fun riding with Wayne and Trish, even though they were faster. After lunch I continued by myself. In addition to tougher terrain, my progress didn't seem as quick because I had used the occasion to switch my cycle computer from kilometers to miles. While I was still in Canada, the GDMBR maps gave distances in miles.

By the time it was 5 p.m., I was on a gravel road near Mount Engadine. I climbed to the top of a hill and saw many "no camping" signs along the way and considered my options. There was a small stream nearby, and so I decided to hide behind some trees into the woods. Hopefully, nobody would bother me about the no camping restriction.

The following morning I was on the road early. It was cold as I descended the rest of the hill. At the bottom I saw two other cyclists breaking their camp at the bottom of the hill. I would meet them later, and I learned they were fined $50 for camping illegally. It was a good thing I left early.

Cycling on the second day was easier, as it included a longer section of gravel road as well as a few sections of pavement. There was even a bike path when I came to a provincial park. The bike path was closed, with signs warning of bears. There had already been signs for bears the previous day. I had a bear canister to protect my food but decided to be extra cautious and purchase bear spray as well. In Canada bear spray is classified as a weapon, and hence I was required to sign an extra declaration when I purchased the bear spray.

After this the route went up a single-track trail up and over Elkford Pass. It would have been much farther to go around than crossing 10 kilometers on the trail. I had enough time and ended up walking most of the trail both up and down. There was a short stretch of 18% grade uphill and one with 14% downhill, but most of the grades were easier.

Once I was over Elkford Pass, the route was still a rough washboard gravel road but easier to travel as I reached the small town of Elkford. It had taken two days of cycling for me to travel what tour divide racers typically cover in an afternoon and evening, but it also felt as though I had already come a long way.

After Elkford there is a choice between an older GDMBR route (the Fernie Alternative) and a newer and more challenging section of trail. Even a few days into the ride, I learned that I was at least as happy traveling on better surfaced roads even when that meant they were also busier. Some enjoy backpacking as a way to "get away from it all," and, while that was nice, I also enjoyed making faster progress and having points of civilization to buy supplies or otherwise visit. So, I took the Fernie bypass and even a section or two of paved roads that paralleled a rougher GDMBR. Following the more traveled routes was a pattern I would continue farther south as well.

Meanwhile, my shoes had been falling apart for a while, and I had used duct tape to put them back together. By the time I reached Fernie, it was time to replace them, and, fortunately, the town was large enough to have a store carrying shoes in large sizes.

After Fernie it was one long day of cycling to cross the U.S. border just north of Eureka. While I enjoyed cycling in Canada, particularly the Icefields Parkway and the Cassiar Highway, it was nice to cross my first country completely off the list.

Across the U.S.A.

After leaving Eureka I cycled one of the more interesting parts of the GDMBR, the Whitefish Divide. Fifteen kilometers south of Whitefish, I took a small road up the valley. It started paved and turned to gravel 16 kilometers later as the route steadily climbed up and over a low pass. The pass was steep enough that I walked the last 3 kilometers.

Just after the pass, as I headed down, I noticed a bear running ahead. The encounter surprised both me and the bear, but clearly the bear had a head start. I paused briefly to let the bear run away and, after that, made sure to ring my bicycle bell when I came to corners I couldn't see around. Close to the bottom was Tuchuk Campground. It was early in the day, but Tuchuk was one of the better places to stop. In the evening another cyclist also stayed. She was slower than I was, but descriptions here clearly told me she was a determined cyclist and a "tough cookie" with her riding. She had ridden several parts of the route that I had cycled on nearby paved roads instead.

I met four cyclists on the GDMBR that day, and this was about average. The overall route is popular, and there is a narrow window of time before it gets too cold in the north but after one will avoid the worst heat in the New Mexico parts of the route. There were more cyclists on this route than on other roads I had cycled.

Even though it was still late summer, it got several degrees below freezing the next evening when I climbed another low pass to get back from the Whitefish Divide. The roads on this second day included several sections with rough washboard roads that slowed my pace considerably. In the afternoon a front came through with light rain and then colder temperatures. I stayed at the campground and was happy to find bear-proof containers in which to stash my panniers.

My third cycling day from Eureka was easier, as I was almost at the top of the pass, and hence the day ride was mostly downhill. In addition, the road started rough but steadily improved and then was paved the last kilometers into Whitefish. In this part of Montana I was fortunate to meet my sister-in-law Natalie one morning and on a different evening visited with Tim Travis[15]. Tim has done a lot of travels by bicycle in approximately a decade of cycling and has written multiple books under the Down the Road in …" sequence. We had been in contact via Facebook, but it was now nice to put a face with the electronic name.

It turned out that the Whitefish Divide was the last major part of off-road cycling I made along the GDMBR. I realized that I was at least as happy riding the paved routes nearby. In addition, I had a sense that fall was coming and wanted to get further south before it became too cold. Through the rest of Montana I worked towards a goal of crossing Yellowstone not too long after Labor Day weekend. I didn't take any rest days here but did have several shorter rides, including the day I cycled into Helena. I enjoyed the towns of Lincoln, Boulder, Seeley Lake and Whitehall and would typically arrive midday after a not too difficult ride. This gave me time to relax and wander through the small towns.

---

[15] Tim Travis, http://www.downtheroad.org/

I did take a rest day in Ennis, Montana, on Monday of Labor Day weekend. A storm was coming, though, and it was nicer to stay warm and dry than cycling in the rain. Labor Day weekend was the annual fly-fishing festival, and I was fortunate to find a motel. I also realized the day I left Ennis that as the valley climbed, it would have been snowing rather than raining.

From Ennis it was two days riding to West Yellowstone near the western entrance to Yellowstone National Park. After one of the most expensive motel stays I had had since leaving Prudhoe Bay, I cycled into the park. The roads were narrow, but the traffic was slow, polite, and respectful. I took my time as a tourist, stopping to see geyser basins, mud pots and fumaroles. I also made an obligatory stop to watch Old Faithful erupt. Somehow, it wasn't as big an event as I recall from earlier trips.

In the evening I found my way to the park campground near Grant Village. The campground includes a bicyclist only area, but I had made online reservations for a normal spot #172. I settled into my spot and was already asleep when I noticed a car pull into the spot and two people get out to start also setting up camp in my campsite. I got out of my tent and sorted things out. The new arrivals had a reservation for spot #174 nearby, but when they didn't arrive until 11 p.m., squatters had taken their spot. They thought my spot was empty since there wasn't a car and my bicycle was otherwise beside the picnic table. Once we figured this out, I had them sort things out with their squatters.

After Yellowstone National Park came Grand Teton Park. In 2016 several large fires were burning, including one that had recently come through the area I had just cycled. Interestingly enough, this same area was last inundated by fire in 1988, when I had also visited.

From Grand Teton I headed southeast towards the Colorado Front Range. I had some longer days cycling, including a ride over Togwotee Pass into Dubois. I was fortunate with tailwinds on that day as well as the following day cycling into Lander. I was now following the route of the Adventure Cycling Transamerica Trail and met a few cyclists riding this route and working to cross before colder fall temperatures. There is a bicycle shop in Lander, where I was warmly greeted, including their offering an ice cream bar and chance to add my account to their scrapbook journal. I appreciated their efforts and particularly found it interesting to read accounts of others who had traveled the same route.

The following day I stopped in the small town of Jeffrey City, where the hospitality even topped that of Lander. The community had a history with cross-country cyclists, particularly after uranium mines and then their only motel shut down. Locals offered the church as a place to camp, and a local pottery business also let people camp nearby. The Split Rock Bar and Café was the only establishment otherwise open during the day. For their hospitality Jeffrey City won an award from Adventure Cycling[16]. The motel was open again under new ownership. I stayed there but also talked with the pottery guy, who offered me a place to stay as well.

By the time I reached Rawlins, I made further plans for a short intermission in Colorado. My plan was to rent a car in Laramie for a week. I would bring my bike into a shop for service, visit my parents and participate in the annual Pedal the Plains ride. Those plans became even more important on the day I left Rawlins. My bicycle was running smoothly as I slowly went up a hill. I downshifted and suddenly my hub stopped working. It was the same failure I had had earlier near Smithers with the same type of Phil Woods hub. I had now seen this failure four times (New Zealand – 2001, Thailand – 2007, Canada – 2016 and U.S. – 2016), so this was a problem where I needed a more reliable solution.

Shortly after my hub failed, a pickup came past, and I experienced more Wyoming hospitality. The couple brought me to the town of Medicine Bow, where I stayed in the old hotel. This had been my original destination for the day. I asked the waitress if she knew of people who might be traveling to Laramie. She asked around, and some other locals had plans for their weekly shopping trip the following day. Overall, it all worked out for me to pick up the rental car I had reserved earlier and take my week break in Colorado.

I brought my bicycle to Lee Sports in Fort Collins and asked them to open the hub and diagnose the failure. I also started an email conversation with

---

[16] The June Curry Award: https://www.adventurecycling.org/resources/bicycle-travel-awards/june-curry-trail-angel-award/

Sugar Wheel Works in Portland about other hubs that might be more reliable. Lee Sports later told me they opened the hub up, cleaned out the grease and applied new lube and everything worked again. That was both reassuring and troubling--reassuring that nothing major was wrong, but troubling because I didn't have the ability to do this service on the road and the hub had failed multiple times. In my conversation with Sugar Wheel works, we decided to use a DT Swiss Tandem hub. It had the advantage of being much easier to service in the field and is designed as a strong hub for tandem bicycles.

After a nice ride in Pedal the Plains and visit with family, I drove back to Laramie, dropped off my rental car and continued the trip. This next stretch brought me through the Colorado mountains via Walden, Kremmling and Copper Mountain. All were familiar haunts from previously living and cycling in Colorado. Fall was in the air, and the aspen were beautiful shades of yellow.

Expedia travel service has a mystery hotel option. One is shown a rough area and a price but not the specific hotel. Summit County is a resort area, and while it wasn't yet ski season, I looked online to make sure I would find a reasonable deal. A condo at Copper Mountain Ski area popped up, and I was intrigued enough to make a reservation. A storm was forecast to come through the area, so I made the reservation for two nights.

Once I paid for the reservation, I learned the details. I first needed to go to Dillon to pick up an electronic key. Dillon was 20 kilometers from Copper Mountain, but, fortunately, on my route. I was pleasantly surprised to find my lodging was in the middle of the ski resort. It was still "mud season," with the resort not scheduled to open for at least another month. However, I was still high enough in the mountains that it snowed several inches on my rest day.

Copper Mountain was at 2950 meters (9700 feet), and I had another 500 meters of climb to the summit at 3450 meters (11,318 feet). This was both the highest point so far on my trip as well as the coldest. Fortunately, the sun was shining, and it was bright white with newly fallen snow. It was particularly cold on the way back down, but Leadville wasn't much past the top of Fremont Pass.

2016 was an election year, and it was interesting to see the signs along the way as well as how they differed between states. While the presidential race between Trump and Clinton had the most visibility on national news, I saw surprisingly few presidential signs on my ride as compared to those for more local races. There was one particular property on my way down from Fremont Pass with multiple Trump signs as well as issue-related signs about guns. Later, I saw some Clinton signs in properties near Santa Fe. However, these were more the exception than the rule. Instead, these were my central impressions:

1. Alaska was early in my trip and earliest before the election, and the Senate race was most prominent.
2. Montana seemed to emphasize the local House and Senate races with campaign signs and the statewide elections and their U.S. House race with TV coverage.
3. Wyoming-- I saw few people and similarly few campaign signs.
4. Colorado-- county races for commissioners seemed to be most popular.
5. New Mexico concentrated on a mix of local candidates.
6. Arizona had more signs than New Mexico, particularly related to several ballot issues.
7. California's ballot initiatives got the most press coverage, but I also saw signs for congressional races and some local candidates.
8. Oregon had several high-profile ballot issues heavily advertised on TV.

In addition to observing campaign signs, I also saw the televised presidential debates. The first of these occurred the evening when I cycled to the Great Sand Dunes RV Park in the San Luis Valley. This campground was next to a hot springs thermal pool. I took advantage of this for a nice long soak before watching the debate in the evening.

I finished my ride across Colorado in the flat San Luis Valley by the small town of Antonito. The town had almost as many medical marijuana businesses as restaurants, but fortunately I found both a restaurant and a supermarket that were open. Also in my cycling across Colorado, I had pretty much abandoned the off-road parts of the GDMBR and now followed main roads via Santa Fe and Albuquerque. The New Mexico parts of the GDMBR are among the most challenging, and I figured I was firmly in the bike tourist camp instead of the bikepacker camp.

I ordered a few new maps from Adventure Cycling for their "Southern Tier" route. The entire Southern Tier goes from San Diego, California, to Saint Augustine, Florida, and has seven maps. I bought only the last two leading to San Diego and had them sent to the post office in Socorro, New Mexico. I had mostly cycled this route 16 years before in 2001 but figured it was important to have updated maps. By now it was mid-September, but I had crossed the highest passes in Colorado and wasn't as concerned about extreme cold.

I had cycled most of the roads on my Colorado section before, but my New Mexico routes were mostly all new. The cycling between Santa Fe and Albuquerque was particularly scenic. Parts were marked as the "Turquoise Trail" and other parts were segments of historic Route 66. There were hills and scenic little towns to cross before reaching a larger metropolis at Albuquerque.

After Albuquerque my route took me along the Rio Grande Valley, which happened to also be the route taken by Interstate 25. I mostly stayed off the interstate by using secondary roads, but just north of Socorro was a 26-mile stretch without good paved alternatives. The signs on the interstate were ambiguous, telling me both that bicycles were prohibited and and that bicycles should stay on the shoulder. I entered the interstate after passing a county sheriff vehicle, so I figured I was probably fine. I had a nice little stay at a little RV park in Las Casitas. It was just a short ride the following day to Socorro, where I also picked up my maps.

From Socorro it felt as if I was entering the home stretch-- just a ride westwards across the rest of New Mexico, Arizona and California to reach San Diego. The morning I departed, however, the winds reminded me not to get overconfident, as there was still serious cycling left. It took me four hours to cycle only 43 kilometers. There was 600 meters (2000 ft.) of climbing involved as well, but the wind was what slowed me down most. It was a high, dry and mostly treeless plain that I cycled for the next several days to the Arizona border.

I had several additional days at higher elevation before a tougher ride coming down into the Phoenix area. The landscapes changed dramatically from pine forests near Forrest Lakes to saguaro cactus before reaching Phoenix. More than 2000 meters of descent (6677 feet) but also more than 1000 meters of climb (3550 feet) in one day brought me to Fountain Hills on the outskirts of the Phoenix metro area. It was mostly four lane highway with good shoulders and gentle grades, although I did walk one short section. I was now also on the Adventure Cycling Southern Tier route.

I spent one full day crossing Phoenix on smaller roads and bike paths and then was outbound again via Wickenburg. This area was known as a place for snowbirds to flock to with their RVs. Signs posted amenities, including activities, church, seasonal rates and, in selected parks, the Canadian flag. Locals told me that the town of Brenda had 200-300 year-round residents and 800-900 residents in peak snowbird season. Snowbirds had started arriving, and almost all would arrive before Christmas. Snowbird arrivals also meant that restaurants were now open again.

As I crossed the town of Quartzite, I saw another reflection of the large snowbird population. One of the candidates for mayor made sure his campaign signs prominently listed "full year resident." Such a statement is naturally assumed most anywhere else, but in Quartzite it was important to call it out.

From snowbird country I crossed the California border at Blythe. On this next section my Adventure Cycling maps warned that "services are extremely limited between Brawley and Palo Verde and may be closed seasonally. Plan accordingly and carry food and water." Google told me there was a store in Glamis, where it might be possible to resupply, but this store closed at 3 p.m. This set my goal for the day – to arrive before the store closed and camp nearby. Fortunately, winds cooperated, and I made it with more than an hour to spare.

Glamis is in the middle of an area of large sand dunes. There are many who come here to play on the dunes with ATVS and dune buggies, particularly on the weekends. It wasn't a weekend and not high season, so the area was quiet. Store owners were friendly, and when I asked about camping places, they told me I could camp under the awning next to the store. The following day was a shorter ride first to Brawley and then to El Centro. I was now within 200 kilometers of San Diego.

El Centro is slightly below sea level. There is a climb leading up and over the coastal range to get to San Diego. There is a solid climb of over 1000 meters, where most climbing is on the shoulder of the interstate highway. Cycling blogs I found online described this climb as one of the more difficult parts of the Southern Tier route, with rough roads, extreme heat, high winds and a few narrow bridges.

After reading these journals, I was prepared for the worst and was pleasantly surprised. The roads leading to the climb had rough parts but also a small section of new asphalt. Temperatures never got much over 30C (86F) for my climb. Along the interstate were 19 emergency stop locations, each with a large barrel of water. The water wasn't drinkable but instead could be used to fill an overheated radiator. My bicycle didn't have a radiator, but I used the water for a similar cooling effect by splashing it over my shirt to get cool. Slowly but surely, I climbed the hill, and near the top I saw the Mexican border for the first time. I would parallel the border until San Diego, but in this section it was marked by a prominent large metal structure.

Jacumba Hot Springs was another slightly fancy resort area. Fortunately, the resort hotel wasn't as expensive as I expected. It was a nice place to stay before two days of cycling across the hills and into San Diego. The first of those days I went up and down multiple hills and into the small town of Pine Valley.

In Pine Valley I was in a familiar area again. Pine Valley is the traditional end of the first day cycling on the "Christmas Bike Ride" put on by the Hosteling International chapter in San Diego. I had done this ride five times before, in 2002, 2003, 2006, 2009 and 2015, though in the opposite direction. On the Christmas ride it takes all day to slowly climb from sea level to Pine Valley. Now I rode in reverse and into the city.

In San Diego I tallied up my numbers for the first part of the trip:

- 8293 kilometers (5153 miles)
- 62,268 meters of climbing (204,290 feet)

- 124 days on the road

Looking backwards I had come a long ways but looking forward had even further to go. I was now going to take a five week break until after Thanksgiving. This would let me adjust from learnings of the first parts, sort out my equipment and otherwise prepare to ride across Latin America. My specific plans included going up to Portland on Amtrak to retrieve a newly constructed back wheel, returning to Austin for several weeks to vote and otherwise spend time in the city, driving to Colorado to have Thanksgiving with my parents and then driving back to San Diego to continue the trip.

Mexico

Mexico is a scary place. At least it seems that way if you read the travel advisories from the U.S. Department of State or the British Foreign Ministry. Phrases like "kidnapping," and "gun battles between rival criminal organizations," along with "defer non-essential travel" or "limit travel to daylight hours on major highways" caught my attention. While I had visited several Mexico/U.S. border cities, I had more experience with countries farther away, such as Armenia, Russia, India, China, etc.

Now some of the advisory language was just the way the State Department of one country may write travel notices, as even the U.K. notice for the U.S.A. contains a few sections for concern. What made the Mexico advisory unique was the level of state-by-state detail. For example, both India and Mexico have roughly the same number of states (~30), but India's advisory only lists a few states with cautions, while the Mexico advisory lists each state, at least half of which include some form of cautionary language.

In addition to the official travel advisory, I also read half a dozen books written by cyclists crossing Latin America and somewhere around 100 blogs. The blogs and books painted a different picture. In total, out of more than 100 accounts, I found two describing crime issues in Mexico, one south of Mazatlán and one in Chiapas. In all these accounts there were approximately a dozen incidents total, half in northern Peru, two in Mexico, two in Colombia and two in the rest of Central America. So I had some reason to be cautious from a risk standpoint, but not overly concerned.

I planned my Mexico cycling route with this plan in mind: cross the border near San Diego, cycle down the Baja Peninsula and then across via the highlands of Mexico via Guajajára to Oaxaca and then on to Guatemala. I read multiple blogs of cyclists traveling the Baja Peninsula and got additional confidence reading their accounts and also a nice list of potential places to stay. I also decided to cross at a minor crossing at Tecate instead of the larger crossing at San Isidro. After a nice Thanksgiving holiday with my parents in Colorado, I drove to San Diego for the next phase of the trip.

After dropping off a rental car, I loaded my bicycle for the next phase of the trip. I had added a front rack, which allowed me a smaller set of front panniers in addition to my two rear panniers. The bike felt heavy again, particularly as I climbed approximately 1200 meters on my ride from San Diego to the border town of Tecate. I could see the border fence, with Tecate, Mexico, behind.

I cycled to the border. Nothing was required to cycle out of the U.S.A., and other than a quick passport check, I could have cycled right past the border into Mexico as well. I knew I would later need a "FMM form" to travel beyond the Baja Peninsula, however, so I made sure to ask. It was a three step process: complete a form, pay a fee and return the form along with a receipt to get the FMM stamped.

While there are hotels in Tecate, I had made it easier by already making Expedia reservations at a place 10 kilometers outside town. I cycled through town, and before I knew it I was already climbing the hill out of town. Wow! That was easy.

My first full day cycling in Mexico was just about as easy, with roads better than I expected. This road had good shoulders, with just a few kilometers of road construction. This brought me over several hills and down into a small town of Guadalupe, where I had lunch. There was a nice taco stand with covered seating and a place to lean my bicycle. After 90 kilometers I reached the coast again with a busier Highway 1 coming down from Tijuana. This brought me into middle of Ensenada, where I had my second (and last) hotel reservation.

I walked through town and tried to buy a SIM card for my phone. While I succeeded in buying a SIM, somehow I had difficulty in getting the configuration right or having the phone service work for more than one day. This was a skill I would later learn, including making sure not to leave a particular tienda until the service representative had put in all the configuration information needed to make the internet connection work.

Over the next three days, I developed my Baja Mexico cycling legs and grew in confidence. Route-finding was easy, as it involved following Highway 1 southbound. One small section of 25 kilometers was very narrow, with not quite enough room for two trucks and a bicycle to pass together, but, otherwise, the road was fine. The road generally crossed from one agricultural valley to the next with occasional desolate areas in between. In the evenings I stayed in hotels in towns I had learned about from other blogs. During the days I found small restaurants for lunch and a tienda to buy supplies for breakfast meals. These three days brought me to El Rosario.

El Rosario is on the northern side of a 360-kilometer gap without many services, as the road crosses the desierto (desert), the central region. The road continued to be narrow, but the amount of traffic also decreased significantly. On the first day I left early and climbed several hundred meters up the hill past giant cirios catci. These cacti were 10-15m. high (33 to 48 ft.) and some looked like inspirations for Dr. Seuss. After 46 kilometers I came to my first "loncheria," a small house where I could buy a drink or a snack. Over the next four days, these loncheria were primary places to get food along the way. Later that afternoon a headwind picked up, and I was happy to reach a small café and checkpoint at 87 kilometers. The café at San Agustin also had a campsite, where I pitched my tent. Camping was fine, though somehow I must have pitched the tent on top of some thorns, as my thermarest air mattress was deflated by the middle of the night.

The second day after El Rosario was at least as desolate as the first-- beautiful cycling through Valle de Los Cerros but otherwise desolate. Once again the wind picked up by afternoon as I reached a small loncheria at Rancho Chapala. With my broken Spanish I asked if I might camp close to the house and out of the wind. I was pleased with some shelter from the worst of the wind as well as a filling lunch. By evening I was hungry again and struggled with my order. What I wanted to say was, "I would like to have what those two men had for lunch." Unfortunately, the men were no longer around, and I didn't yet know past tense conjugations – so my pantomime also didn't help. In the end I had to fall back to a simpler, "What do you have?" and pick something that sounded good.

The wind picked up through the night and was strong when I left the following morning. Fortunately, half a dozen kilometers after leaving the Rancho Chapala, I seemed to clear an open valley, and winds were much better. Two otherwise uneventful days brought me to the edge of the large gap and to the larger town of Guerro Negro. A week on the road and I had grown more comfortable cycling this part of the Baja Peninsula.

Guerro Negro also marked the border to Baja California Sur. I had crossed my first state in Mexico. There wasn't much to the border crossing other than a sign and an agricultural inspection that I could cycle past without stopping. I met several cyclists in this next section of road, as the highway crossed over the peninsula from the Pacific Ocean over to the Sea of Cortez. Crossing this peninsula would take me three days cycling.

In the small town of El Marasal, I walked over to the bank to get money from the ATM. Somehow, neither of my debit cards seemed to work. This put me slightly on edge, since often the small motels wouldn't take credit/debit, and hence I would need to watch my remaining cash carefully.

On my third day crossing the peninsula, I spotted another cyclist ahead. While I had seen half a dozen cyclists so far, they were often faster than I was. This cyclist seemed to be slower, so I gradually caught up. I met Corrine a short while later. We cycled together much of the rest of the day until it came time to descend from the plateau down to the seashore. I knew I was slow at descending and hence encouraged her to ride ahead.

It was a few days of cycling along the Sea of Cortez until the road would climb again to the city of Ciudad Constitution. I made it a short day to Ligui, close to the base of the climb – so I could start fresh the next morning. Ligui doesn't have a hotel, and cyclists are typically directed to camp at the beach. I found the small road to the beach and found it rather undesirable. At midday it was still hot in the sun, and there seemed to be plenty of flies. I returned to the village and met a police officer. I asked him about camping possibilities on the basketball court in town. He first told me about the beach again and looked skeptical when I described it as unsuitable. However, he also told me there would be an evening gathering, and after this was over, around 7 p.m., I could camp on the basketball court.

I set up my tent half hidden behind a baseball dugout on a neighboring field and then listened as towns-people gathered. It seemed to be some sort of celebration, with speeches by local dignitaries, as well as a raffle that gave some children new bicycles. My spot behind the dugout was comfortable enough that I never did move to the basketball court. This was good since the following morning they came at 5 a.m. to turn lights on and clean everything up.

After climbing the hill it was mostly flat to Ciudad Constitution. This larger town was the site of my first rest day since San Diego. I bought a ferry ticket and made further plans for the next weeks. The start of these plans was a two day ride to La Paz.

La Paz is capital of Baja California Sur and a big contrast from the small towns I had traveled through. There were many more large box stores and other chains. Also, I got a sense this area was commonly visited by tourists, while the other places might have a small number of tourists driving through all the time but few staying for long. I had roughly a week before I had a ferry ticket to Mazatlán on the mainland of Mexico.

I decided to visit the Connors. Mike and Peggy have a home in Los Barriles, approximately 100 kilometers south of La Paz. I had worked with Mike for many years at HP, and he was my boss both in Massachusetts and Colorado (one of those to whom I was grateful for allowing me a leave to bicycle across Canada as well as across Russia). It was a hilly ride but then a relaxing time in Los Barriles, where I ended up spending two days. We went to the local tire shop and used their large water tank to find holes in my thermarest. I patched these up and would later learn that this stopped perhaps half of the leaks – so it was better than before but still required adding air every three or four hours.

Mike was kind enough to drive me back to La Paz, where I spent a few days in the old town just before Christmas. On Christmas day itself I cycled 17 kilometers out to the ferry terminal, where I took the ferry to Mazatlán. Boarding was simple enough, and I almost had cycled past the passport checkpoint when they called me back.

The ferry was overnight, and I reserved a cabin. My ticket included both an evening meal and breakfast the next morning. These were cafeteria style with a standard menu. After this I spent the rest of the time in my cabin and had a restful night sleep before waking up as we approached the mainland.

Mazatlán was the start of a hot and humid section. It wasn't too bad at a hotel right along the beach, but the next morning, as I departed on the highway south of town, it was a sharp contrast from the Baja Peninsula. In this section I got on the road early and tried to get much of my cycling done by midday.

On the first day I had a choice between the libre (free) and the cuota (toll) highways. While the cuota had higher speeds, it also had better shoulders and was a smoother surface. The libre was usually without shoulders but did go past more of the small villages and towns. While I saw a "no bicycling" sign on my first day on the cuota, I had no problems either when I encountered policia or when I came to a toll booth. Often the toll booth workers would direct me to bring my bicycle to the right side along a sidewalk so as not to trip an alarm.

In addition to the wider shoulders and smoother road surfaces, the toll roads were well-traveled, and the travel advisories seemed to favor them over small, off-the-way roads. As a result, for much of the route between Mazatlán until close to Mexico City, I took the cuota.

Hot afternoons meant I reached the small towns early enough to find a hotel and relax in the cool shade. I used Google Maps and other cyclist blogs to find these places. In the small town of Escuinapa, I couldn't find a hotel at first but then noticed a sign and asked an older woman nearby. The room was only 150 pesos ($7) but also not fancy. It, however, did have a ceiling fan and cooler concrete walls.

In the town of Ruiz I had a nice hotel picked out from other cyclist blogs. High temperatures that day were near 37C (97F), and I was fortunate to reach the town at midday. My chosen hotel was half a dozen kilometers off the cuota on the other side of town. I rode through town, across the cobble stones and the railroad tracks only to discover the hotel was full. No worries, I had passed a different hotel near the center. Unfortunately, it was full as well.

I ended up back near the cuota where I had passed a somewhat strange looking hotel. In front of each room was a garage area with curtains where you could discretely park your car. The room had no windows and other than a bed and TV not much inside the room. As I traveled further through Mexico and Central America, I would pass more of these "love hotels" where people could discretely meet.

From Mazatlán to Ruiz, the terrain was mostly flat. After this the city of Tepic was ~1300m (4000ft) and a good day of climbing. The climb sounded arduous from blogs I read, so I was on the road early and my hotel was right next to the cuota, allowing an early departure. Fortunately, I had done much of my climbing before it became too hot. Overall the ride was easier than I expected and the grades rarely exceeded 6%.

I reached Tepic on December 31st, New Year's Eve. The city was busy with venders selling fireworks and other goods, shoe shine stalls and a lot of food. I decided to take a rest day here for New Year's as I wasn't certain what would be open or closed on January 1st. Even though I had a rest day ahead of me, I was soundly asleep before midnight

Over the next weeks I cycled across the highland areas of Mexico. Elevations gradually increased from 1300m to nearly double and eventually briefly to over 3000m. With that change in elevation came a welcome change in temperature as well. I no longer had hot humid afternoons, and on some mornings it was even near or just below freezing. There were long stretches on the cuota toll roads with night stops in the small towns near the freeway. The towns were initially busy, but as I came to the state of Michoacán, they seemed deserted until after dark, when locals would come out.

Three days after Tepic (population 300,000), I came to the large metropolitan area of Guadalajara. The city has a population of 1.3 million with more than 4 million in the metro area. Other cyclists had written of a challenging ride of ~25 kilometers after one left the cuota so I mentally prepared. The roads were busy and initially the shoulders were narrow. As I cycled, I kept an eye out for potholes or hazards ahead while also keeping an eye out on a small mirror attached to my glasses. This took concentration, but overall traffic was well behaved. After reaching the center of the city, I wrote in my blog, "(1) Mexican drivers are more patient and polite to touring cyclists than American or Canadian drivers and (2) despite that, I will be happy to bypass Mexico's largest city (Mexico City), as it still takes a lot of concentration to carefully make your way into these big cities."

An example of Mexican politeness came when I unexpectedly found myself in a tunnel after the road went underground. I noticed the car behind turned on its flashers and slowly escorted me through the tunnel. There was no quick pass or angry honk, but instead an escort for which I was grateful.

When I did hear honks on the road, they were most often friendly quick toots, rather than a long "Get out of my way" honk. I also got my share of thumbs up signs when motorists noticed my bicycle laden with touring gear. When I stopped in rest areas along the cuota freeways, curious motorists would also sometimes ask about my journey. It left me feeling positive about Mexico and Mexican drivers I met along the way.

In Guadalajara I took my bicycle to a local bike shop for maintenance. It was still riding well, but the city provided a good opportunity to check and replace worn parts like brake pads and my chain. The shop had mostly the same bike parts as in the U.S.A. Prices of parts were similar, though labor was considerably less.

Cycling out of Guadalajara was easier than cycling into the city. Some of this was perhaps because I was going outbound in the morning when commuters were still cycling inbound. There was a brief period when I rode on a three or four lane highway with a lot of traffic. It was always difficult to see if the rightmost lane was a shoulder or a travel lane, since it was generally used by either slow traffic or small minibuses that would pull over for passengers. However, the busiest sections didn't last long, and soon I was on a two lane highway with a reasonable shoulder again.

After Guadalajara the next state was Michoacán, a state about which the travel advisories warned. Major highways were safer, and the advisory warned about the smallest roads. I took some small roads into the capital of Morelia and didn't really notice anything out of the ordinary. What I did notice was that villages where I stopped seemed rather deserted. In one of these villages, I knew there was a hotel, but it took some effort to find it. Fortunately, I took a digital photograph of a sign with the hotel name and showed it to locals, who recognized the sign and brought me to the hotel. Along the way I could practice my Spanish, and they could practice their English when we passed by some farm animals. We didn't always know the respective words, but by pantomiming as well as making animal sounds, we could relate the words to each other.

I arrived at the hotel, but nobody was there. I rang the bell, but there was no answer. I waited for a little while and tried the bell again, before noticing a sign nearby with a telephone number on it. I called the number and, in my broken Spanish, explained that I was a tourist inquiring about a room. The proprietor responded that he was on his way and would be there in 20 minutes. A basic telephone conversation was an interesting test of my Spanish, and it felt good that my Spanish was good enough to figure things out.

By the time I reached Morelia, I was in email contact with another cyclist, David, from Montreal. We had both participated in online bicycle forums, and David knew of my trip from a link to my blog I had posted. He coincidentally had another Mexico/Central America trip fall through and was curious if I was open to cycling together for some weeks.

For several reasons I was open to the idea of cycling with others, particularly in an area that had travel advisories and where my Spanish wasn't strong. The challenge is figuring out if there is a match that will work well for both parties. So, we'd exchanged information and thoughts via email and the evening in Morelia also had a Skype call. Our conversation went well, and we agreed to meet later in Mexico and then cycle from there to Costa Rica. As we worked out both the calendar and cities in Mexico with good airport connections, we settled on Oaxaca as our meeting point. I would have a little time before David could reach Oaxaca, so I found a language school online and registered for a week of Spanish classes.

Another decision I made early in January was to sign up for part of the TDA South American Epic bicycle ride from Puerto Montt, Chile, to Ushuaia, Argentina. The TDA ride was scheduled to leave Cartagena, Colombia, in July and reach Puerto Montt in November, so I planned to ride only the last 20% of South America with TDA. These were my reasons for this decision:

- TDA could be a good "backstop" if for some reason I found myself traveling more slowly than I anticipated. In this case I would already be registered but would ask if I could join earlier.
- TDA had a fixed end-day of December 21st, so I could make more definite plans for after my trip.
- The Carreterra Austral region of Chile was beautiful but also more challenging than the Argentinian side of Patagonia. A supported ride would bring me through the more challenging bits.

Three days of cycling after Morelia brought me first to end of the cuota and then over my highest elevation of 3000 meters to the city of Toluca. I decided to bypass Mexico City itself and instead ride further to the south. At one point I came across a group of religious pilgrims walking the other direction along the highway. I stopped to get a photograph, and they struck up a conversation. We were both interested in our respective journeys. What I found interesting is that such a quick conversation often leads to a selfie photograph with a phone and then an exchange of Facebook contact information to trade the photos. The world is truly becoming a smaller place.

In addition to a 3000 meter elevation, this part of Mexico had many smaller hills as well. In the town of Cuernevaca, the downhill grades exceeded 11%, and I carefully rode my loaded bicycle, squeezing the brakes frequently. At one point it was steep enough that I got off and walked a short stretch downhill instead.

As I entered the southern state of Oaxaca, I saw more protest signs that said, "No Al Gasolinazo!" as well as signs of a teachers strike. The reference to gasoline was triggered by two events: the decline of the peso against the dollar and also deregulation of the price of gasoline. The combination had sent prices rising significantly.

As I left the small town of Asuncion Nochixtlan, I came past a large burnt up bus in the middle of the road. In the preceding June, a group of protesting teachers had erected these roadblocks in a dispute with the Federal Government over education reforms. Exactly what happened next is disputed, but efforts to clear these roadblocks resulted in 8 deaths and almost 200 injured. Banners had been erected on the burned-up bus with the name of one of those martyred, and there were also several burned-up trucks. All were still in middle of the road while traffic went around. Later, in the city of Oaxaca, I also saw several peaceful protests through the main square and an area where protestors were organizing.

I reached the city of Oaxaca at the end of January. I had a week here before David would arrive and spent the first weekend as a tourist visiting the impressive archaeological site of Monte Alban. This site was where the top of a nearby mountain was cleared and then temples and other buildings erected.

Also in Oaxaca was a Spanish language school, where I signed up for a week of classes. We started with a self-assessment test after which I was placed in a group with others at a similar level. I would roughly describe it as "had some past class familiarity with Spanish but can use a more formal grammar and vocabulary refresher." My self-assessment was that I had enough "survival Spanish" so I wouldn't starve or not be able to get a room, but I was also a long way from being able to sustain any type of reasonable conversation. The class helped me brush up on skills and provided some structure to my week. Class hours were in the morning, and two of the afternoons, we had an "excursion" to local sights in Oaxaca.

In addition to the class, I also used it as an opportunity to bring my bike in for further service.

David arrived on a Friday evening, and by Saturday morning we were on the road again. We mapped out a route that took us farther on the highlands before descending near Tehuantepec – crossing a windy stretch and then climbing back through Chiapas State and to the border with

Guatemala. Our first day cycling was straightforward and mostly flat. We developed a rhythm of leaving not too late, getting a lunch along the way and then finishing by early afternoon – and would keep up a similar rhythm for the remaining weeks as well. I was pleased to find that our speeds were fairly matched, with neither much quicker than the other and hence having to wait for too long. On the later days as the route became steeper, my cautious descents caused David to occasionally have to wait but hopefully not for too long.

Our third day from Oaxaca brought us to the little town of La Reforma. We knew from reading other cyclists' blogs that there wasn't a hotel in town but that others had stayed on the town basketball court. The court was easy to find; it was right in middle of town with a large cover. Municipal offices were nearby but closed. However, we asked around at the local store and with people we met, and the locals told us it was fine to pitch our tents on the platform above the court. I think most everyone in town must have known we were there.

It was a noisy night with roosters crowing, trucks nearby and locals in search of a wifi connection coming over to browse the internet and chat. I still slept well, with exception that I accidentally rolled over onto my glasses and and they broke off at the temples. I fortunately had a set of prescription sunglasses with me. However, until I got my glasses repaired a month later, I used my sunglasses all the time, leading to some dark nights walking.

After La Reforma we descended all the way to sea level and the town of Tehauntepec, where it was considerably warmer again. In addition, the area is notorious for high winds, as there is only a low 250 meter high pass between the Atlantic and Pacific Oceans. We had our share of winds in this section as well, though perhaps less than average. When we talked with locals, they talked of a very recent period with much more wind. The combination of wind, heat and a long gap between known towns had me anticipating the worst with a hot windy campsite beside the road. I was thus pleasantly surprised when we found a nice little hotel in Santiago Niltepec. This allowed us one more day on the flat windy plains before our climb back up the hills on the other side of the windy bowl.

That next morning we were on the road by 7 a.m. and didn't finish until 5 p.m. It was a long slow climb up the hill, and I wasn't feeling 100%. A cookie break and seeing the sign for Chiapas State both definitely helped. We stopped at the top of the hill for a nice filling lunch, and I had plenty to drink. After this it was flatter but still a long, slow ride.

In Cintilapa there was a big festival going on. The first hotel we found was all booked up. The second only had a single bed. The third was right off the square in an extremely noisy location. Eventually, we circled back and picked the hotel with a single bed. David offered to take the floor, and I accepted that offer and slept on the bed. After a long ride it was nice to finally rest.

The following day was not much easier,not so much the climb, but we had to cross the major city of Tuxla as well as make some steep descents on a crowed road into Chiapa de Corzo. This small town had a touristy center with archaeological ruins nearby. By now we had been nearly a week on the road together and had a day with significant climbing ahead of us. Both were excuses to take an easy rest day.

After our rest day we started on the road early. In total, that day we climbed 1836 meters or a little over 6000 feet. This started from a little over 400 meters to over 2200 meters before dropping back. Fortunately, the grades were steady and not too steep, and we were on a cuota road with a wide shoulder. The change in temperature was noticeable, from a hot rest day in Chiapa to a cold and rainy arrival in San Cristobal. It was also interesting to see the variation in the hotels. In the highlands thicker blankets were on the beds, and in the lower areas air conditioning was a premium over fans.

After San Cristobal we had just a few more days riding in Mexico to reach the border with Guatemala. The terrain continued to be mountainous. On the last day before the border, I had slowly descended nearly 15 kilometers and was in an area that started to flatten out when I had severe vibrations on my rear brake. I wasn't quite sure what had happened but noticed the wheel would barely turn. I stopped and made a better assessment and was able to at least get the wheel rolling again.

David was ahead, and I showed him the situation. We took an early lunch stop and put the bike upside down to see if we could figure things out. We got things rolling more smoothly, and a short while later we found a motorcycle repair area where we showed the mechanics the bike. This led to taking the brakes apart and learning the clip had bent, leading the pad to no longer fit smoothly. I had spare brake pads as well as a clip, though it still troubled me not to know the cause of the original failure.

The combination of some extra time working my brakes and a hot afternoon brought us to the border city with Guatemala at the end of the day. There was a small hotel there, and the first town in Guatemala was another 10 kilometers up the hill. Rather than cross the border that evening, we spent one last night in Mexico.

Overall, I enjoyed my cycling in Mexico. I had taken a cautious approach after reading travel advisories that made Mexico sound like a dangerous area. However, in my entire two months cycling across a dozen states, I never felt as though I was in an unsafe situation. I was also pleasantly surprised by the motorists and thought the traffic was at least as well behaved in Mexico as in either Canada or the U.S.A.

One more restful sleep, and then David and I would cross over to Guatemala.

Guatemala

Honk! Honk! "Out of the way, here comes the chicken bus!" we heard. Just after that a large decorated school bus came zooming past. It was still at a safe distance, but I was glad I had my mirror to watch. Over the next week and a half, I used that mirror often.

Things changed almost immediately at the border. Compared to Mexico, I found Guatemala to be a noisier, hillier, colder and poorer country. Even the names used to warn of speed bumps changed from "tope" to "tumulus." In Mexico people had a reserved sense of curiosity as we passed. In Guatemala the kids would run out yelling, "Gringo! gringo!" calling a lot more attention both to us and to themselves.

Before crossing the border, we went to Mexico to get an exit stamp. I had carefully saved my FMM card and showed it to the guard.

"Where is your receipt for the FMM?"

I remembered paying for the FMM and getting a receipt, but also somehow remembered turning in that receipt to get the completed paperwork. In any case that was two and a half months ago, and I no longer had a receipt. The guard informed me it would cost me 500 pesos (~$25). Somehow this seemed like a scam, and I was tempted to just leave without getting a stamp and see if I could enter Guatemala without having the Mexican exit stamp. Later reading of other cyclist blogs indicated others had done this, but I was a bit more cautious, particularly since the border was several kilometers farther uphill. I reluctantly paid my fee, though not without letting the guard know I thought he was scamming me. Sigh.

The last kilometer before the border we passed a bunch of small shops, followed by the border zone. A money changer approached me. Banks in Guatemala will also exchange money but not always Mexican pesos. So, I negotiated an OK, but not exceptional, rate and exchanged the last of my pesos for quetzals. A few kilometers farther we stopped at a bank to withdraw some more money from an ATM.

Over the next two days we cycled up a stunningly beautiful valley. Eventually, we would crest over 3000 meters again, and it was cold enough that I would get out my wool hat and mittens. Until Guatemala City, we had several sections on the Pan American Highway. It was a busy four lane highway but was paved, and grades weren't as steep as those of the smaller, sometimes gravel roads. The road did keep getting busier and busier as we approached Guatemala City, our largest metropolitan area since Guadalajara.

The day before we reached Guatemala City, we had difficulty finding a hotel until we saw an "events center" that seemed to specialize in weddings and similar affairs. The price was also rather expensive, though we were able to negotiate a lower rate.

From here there would be a longer descent into the metropolitan area. I wasn't looking forward to the descent, anticipating a combination of steep downhill on a very busy highway with no shoulders. That morning as we crested the hill, I encouraged David to go ahead and not necessarily wait for me, though he still did that at various strategic points. We also had a tentative rendezvous point at a particular hotel we had randomly picked near the city center.

The descent turned out better than I expected, as there were shoulders for most of the steeper downhill stretches, and it never became very busy. I concentrated on taking my heavily laden bicycle slowly down the hill, including riding my brakes somewhat often. I could tell that the pads were well worn. Close to the bottom the shoulder went away, and it was more chaotic because there was more traffic but the road hadn't yet widened to three and four lanes, as it did later.

I half expected David somewhere along the way but didn't see him. However, I also concentrated mostly on the road, as it was still rather busy. When I got to the turnoff from the main highway onto smaller roads going to the center, I was somewhat surprised that David must have gone ahead. I walked a bit here to figure out how to best make a left turn from one busy road to another, when to my surprise here came David from behind.

Apparently, David had stopped and waited for me and waited for quite a while. Eventually, when he didn't see me, he decided to proceed to our rendezvous point. Somewhere during that waiting period, I had passed, and neither of us noticed the other – I know I was busy enough just keeping track of all the vehicles on the road to do much scanning along the sides. It would have sorted itself out since we had a rendezvous point, but it was still nice to connect before reaching the center.

Once we found the rendezvous hotel and inquired about rates, they were reasonable enough that we checked in for two nights. After this first order of business, we needed to find a bike store, both to take care of my now worn brake pads and to investigate what happened my last full day in Mexico when the brakes dramatically shuddered. The first shop we found was one that sold bikes and parts but didn't do service, but the second one was a very professional shop with good mechanics. In short order the bike was updated with rotor and new pads, and I felt reassured it would ride better.

After a relaxing rest day wandering through the city, we headed outbound again. It was easier to leave the city than to enter, and while we started on the busy Pan American Highway again, it gradually became calmer.

One of those afternoons we experienced the kindness of strangers in Guatemala. We had eaten lunch at a roadside restaurant, then descended to the bottom of a canyon before starting a slow steady climb for many kilometers. It was getting hot.

Up ahead I noticed a car stopped the other direction on the road. I didn't think much of it as sometimes drivers pull over. However, as I came close, the driver came out and ran over carrying two bottles of cold water. Wow, just what we needed! We thanked him, and then he somehow went back to his car to bring over two more bottles. That was unexpected, and we thanked him again. The driver then left, and we slowly continued up the rest of the longer hill feeling refreshed.

As we reached the crest of the hill, who should arrive but the driver again. This time he was carrying two cold cokes. It was even a bit strange to have him help us three times, but it was also hot enough that we didn't refuse.

The last two days in Guatemala, we left the Pan American Highway and followed a much smaller road. On previous nights we had stayed in little villages along the way and were fortunate to find the village of Jocotan not far from the Honduras border.

In Jocotan, as well as in other villages, we had developed a routine. First find a hotel. Next, get clean. After that, walk through town to get something to eat as well as find a grocery. Buy a standard set of items at the grocery for evening as well as for the next morning. My list frequently included bread, fruit, a can of tuna and some juice as well as a coke. After this the procedure was to update my blog, look at the internet (when we had wifi) and otherwise relax for a not very late night.

Overall, Guatemala was an interesting country but also a shorter ride—a ride that we crossed within two weeks. Next on the list would be Honduras.

Honduras
Honduras was a pleasant surprise and one of my favorite countries.

As we cycled up to the border, I wasn't certain what to expect and my expectations had been set low by travel advisories and what I had read. One report listed Honduras as the country with highest per-capita murder rate in the world. Another pointed out there were parts of the northern triangle (Guatemala, Honduras, El Salvador) from which as much as 10% of the population had fled, some to Mexico and others seeking asylum in the U.S., although Guatemala had been fine.

There wasn't much of a village on either side of the Guatemala/Honduras border, but there was a steep hill where my odometer reached up to 12% grades. There were several kilometers of trucks waiting. Before crossing the border, we spent some quetzals on lunch. After that we quickly checked out of Guatemala and worked through the formalities of entry into Honduras. These included a quick "health consultation," though with my limited Spanish I think it was mostly a quick visual once-over to ensure that I looked healthy and an entry stamp.

Cycling away from the border, we came across some nice women from the tourist office making a quick survey, and after that Honduras only became better. We cycled a few more hills and into the town of Copan Ruinas.

Over the next days we would see subtle changes that came with a new country. Gasoline was priced in liters again after gallons in Guatemala. Small stores were more often named "pulperia" rather than "tienda." We still saw some large buses, but they were less flamboyant than the chicken buses in Guatemala.

The roads we took through Honduras were mostly smaller roads than in Guatemala. This meant less traffic but also some steeper hills. I didn't mind the 12% uphill grinds if they weren't long and didn't happen too often, though the steep downhills were more a challenge. I did notice that there were sometimes larger gaps between small restaurants, which made it more important to buy lunch and breakfast items in the small towns.

In both Guatemala and Honduras, these small shops would occasionally have arcade style video games. It seemed as though the xbox/playstation market was a lot less than in the U.S. and even Mexico. Overall, Honduras seemed less "loud" than Guatemala, not just the buses, but also the kids. While kids might still yell, "Gringo!" it was less common. In one spot, we met some boys and asked them why they weren't in school on a Thursday. They told us they went half days and that school was very important to their future.

From Copan Ruinas to Tegucigalpa was a very hilly ride on roads that were small but generally in good shape. Many cycling days exceeded 1000 meters (3300 ft.) of climb, despite averaging 50-60 kilometers per day. It took about a week, including one day as a rest day.

The day we cycled to Siguatepeque we had 1075 meters (3520 ft.) of climb along with 1647 meters (5404 ft., more than a mile) of descent. I could feel my brake pads being very worn. Fortunately, we were coming to a larger highway, where I hoped we might also see fewer extremely steep grades. Close to the road intersection was a somewhat fancy "business" hotel. The rates were slightly more expensive than our small town hotels, but we weren't in the mood for a long exploration into the city, so we stayed there. As David went to check in, some local TV reporters came up. It was an oral test of my Spanish skills as I spoke to the camera, answering the customary questions about our travels. I'm not sure if it ever showed, but I've now spoken more Russian and more Spanish than English to TV reporters.

It was two days on a larger highway cycling into Tegucigalpa. Since the countryside isn't flat, our cycling into the city had steep hills and some of the most challenging cycling yet. I could tell my brakes were not as effective, and the busy roads made it more challenging. Fortunately, after some harrowing riding, we found our way first to a bike shop and eventually to a hotel. The bike shop replaced my brake pads, and this made a huge difference.

One thing I did notice in Honduras, was more guards armed with shotguns. We didn't walk far in the city at night after dark, but neither in the city nor in the smaller towns did I ever feel unsafe. However, I did find it interesting that even store delivery trucks with milk or bread might be accompanied with a guard carrying a shotgun.

It was a busy ride on the ring road around Tegucigalpa before reaching smaller roads outbound on our way to the Nicaraguan border. It was election season, and, in addition to signs and banners along the way, some caravans of enthusiastic campaigners came past in cars, trucks and buses. We spent one last night in Danli, not far from the border, and our roughly two-week ride through Honduras was complete.

I'm sure Honduras has difficulties, including some drug-related violence. We didn't explore the most dangerous areas, but other than seeing guards with shotguns, we never had a sense of unease. The people in Honduras we met seemed genuinely friendly and not as likely to call attention to us as those in Guatemala. I also think our route through Honduras was more ideal than that through Guatemala, as it went along smaller roads and through smaller towns. It was hilly, but we also mostly stayed at higher altitudes, which meant cooler temperatures. Our days of cooler riding were numbered, however, as we would go back through lowlands in Nicaragua.

Nicaragua

Nicaragua is clean, and they separate their recycling! Our first impressions as we crossed the border were helped by a lack of trash on the road sides as well a smooth road descending down towards Esteli. We were now formally out of the "northern triangle countries." While I never ran into danger in either Guatemala or Honduras, I indirectly noticed the effect because Nicaragua had more tourists, first in Esteli and then definitely in Granada and along the coast. It was almost as if some tourists "discovered" Nicaragua as a beautiful but less expensive alternative to Costa Rica.

We no longer had our posters and rallies for the upcoming Honduras election. These were replaced with big signs about Daniel Ortega. He had been in power perhaps twenty years, and his last campaign had been several years earlier, but there were still signs throughout for both Ortega and the red and black of his coalition.

Our second night in Nicaragua we reached the town of Esteli. The locals had an evening bicycle ride. While we didn't participate, we were out on the square when they left. It was interesting to see the cyclists.

From Esteli to Granada was too far to ride in a day, and we didn't know of any hotels. It was not a big problem to camp, though we were now also reaching lowland areas with hotter temperatures. We set off in the morning with the plan to at least reach the town of Puertas Viejas and then ask around.

When we reached Puertas Viejas, we stopped and had a mid-afternoon meal at a roadside café. As expected, the locals told us there were no accommodations in town. A truck driver was having a meal at the next table, and he told us there were also no accommodations in Las Maderas, 22 kilometers farther down the road. However, he did know of a hotel 8 kilometers after that.

An idea entered our mind. What if we got a lift on that otherwise empty truck? It seemed like a good idea at the time, and the driver was friendly and willing, but he was going to finish his meal first.

We waited until the driver and another passenger finished their meals. All of a sudden there was a quick rush to get everything loaded. I wheeled over my loaded bicycle and started detaching the panniers to put them in the truck. David also got his bike ready. Then I quickly went back to pay the bill, as David didn't have enough change. Whew! It was quick, but we were soon loaded and on our way.

We had gone just a few kilometers when I looked around and realized I had left my Camelbak at the café, just beside the table. Uh oh. Not only did the Camelbak have my water but also my passport and some other valuable items. I let David know and rather than interrupt the driver from the back of the truck, we decided to continue on to our stop and then find a way to return to pick it up. Hopefully, it would still be there.

Another 35 kilometers later, the truck stopped at the small town. By now I had had enough time to get worried about my missing valuables. David helped explain the situation to the truck driver and soon the driver was also helping to find a solution. They tried calling the women who worked at the café, but there was no answer. The driver spotted a friend who was getting gas, and after explaining the situation and negotiating a price, the automobile driver was willing to go back. David and the truck driver both accompanied the motorist while I stayed back to watch the bikes.

It took 75 minutes, but they returned with the Camelbak. Whew! The women at the café had noticed I had left my bag almost immediately, but by that time the truck was already gone. They had kept it there.

By now it was getting dark. It turned out there wasn't a hotel right in San Benito, though some locals told us of a possible place another few kilometers down the road. With flashing lights and slow cycling, we reached an otherwise marginal guest house and settled in for the night.

The following day it was a short ride to Granada. We took a relaxing rest day there, and I was even able to get my glasses fixed by a local jeweler. No more wearing my sunglasses at night!

Granada was close to sea level and hence hot again. In addition, the entire country is low and flat here, which allows winds to whip across the country. This meant many more windmills in the countryside to generate electricity, but it also meant windy conditions. I tend to be more of a morning person than David, so I was out early the next morning to try beating both the heat and the wind. I finished my riding that day by 11:15 a.m. and found a cool spot in a Burger King to wait for David to arrive.

That afternoon we walked to the grocery, where I was surprised to find some tourists paying their bills with U.S. dollars. Apparently enough tourists come to this beach area of Nicaragua that the dollar was also an accepted currency.

Just one more day and we would be across the border to Costa Rica, making Nicaragua the country I spent the shortest amount of time traveling across.

Costa Rica

Costa Rica was the seventh country on my journey. By now I was more goal-driven to reach Panama City by end of March and hence chose mostly to follow the roads down and along the Pacific Coast. This area is more developed than the Atlantic coast, and it is also mostly at sea level, so I had some hot days of cycling.

Immigration was more bureaucratic than average, but soon we had exchanged currency and were on our way. David and I cycled just three days before reaching a turnoff where we would split. David would visit friends in the general area of San Jose, and I would proceed farther along the coast. Those three days I alternated between a somewhat wide new highway and the older highway with a narrow shoulder but still the same amount of traffic. Other cycling journals either made it sound like a horrible highway or had recommended an alternative via the Nicoya Peninsula. With our expectations set low, it turned out just fine.

As we reached the intersection of highways, we said one last goodbye. I had enjoyed our six weeks of travels together. We turned out to be well matched in cycling speeds, and both of us were easy going enough to figure out how to navigate the adventure together. I was also appreciative of David's much better skills in Spanish as well as his mechanical aptitude that together helped keep my bike running through several sets of brake pads.

After we split I cycled a few kilometers farther and spent the rest of the afternoon at an aged surfing style hotel. The following several days I cycled along a much more developed coast and ended up staying in little beach resort communities of Jaco, Quepos and Palmar Norte. The roads were flatter and my speeds quicker as I tried each day to get as much cycling done as possible before it turned hot. Otherwise, I had an uneventful cycle ride through Costa Rica. I think it is a country I could return to again, though this time perhaps I would go more off the beaten track as those smaller places were what I had enjoyed about Mexico, Guatemala and particularly Honduras.

Panama

Now I was heading to the Panama Canal! I had a bit of finish line fever as I approached the immigration checkpoint from Costa Rica to Panama. Just one more country and I would reach Panama City, my end goal for cycling North America.

There is no road between Panama and Colombia. Instead, there was a 100-kilometer-wide section of swamp, jungle and more dangerous "end of the road" terrain known as the Darien Gap. While people have been able to cross the Darien Gap on foot and canoe, it is an entirely different level of adventure. Instead, almost every cycle tourist who wants to cross will either fly between Panama and Colombia or find their way to the coast and then take a boat to cross via the ocean.

I decided to fly, and since I was flying anyways, had booked tickets to fly first from Panama City to Denver and then a week later from Denver to Cartagena, Colombia. Having a plane ticket also satisfied one thing I might need in crossing the border, "evidence of onward passage." The clause of requiring evidence of onward passage is in the official immigration policies of several countries, including Costa Rica and Panama. Cycling blogs seemed to indicate it was most often enforced cycling into Panama. I had the key piece of documentation, though it turned out that when Immigration saw my loaded touring bicycle, they considered that by itself to be sufficient evidence.

In Panama I once again saw the contrast between the larger, direct Pan American Highway and smaller roads and cycled some of both. The first two days first to David and then to Las Lajas, I was on the big and sometimes busy highway. I did benefit from road construction going to Las Lajas, as the new lanes were already paved, but all traffic was directed instead onto just one side. As a result I had a nice new wide cycleway all to myself.

In Las Lajas was a nice little resort hotel. Like Costa Rica, Panama seemed to have more upscale hotels that catered to tourists. I had carefully asked the prices to avoid the most expensive places. The Las Lajas hotel was nice enough that I spent an extra day, but not so nice that the price was too expensive. After this I ended up on much smaller roads that were hilly, but my favorite cycling was in Panama as there was hardly any traffic and the roads wound through small, natural areas.

From Sona to Santiago I was back on the larger highway and from there just a few days cycling to Panama City. I had known before that Costa Rica was a wealthier country than others in Central America, but as I cycled through Panama, also realized that Panama was wealthy as well. I passed multiple small housing developments that appeared to cater to expats who would build and live there. I know it wouldn't be an area for me, however, as the afternoon temperatures climbed.

I had one last day on Farrallon Beach, where I passed several very expensive hotels before finding a not very expensive hostel. In these smaller hotels I sometimes had to negotiate whether I was allowed to bring in my bicycle. Farrallon Beach was an area where I was more nervous than average about someone tampering with the bike and was pleased that one of the hotel managers let me take my bicycle in. I quickly brought it inside, only to discover that they had changed their mind. However, now the bike was in my room, and a different manager seemed to think it was still OK. I decided to let them sort it out and instead closed the door.

My last day cycling into to Panama City was also the most hectic. As the traffic had steadily increased, I had taken smaller roads than the main Pan American Highway but was directed back to the highway for the last kilometers. Initially, the highway had a nice wide shoulder, so I didn't mind three lanes of high speed traffic to my left. However, soon I found with increasing frequency that trucks were parked on the shoulder. I would check my mirror and quickly ride across the gaps. Whew!

As I got close to the city on a smaller road, I think I figured out what was going on. It seems that during the peak rush hours, some roads surrounding the city have their directions reversed to enable more commute-bound traffic. In addition, they may also prohibit trucks during those hours. The result might make for a smoother rush hour – but all those trucks parked on the shoulders of the highway also make it tougher for cyclists.

However, I was soon through the worst traffic areas and then across a high bridge crossing the Panama Canal and into the middle of the city. I had made it through North America and to my goal. By the numbers I had now traveled:

- 14,884 kilometers (9,248 miles) from Prudhoe Bay to Panama City
- 206 cycling days spread out over a little more than 9 months
- 130,600 meters of climbing (428,600 feet or 81 miles)
- 5 flat tires, 5 sets of brake pads, two hubs and one derailleur

I still had a week left before my flight would leave and just a few things on my TO DO list: to get a duffel bag for my flight, to get a box for my bike, to visit the Panama Canal and otherwise to get myself set for a ride across South America.

During that week I figured out the subway system and the buses and got myself out to Miraflores Locks to observe ships crossing the canal. However, the most interesting thing I did was take a boat tour across the Panama Canal. There is a company that has a once -a -week boat trip. It goes halfway across the canal, and once a month it does a "full transit" from the Pacific Ocean to the Atlantic Ocean. As luck would have it, the week I visited was a full transit week and hence I signed up for an all-day trip.

I was picked up from my hotel at 4:30 a.m., and we then gathered perhaps 100 tourists for a 6:00 a.m. departure at the docks. We first sailed underneath the Bridge of the Americas that I had cycled across coming into the city and shortly thereafter went to Miraflores Locks, the first of three locks for the day.

Our tourist boat had three decks but was still small compared to ships normally crossing the canal. Hence, we needed to piggy-back on another larger ship to use the lock. Fortunately, morning ship traffic was busy, and there wasn't much of a wait before we entered the lock and the first of our 26 meter (85 foot) rise to the interior lake. A second set of locks a little while later brought us the full height.

Once we were at elevation, we sailed over the top of the "continental divide" as well as the steepest areas of excavation that were needed to build the canal. After passing the narrow, steep area, the waterway opened to a nice broad lake. We stopped here to let those on a halfday trip disembark and then spent the next several hours slowly cruising across the lake. It was interesting to see the large cargo vessels. The sizes of the largest ships possible had increased just a few months before with the opening of several newer and larger locks.

On the other end were locks that would bring our ship back down to sea level. While we had minimal waiting time on the Pacific side, our luck wasn't with us on the Atlantic side, and we spent two hours waiting until a companion ship arrived and we could go through the locks. After this it was a short sail to the port area and then a bus back to Panama City.

Overall it was a long day when I arrived back at the hotel at 8 p.m., a little over 15 hours since departure. However, overall, I found the experience to be well worth the time I had spent.

I now had just a few days before flying to Colorado, a week in Colorado and then a return to my bicycle trip starting in Cartagena, Colombia.

2017 - Tales from across South America

Colombia

While I didn't know it yet, Colombia would turn out to be one of my favorite cycling countries. For now I was just happy to have arrived, complete with bicycle, and be cooling off in a hotel along the Atlantic coast in Cartagena. The afternoon was hot and humid, as afternoons would be for the next week until I started the big climbs through the Andes Mountains.

In the past Colombia had had a reputation for having warring drug gangs and kidnappings. However, things had simmered down in the last few years, and very recently the FARC rebel group had made peace with the government and was in the process of becoming a peaceful political organization. The U.K. Foreign Service and U.S. State Department still advised against travel in parts of the country. However, the U.K. also provided a "green" route along the main highways from Cartagena, Medellin, Cali, Popayan and Pasto. It was in this zone that I had plotted my route.

My readings of other bicycle travelers' accounts also uncovered two incidents not far from Cartagena, one just a few months before, where a bicyclist had been held up by a thief. Hence, I decided to leave Cartagena early on Easter Sunday morning and stick to the main highway. As it turned out I was hardly the only cyclist out for a weekend ride and never came to any situation in which I felt unsafe. Safe cycling with many others on the road was a pattern that would continue for the rest of Colombia.

The landscape was green. It was rainy season. Over the next month I cycled through some strong showers. However, on this first Sunday riding, the skies stayed dry. After I crossed Cartagena, a city of more than a million, I entered a four lane, divided highway. There was a toll booth with a narrow lane for both bicycles and motorcycles. Here and elsewhere through South America, cyclists were allowed on the toll roads and not charged. I saw more than a dozen cyclists on this road.

By 11 a.m., it was already over 30C (86F) and humid. I had reached a road intersection with a restaurant and nearby small hotel. It was still early, but I decided I would spend the heat of the day in the hotel with air conditioning. I also continued this pattern through the next week. Relative to other countries, Colombian hotels were not very expensive and also relatively uniform in their prices. I paid 30,000 pesos or ~$11 U.S. for that hotel night. This was in contrast to what I would find later in Peru, where there was a much larger range of both inexpensive and expensive hotels.

My Mexican Spanish failed me at times, as I found many Colombians tended to talk more quickly. However, most all of the simple conversations about buying things, reserving hotels or getting directions were still not difficult. Also, I found a smile went a long way, and Colombians I met were generally friendly.

Over the next week I continued with the pattern I had started: on the road early and stopping by midday to find a small hotel. The terrain varied between very flat and some areas with small rolling hills. The roads were smoothly paved, not too busy and generally had good shoulders.

On my second day I encountered a long backed -up line of trucks and vehicles. I cycled in the left lane to the head of the traffic jam to see what was going on. Apparently, a set of protestors had piled branches in the road and had stopped traffic in both directions. Nearby were half a dozen police officers. They saw me with my loaded bicycle and motioned me to carry the bike along the side and over some of the branches. I carefully walked over and kept my eyes wide open as I crossed the barricade. While trucks and even motorcycles were stopped, somehow it was OK for a bicycle tourist to pass. Another two hours later a flood of cars and trucks came past, telling me the protest had also ended.

 After a week of cycling, I came to the Rio Cauca and the small town of Taraza. Along the road were multiple jets of water squirting up in the air. Signs said, "Lavadero." I soon observed these were popular places to stop and thoroughly wash a truck or automobile. Some of the jets had high enough pressure to send them squirting ten meters high. I think some of this came as the Rio Cauca valley was narrowing, with higher hills to build up water pressure.

The big climb began half a day past Taraza, where the elevation would go from 100 meters to over 2000 meters. I stopped at a small bakery at the start of the climb to refuel. From here a consistent 5%-6% grade started out. It was a slow and steady slog. While the afternoon started warm and humid, by the time I reached the small village of Valdivia, it was much cooler. A gas station with hotel rooms for 20,000 pesos was a welcome stop. In the evening and overnight, the rain came down heavily.

While it was still raining lightly in the morning, it was definitely lighter when I set off to continue my climbing for a second day. Along the way I encountered a second backlog of trucks. This time, rather than protestors, it seemed to be rockslides that had blocked the road. Unstable hillsides, rainy season and then rockslides would close the roads multiple times later in Colombia.

After reaching the top of the first big climb near 2500 meters elevation, I came to the small town of Yarumal, where I would also spend the following day as my first rest day in Colombia. After Yarumal it was two days with more downhill than uphill to reach the larger city of Medellin.

Despite being a large city with busy highways and a lot of traffic, I found many cyclists on the roads around Medellin. Some sections of highway were even marked with a right lane only for trucks and bicycles. I found a place near the main commercial district and then wandered through the middle of the big city. Here were supermarkets, SIM cards, restaurants and all the other things a touring cyclist might require.

Medellin was just the start of the larger mountain region. On the day I cycled out of Medellin, I was back climbing slowly over the next mountain range. Traffic gradually subsided as the huge highways gave way to a two lane road going over a smaller pass. At the top was a restaurant where the owner offered to let me camp. However, it was early and the next 40km included 1700m of descent, so I started downhill. The pattern of longer climbs and descents would also continue for the next weeks in both Colombia and Ecuador. Along with the descents came increased heat, though it was never quite as warm as on the plains in the far north.

I celebrated my birthday in the small village of Irra. There was a small hotel right on the main square. Loud music was beating right from the square. I had carried my bicycle and all my gear up two flights of narrow stairs. For the most part, in Colombia I carried my bicycle inside, though at times it was a steep climb.

Over the next weeks the places I stayed varied between smaller towns and roadside hotels. It rained many days, sometimes heavily. However, after the rain it would dry off and become warmer. It was never extremely hot or particularly cold. Many cyclists were on the roads, particularly on the weekends and on the May 1st public holiday.

Near Cali I came into a flatter valley with almost 200 km of mostly flat terrain. There were many fields of was sugar cane. My average speeds increased on the flat terrain. As I came to end of the valley, I had two days with a lot more climbing and a lot more rain through the smaller roads to Popayan. This seemed to be one of the more security sensitive zones in Colombia and major bridge crossings and other strategic points had army soldiers guarding them.

Popayan is known as the white city for the architectural buildings in the middle of the city. Hotel prices were more expensive here, but I found one that was still reasonable. By now my front derailleur wasn't letting me shift into my largest gears. This wasn't as big of a concern because I wasn't using my highest gears as I had with all the climbing.

From Popayan to Pasto was four days of cycling with a lot more climbing but not extremely long distances. I wasn't feeling 100%, and my bicycle with limited gears also wasn't feeling 100%. However, I knew I could take a few days to recover in Pasto before my brother Bert would arrive to join me for the next leg of the trip.

Before getting to Pasto, I looked on my maps to scout out the locations of bicycle shops as well as a hotel near three major bike shops. After checking into the hotel, I went to each of these shops, only to discover that most would close between noon and 3 p.m. or so for an extended siesta. Once they opened, I further discovered that the Pasto bicycle business seems to split between shops that mostly sell new equipment and mechanics that do business not affiliated with any shop.

After bouncing between all three shops, I ended up in the downtown bicycle district. I figured if necessary I would buy a new front derailleur and have it installed. However, the shop took my bike into a back room and came back and told me it was now fixed. I'm not sure exactly what they did and it didn't end up costing me, but I had my gears back again.

On the second of two rest days in Pasto, I cycled across the city to a new hotel closer to the bus station. My brother Bert arrived in the afternoon; we would spend the next few weeks cycling the last small bit of Colombia and then into Ecuador.

From Pasto to Ipiales, the last reasonable sized town on the Colombia/Ecuador border, was 83 kilometers. However, this included 2000 meters of climb/descent, so we split it into two days of cycling. We climbed up to 3174 meters before a long descent to the river below. At the bottom was a bridge guarded by soldiers. Bert was ahead, and by the time I was there, Bert had already gotten them to take a photo of him by the bridge and soon we ended up with a photo of all of us together, soldiers, cyclists and bicycles. The smiles told me that at least this wasn't a particularly tense assignment.

There was a small town of Pedregal with shops, restaurants and a few hotels. Once we learned the hotel in town didn't have hot water, we went a little farther to a small country hotel by the river. There was also a neighborhood restaurant there. It didn't have any signs, but once we asked enough locals, we could find our way.

On our last day in Colombia, we cycled up to the border town of Ipiales. Journals from other cyclists suggested that the border occasionally has long delays. It was still early in the day, so we decided to check things out. There wasn't much of a delay, and overall the crossing was smooth and easy. By the end of the day, I even had a new Ecuador SIM card and had figured out the ATMs.

Overall, I spent 31 days cycling across Colombia. The roads were smooth and often with good shoulders. I saw many other cyclists on the road. The landscape varied between humid plains, colder mountains and wet forests. Lodging wasn't very expensive, and food was easy to find along the way. Despite its past more violent reputation, I never felt unease from either people or from traffic on the road. Overall, Colombia turned out to be one of my favorite cycling countries and one to which I would like to return for more touring.

Ecuador

Where's Bert? Which way did he go? A few kilometers past the Colombia/Ecuador border is a split in the road with a side road going to the town of Tumbes and the main highway continuing straight to bypass the town. I came to the intersection and wasn't quite certain which way Bert had gone. Before we departed, I had mentioned taking the main highway until a later exit – but there was an extra curve that made it not obvious.

I went down the side road for a little bit, thinking perhaps Bert had paused just past the intersection. When I didn't see him after a kilometer, I decided to turn back to the intersection and take the main road. Not much later, I figured we had probably missed each other, so I now concentrated on getting myself to the town center to sort things out. Fortunately, once I got to center of town, the phone connection on my Colombian SIM was still strong enough that I we could communicate via a combination of text messages and email. I had email but my SMS didn't work, and Bert had SMS but no email. It turned out we were within 100 meters of each other. After that point we learned to pre-agree on rendezvous points in case we got separated.

Our route through Ecuador continued a pattern of longer climbs and descents along the Andes Mountains. There were patchwork fields separated by small rows of trees. In the valleys were occasional small towns centered on a large church. For the most part we followed the major highways and had reasonable shoulders, but traffic was not too busy. I noticed more people wearing wool ponchos, and it reminded me of photos I had seen of Peruvian mountain villages.

It took five cycling days to reach Quito. Along the way we crossed the equator. We crossed on a smaller road that didn't have a monument or other marker, so I ended up checking the location on my phone and taking a photo of the surroundings once it started showing south latitudes.

Just before the equator we caught views of Cayambe volcano. At 5710 meters (~19,000 feet), it is Ecuador's third highest peak. The south flank of the volcano is on the equator and is the only place along the equator with a permanent snowfield. Also interesting is that due to the slightly flattened shape of the earth, the summit of Cayambe is the point farthest from the center of the earth.

Those last few days before Quito, I wasn't feeling 100%, and my gastrointestinal tract was giving me troubles. More concerning was that I seemed to develop a saddle sore that made it painful to sit on the saddle for extended periods. Hence, I was looking forward to taking a rest day in Quito and letting my body recover. The combination of saddle sore and steeper grades made my entry into Quito slower than normal.

Quito is a huge city that is situated on a large mountain ridge. The last kilometers passed through the urban area until we reached a frequent backpacker destination near Foch Plaza. We found a friendly hostel and checked in for two nights. During our rest day Bert sampled the local delicacy of cuy (guinea pig).

Despite a day of rest, my saddle sore was still painful. It was infected, and I read on the internet that doxycycline was sometimes used as an antibiotic. I had doxycycline with me as an anti-malaria pill, so I started taking it at the dose I would if entering a malaria zone. We decided to take a second rest day and then went to find a local clinic.

After asking questions from the locals a few times, we found a clinic that could provide a diagnosis. After a short wait I saw a doctor, who cleaned the infected area, confirmed my antibiotic choice and also suggested an anti-inflammatory. This treatment along with rest meant that I was feeling considerably better the next day for our departure. In the next few days I was back at 100%. Taking a two –day break in Quito ended up being the right choice.

It was busy as we left Quito. We headed outbound during rush hour. However, Quito reverses the flow of traffic on some roads during rush hours, so we had only a single busy lane. Within a few kilometers we had left the busiest parts and were back onto our major highway, heading south through Ecuador. Bert joined me for another full day of cycling to Machachi. On the following day we cycled together to the top of the next large pass, where Bert turned back towards Quito as I continued south.

My route continued along an area known as volcano alley. I passed Cotopaxi, Ecuador's second highest point and rode into the larger town of Ambato. Ambato had a great little town square, where I stopped before deciding to continue so I would be on the "outbound" side. After I found myself on a short hill with an insanely steep grade, I pushed my bike up the hill.

A short while later I felt my rear tire go flat. I took a slow, careful approach to unpack everything, diagnose everything and then fix it. I had cycled over glass, and there was a hole directly in the middle of the tire tread. The hole was big enough that small bits of sand and other abrasive materials would likely get in. So I decided to place a small piece of rubber as a "boot" on the inside of the tire to keep this material from causing further flats.

The following day I passed Chimborazo, Ecuador's highest point, which was not far from the town of Riobamba. The primary highway splits here, with a lot of traffic going to the coast and a smaller road continuing south towards Cuenca. I continued on the smaller road, which meant less traffic and also more hills over the following days. Descending into the town of Alausi, my GPS recorded 11%, 12%, 13% and even a brief period of 16% descent. By nature I am cautious, and on the steepest part of that hill, I walked my bike rather than ride the brakes trying to stop my heavy bicycle.

From Alausi to the following town of Chunchi was only 13 kilometers as the crow flies but 35 kilometers on the road. This gave a good idea of the winding road as it passed across steep valleys. Fortunately, there were not many grades over 10%. However, the road was either climbing or descending and very rarely flat. A combination of climbs and spectacular views meant that I stopped often to take photographs.

From Chunchi it was two days bicycling to the larger town of Cuenca, where I found a nice hotel and decided to take a rest day. With all the climbing and descending, I had worn down my brake pads. I didn't need to replace them yet but decided to see if I could at least find some extra pads. I looked in my online map and found a bicycle repair shop not far away.

I walked to where the shop should be but couldn't find it. As I looked over things again, I saw a notice of "Ask inside the Andes clinic." I had seen a medical clinic, so I decided to go back. This time I went inside and started asking around. At first, with the combination of my minimal Spanish and asking nurses, it seemed as if this wasn't the right place. However, I showed them the online information, and with the addition of a nurse who spoke better English than I spoke Spanish, it turned out that some local entrepreneurs had used the clinic as their contact address. We called their number, and they agreed to meet an hour later.

I met the two young gentlemen who did bicycle repair and explained the situation. I showed them a package with a spare set of brake pads I already had and asked if they could find any others in the city. They carefully wrote everything down and then called around. They found a shop that carried them, but it wasn't nearby. We settled on a price, and they agreed to ride out to the store and then deliver the brake pads to my hotel later in the afternoon. Overall, it worked well and was another reminder that repair and sales of bicycles and parts are sometimes separate businesses in Ecuador.

Cuenca is located at 2500 meters. There was another choice of roads here, either a further extension of the road of volcanoes south to Loja and or a road that descends down to the coast. While I enjoyed the views and cooler temperatures that came with the altitude, I had done a lot of climbing over the previous month and was ready for a change. I decided to take the road down via Santa Isabel and Santa Rosa.

Two days cycling with much more descent than climbs brought me to the banana region of Ecuador. Near the bottom the roads took me past long stretches of banana plantations. There was even a small town of Buena Vista with a banana monument in the town square. Some of the bunches of bananas still on the plants were wrapped in a protective packaging.

Santa Rosa was the last town I stayed in in Ecuador. Many of the downtown streets were torn up, and this didn't leave the best impression. However, I was able to find a reasonable hotel with air conditioning. I expected this to become much more important as my planned route through Peru would have long stretches along the coastal highway.

Peru

Cycling across Peru took me a month and a half of riding, longer than the time I spent in either Colombia or Ecuador. It would have been even more time if I had cycled through more of the mountains rather than spending most of my time along the coast.

I had read many journals from other cyclists. As I put together my route, there seemed to be two general choices: stay low along the coast or go up through the smaller valleys in the Andes. The Andes routes had an advantage of scenery, and most riders spoke highly of their travels. The roads were generally smaller, often unpaved and more remote. Higher altitudes brought with them dry conditions and cold nights, often well below freezing.

The coast of Peru was generally flatter, with one main highway that was well traveled and occasionally busy. A surprise for me was the cold Humboldt Current, which kept temperatures in a narrow range that rarely exceeded 25C (77F) or dropped much below 10C (50F) and typically fell in a narrower range. The current also brought prevailing winds from the south that were occasionally strong headwinds, particularly once I passed Lima. The coast was a dry desert, and many sections were without any signs of plants or animals.

The northern coast of Peru also had a nasty reputation as being dangerous for cyclists. In my reading I had read more accounts of cyclists being attacked or robbed in northern Peru than in the rest of Latin America combined. One town of Paijan was particularly notorious. A Paijan story I read a few times involved a lone cyclist being followed out of town by thugs on motor taxis. Once in the quiet rural areas, one attacker would assault the cyclist while others would take his/her belongings.

The lawless reputation, bleak scenery and headwinds caused other cyclists to skip the northern coast, either by taking a bus south to Lima or by spending more time in the mountains. Despite reading these accounts, my plans were to start cycling along the coast, remain cautious and adjust as necessary. I also decided I would find places to stay indoors rather than camping along the road.

In hindsight my expectations had been set low enough that Peru turned out to be a pleasant surprise. I never had occasion to sense any danger, temperatures were pleasant along the entire coast and the riding was easy, with just a few days with strong headwinds. Overall, if I were to rank the countries by my enjoyment, then Peru was still on the lower end – but also more pleasant than expected.

The transition to a more arid region continued on my first day cycling across the Peru border. I left Santa Rosa, which averages 49cm (19 inches), to ride across the border to Tumbes, which averages 31cm (12 inches), and it would become even more arid in days following. Banana plantations gave way to low, scrubby vegetation.

The border crossing was simple and efficient. There was one building that provided both an exit queue from Ecuador and an entry queue to Peru. I spent some U.S. dollars (also currency in Ecuador) at a border café and exchanged others for Peruvian Sol before setting off to the border town of Tumbes.

It was Sunday afternoon, and most of Tumbes was shut down. I found an expensive hotel but not many other places to stay, so I decided to splurge a bit before walking through town to find a bite to eat, get a SIM card and get more Sol from an ATM. After all I had read, I was extra cautious and had that reinforced when someone on the street told me to hide my expensive camera.

Most places were closed, but I found a restaurant that was busy and also was willing to break a larger bill. I ordered chicken but received poultry that seemed much tougher to eat, duck most likely. While they were willing to accept my larger bill, they also didn't end up with quite enough change, so I paid a larger tip than expected. That first afternoon reinforced my "Welcome to Peru" wariness, but fortunately the days became better from there.

The following day, I cycled along the coast to the touristy beach town of Mancora. I crossed over several small beach settlements, where the Peruvian tuk-tuk was prevalent. They seem at least as popular in Peru as places like south India I have visited, and I think some of them may even have been built in India.

Mancora was followed by a not very difficult ride to Talara the next day. Leaving Talara the forecast called for headwinds, and I left early, hoping to beat the wind. My strategy didn't work, as it turned out the wind was strongest earlier in the day and only died down in the afternoon. The day was also made more frustrating by three flat tires.

The first flat was only 10 km after starting, just as the road from Talara rejoined the main highway. I stopped to diagnose the situation and had several onlookers. It turned out that my front tire had run over a thumbtack on the road. I patched the tube and started off but got only a kilometer down the road before the front tire was flat again. This time I stopped next to a wind farm (never a good sign) and tried sheltering out of the wind to swap in a new tube and make a better fix. It held for the rest of the day.

What didn't hold was my back tire, which developed a hole in the afternoon. By now it was hot, and I brought the bike under a tree beside the road. Fixing a rear flat takes some more work, including taking my gear off the bike, turning it upside down and bringing out the wheel. A small hole had developed next to the boot I had placed inside the tire after getting a big puncture in Ambato, Ecuador. As it turned out, I would get a second flat in similar fashion several days later, when I would decide that in the longer run, such a boot can generate friction that eventually creates further holes. With wind, flats and some rough roads, I was happy to get into the middle of Sullana to end what had been a tough day.

The following morning in Sullana, I awoke to a flat rear tire again. Apparently, I had fixed one hole, but there had been a second as well. My departure was delayed, but fortunately it was a shorter day cycling into Piura, and there wasn't much wind. Piura was a larger city, and I had a great little hotel near the main square. As I walked around and got a sense of the place, I thought, "Maybe Peru isn't such a bad place after all."

From Piura there are two choices of roads. The main Pan American Highway goes straight across the Sechura Desert. There is more than 250 km of open desert, with no towns and very few services other than a restaurant or two. The area is notorious for high winds, and cycling journals I read were full of accounts of long difficult slogs into the wind.

The other choice was the old Pan American Highway, which skirted along edges of the Sechura Desert and had a few small settlements. It was a longer route that would likely take three days rather than two but also with better choices to stay or eat. I decided to give this a try.

It was still moderately busy leaving Piura, but by afternoon the road became much quieter. To amuse myself I kept a "census" of how many cars passed the other direction. For each of the following hours, these were my findings:

-   7 a.m. – way too many to count

-   8 a.m. – 68

-   9 a.m. – 44

-   10 a.m. – 29

-   11 a.m. – 32

-   Noon – 4

-   1 p.m. – 5

These numbers also tell the tale of having two main roads that turned off and took with them most of the traffic. Once I passed the second turnoff, it was a longer and lonelier road. It was here that I had another flat in my rear tire. It was once again around the boot, and it was becoming clear to me that the boot would continue to generate further flats. I decided to swap in one of my two spare tires and keep the older tire as a spare.

In another sixteen kilometers I came to the small settlement of El Virrey, where I spent the night. There wasn't a hotel here, so I would need to violate my "no camping in Peru" plans. There was a small dusty park with fence around it. I asked at a neighboring residence/café, and they were fine with my camping there. In a small village like this, most everyone detects a stranger is visiting, so I figured it would be best to be visible right next to the main buildings in town. As a bonus the residence also had a small café, and I was later able to get dinner.

Setting up my tent interested two neighborhood boys, Carlos (8) and Antony (11), who supervised the process and peppered me with questions about my travels. It was a good practice of my Spanish. They hung around for an hour or so before we exhausted both our conversation and my limited Spanish vocabulary.

After El Virrey it was two days cycling to Lambayeque, which marked the end of the Sechura Desert. One day, cycling to Olmos, I noticed many small churches along the route. I started counting and photographing them and reached at least 15 in just a 50 kilometer stretch. There weren't many more houses than churches, and some looked abandoned.

That afternoon as I walked through Olmos, I found the local market street. These streets aren't always in obvious locations but instead are sometimes hidden behind a street or two. As I walked around looking at the bustle of activity, the locals also sized up this foreigner who had landed in their midst. I don't think tourists are a common occurrence in Olmos.

After crossing the Sechura Desert, I came through areas with more sugar cane. The land seemed to alternate between irrigated agricultural areas and dry open desert areas. I crossed the larger city of Chiclayo before coming to section that would contain the notorious and dangerous town of Paijan.

Paijan had a reputation as a violent town, particularly towards touring cyclists, and I wasn't certain what to expect. Many cyclists avoided the town by going through the mountains or taking a bus. I decided I would try it but also take some extra precautions, including asking for a police escort if necessary. I made my detailed plans, including stopping at the last town with a hotel the day before. This way I could cross Paijan early in the day, hopefully before the bandits were awake. I buried my camera and other valuables deep in my panniers and brought up my "decoy wallet" and expired passport to my handlebar bag. The decoy wallet had a small amount of cash and an expired credit card or two that I could give away if necessary.

I cycled across 40 kilometers of bleak desert before reaching the outskirts of Paijan. While I had hidden my fancier camera away, I did clip a small video device to my camelback and started recording my ride. The sun was shining, and the town looked not much different from other towns I had cycled across. On the north end of town, I saw several police cars parked in front of a bar and briefly thought about going in to strike up a conversation about security and ask for an escort if necessary – however, the town looked so sleepy that I decided to ride a bit farther and ask at the police station heading out from town.

I carefully sized up each of the tuk-tuks as they came past, but none of them seemed particularly menacing. There still seemed to be a reasonable amount of other traffic on the road. I kept cycling along, and before I knew it, I was already headed outbound and had likely missed the police station on my map. Not to worry, I continued cycling out, and in a few kilometers came to sugar cane fields again.

In another 10 kilometers I was to the next town and had crossed that hot spot of Paijan without any indication of trouble or other reason for worry. It ended up being much like any other town through which I had cycled.

By the end of the day, I arrived in Trujillo, Peru's third largest city. What I noticed most about Trujillo were the foreign tourists. It seemed strange to be in a town again where English was spoken and Western-looking tourists wandered through the streets. Otherwise, Trujillo seemed like a nice place to visit, but I wasn't quite in a rest day mode yet so ended up cycling another two days before taking my first Peru rest day in Chimbote.

The day before reaching Chimbote, I stayed in the small town of Casma. I wandered through town before finding a small hotel in the back streets. I brought my bicycle and all my gear up two flights of stairs into the hotel room. Some of these small towns and this hotel in particular seemed to be infested with crickets. They would scurry away when I walked in but otherwise were on the floor and along the bed and in the bathroom.

I decided not to be squeamish about crickets. However, a few of them tagged along with me on the road. I noticed this at the Chimbote hotel, when I went to retrieve my passport and a cricket hopped out of my pannier. The desk clerk looked at the cricket and then looked at me strangely but still rented me a room. Later, in that room, a second cricket popped out as well.

While the coast of Peru had been arid, it became even drier by the time I reached Chimbote, where the annual precipitation is 12mm or less than half an inch. One travel website warned, "May is the wettest month. This month should be avoided if you don't like much rain." Clearly this was a relative statement – since average May rainfall is only 3.7mm. or $1/7^{th}$ of an inch for the entire month. This is arid enough that the countryside is completely without plants, and there is not a spec of green to be seen.

It took four days of cycling through these arid regions to reach Lima. The cycling wasn't particularly difficult, and the road was good, with gradually increasing traffic. One of those days I stopped to take a photo of an interesting sign when I noticed a small bus ahead. It looked interesting and almost cycling-related.

I spotted a Tour D'Afrique (TDA) label – the group I would join five months later in Puerto Montt, Chile. The staff was driving the bus from Brazil to Colombia to start the trip another three weeks later. They had coincidentally stopped along the highway not far from where I also stopped to get my photo. I waved hello and received a return greeting from Yanez. Yanez was cook on the TDA Africa ride in 2013 and was now also a cook and bus driver for this trip. We caught up briefly before going our respective ways.

The city of Lima has 9 million inhabitants and would be the largest city I would cross on my trip. I carefully planned my entry, as other cyclists described it as a chaos to ride. While sections of the city were busy, and I spent nearly 10 kilometers in stop-and-go traffic, it turned out that Lima was not the most difficult city riding of my trip. If I were to rate my "top 5" chaos cities for cycling from my trip, it would be as follows:

1. Tegucigalpa, narrow grades and fading brakes

2. Panama City, high speed traffic and trucks parked on the shoulders

3. Guatemala City, general chaos and peek-a-boo shoulders

4. Guadalajara, sprawling and constant need to keep adjusting to traffic

5. Lima, big and spreading

So it wasn't an easy or necessarily pleasant ride, but I had also been through worse.

It all started pretty calmly as I followed the main highway. Prior to Lima there was a split in the road, with the main highway going up and over the hills and a marked truck bypass along some steeper hills on the coast. The bypass route or Serpentine Highway was two lanes and had no shoulders and many trucks, but the speeds were necessarily lower, and it would avoid at least 400 meters of unnecessary climbing over some hills. There were large signs on the Serpentine Highway saying, "No Ciclistas" as well as no motorcycles. I ignored the signs and even passed a police car, but the police didn't seem to mind my heavy touring bicycle on the road.

After the Serpentine Highway I was back to the main road, which had now picked up a third lane each way and was turning into a toll road. At first it had shoulders, but eventually the road kept getting busier and adding another lane. While I wasn't yet near the center of Lima, I decided to get off this highway not long after I passed a toll booth.

My timing wasn't perfect, as there was a narrow canal that directed all the roads off to the right and away from where I wanted to go. These were poorer neighborhoods, with many run down buildings and not on the normal tourist circuit. A few kilometers later I was able to cross this canal and take surface roads heading more towards the center of town.

For another ten kilometers the roads weren't too busy, but then I reached a very congested area. It was midday and not yet rush hour. My road didn't have as much traffic, but there were multiple crossroads, and the larger of these had lights that backed up traffic for multiple light cycles. It took me an hour to travel only six kilometers or about the same pace as I could have walked.

Once I came through the largest area of congestion, I reached the older city center, where the roads and traffic were improved. I was able to cross the main parts of town to reach Miraflores. There was a large contrast between Miraflores and the much poorer neighborhoods I had passed through earlier. I had picked my location partially based on other tourist journals and also partially because there were multiple Western type bike shops. I found a nice hotel and checked in for what would be three nights and two rest days.

At Lima I had traveled 1/3 of my expected distance across South America and decided this was a good location to get my bike serviced and replace worn parts. I scoped out the nearest bike shop, and it seemed reasonable, so I came back with my bike. I asked them to replace the chain and cassette and also put in new brake pads. While the relatively flatter coast of Peru meant I was wearing through my pads more slowly than in Central America or Colombia or Ecuador, it was still good to leave with fresh pads.

In hindsight my choice of bike shop wasn't ideal. Peru seemed to be another country where not every bike shop has a big service department but instead focuses more on sales of bikes and parts. As a result, the mechanic I had was not the most experienced and seemed to struggle a lot getting the pads into and out of the brakes as well as adjusting them. However, the bike seemed fine on a short test ride, so I was ready to go again.

I took my second rest day as a tourist, including a bus tour on the "Mirabus" ride around town.

Leaving Lima was almost as hectic as entering, though for different reasons. At one point I found myself on a major high speed highway needing to cross several lanes of traffic. I waited for what seemed like a long time before making a suitable opening and then dashing across. After that somewhat harried highway ride, I was back on city streets for a while before taking the toll road south out of town.

The following days south from Lima went through areas that were sometimes agricultural, sometimes desert and sometimes fancy little beach resorts. However, unlike the area north of Lima, the main highway didn't go through these resorts, so they seemed more like small gated communities off the main highway. The traffic also gradually became less.

Over the next six days, I once again I stayed in a mix of small towns and occasional highway-side hotels before coming to the small town of Nazca. Nazca is famous for the Nazca Lines, huge constructions in the desert south of town. They are perhaps best seen from an airplane low overhead, but I tried to see what I could from the view tower and cycling along the road. I was tempted to take a small flight, and others would later tell me what I missed.

Nazca marked another major fork in the road. My original plan had been to climb the mountains here to Cusco. Cusco is an interesting town, typically a jumping off point to see Machu Pichu. However, after reviewing the elevation profiles, I decided I would continue following the coast for another 400 kilometers to Arequipa. From here I would then climb up to the Altiplano but on a route with much less up and down along the way.

It was along this stretch of coast that I first started meeting the pilgrims. They were walking along the highway against traffic. Typically, they would come two or three at a time. Some had small strollers to carry belongings and also images or dolls of their deity. A few carried along a heavy wooden cross that was rested on one shoulder with a small wheel behind for the tail. I kept meeting them for most of a week. I would greet them, and, for the most part, they were friendly.

After Nazca the highway became quieter and the towns fewer. In January 2018 this area would be hit with a strong 7.1 earthquake. Earlier in my trip, I had come past another area in Pueble, Mexico, that would also be hit with a 7.1 earthquake in September 2017. As a measure of how much less populated the area was, the Peru earthquake killed 1 person and the Mexico earthquake killed 370, despite being the same magnitude.

The last few days along the coast had some of the strongest headwinds I had encountered so far. At times I found myself pushing hard in my lowest gears on level ground and barely riding at 8 km/hour. I watched my time carefully to make sure I would be able to reach the next town before dark, as towns were also spread farther apart.

From the town of Camana the road veered away from the coast, and two days riding brought me to Arequipa. Arequipa is Peru's second largest city and was one of the more pleasant places I visited. I spent two rest days there. It was time to bring my bike back to the shop. One of my front brake pads had fallen out along the road. I wasn't sure exactly when or where it happened, but I noticed it when trying to brake and finding it much more difficult. My best guess is this still related back to the poor service job in Lima, as I had also needed to readjust my brakes several times after that. Fortunately, the bike shop in Arequipa did a better job.

Arequipa is at elevation 2300 meters (7600 feet). In the days following I would now ride up to the Altiplano to climb over 4500 meters (14,800 feet). This would take me five days of cycling – in part because of distance and in part because I wanted to be careful to avoid climbing too fast without giving my body time to adjust to the altitude.

In addition to being at a higher altitude, the Altiplano also has a large swing in temperatures, with nights well below freezing-- minus 10C (14F)-- and days closer to 15C (59F). When I originally planned my trip, I had prepared myself for temperatures down to minus 6C (20F) and my sleeping bag was only rated a few degrees colder. On the way to Arequipa, I met a pair of German cyclists and asked them how cold it had been on their riding through Bolivia, and they told me the coldest was close to minus 15C (5F). Fortunately, as part of this conversation, they also offered me a lightweight extra sleeping bag they no longer needed. I offered to pay them for it, but they wouldn't take anything.

I took my two rest days in Arequipa to prepare for the trip and otherwise rest at the lower altitude. It would be another five days before I was in internet contact again, the longest gap I had had since northern Canada.

On my way cycling out of Arequipa, I was doored. It was busy on the road leading out of town, and I was riding along the right shoulder. At one point I saw a lone car parked on the right and moved left to pass it. I didn't move quite far enough, however, as just when I came to the car, the door swung open. I was far enough out that the door missed me, but I hit it with my right front pannier. Before I knew it, my bike was knocked over on the road and I was mostly upright beside it. I had jumped just as the bike went down.

Now it was time to assess the damage. I was without so much as a scratch, but the pannier had burst open. My bike bell had broken, and my front brake pad had fallen out, but otherwise the bike looked ok. The car driver was apologetic, but I still had a problem in that the pannier was ripped in a way that would no longer hold the contents. Overall, the collision happened relatively slowly since the road was uphill and I was climbing.

There was not much else to do but to walk the few kilometers back to the bike shop and see if I could get the brake fixed and do something about the pannier. The bike shop was able to fix the brake. The shop didn't sell any panniers, but they told me about a luggage repair shop nearby that might be able to do the repair. I found the repair shop, and two hours and <$10 later I was on my way again. I made a short ride up to the village of Yura, where there was a hotel.

From Yura I spent a day cycling up the hills to reach 4000 meters (13,200 feet). This would bring me through most of the elevation gain on a slow steady climb that rarely exceeded 7% grade. I was slightly concerned that I might be gaining elevation too fast, but there weren't other good alternatives. As it turned out, the alternatives at my destination weren't ideal either. The road went past a toll booth and nearby were half a dozen shops and a local police station. I asked at the police station if I might stay inside, but they didn't have any room.

A little past the toll booth were several houses, including one with barbed wire in front by the road. The house looked abandoned, and there was good flat concrete in front and some shelter from a cold biting wind. I asked the neighbors in the adjoining house, and they told me while it wasn't their house, they were fine about my I staying there. There was road noise from the nearby tollbooth, and I was clearly out in the open but otherwise happy with my camp location.

Shortly before sunset I walked past the shops and got something to eat. After sunset the temperatures quickly plummeted, and it seemed the shops also closed up as everyone went inside to get out of the cold. The temperatures that night would get down to at least minus 6C, and I was happy I had the second sleeping bag, as my water bottles froze.

At 2 a.m. suddenly bright lights were shining on the tent, and car horns were honking. I was awakened and not quite sure what to do, so I came out of the tent. It turned out the little house wasn't abandoned, and the residents had come home at 2 a.m. to find someone with a tent camping right in front. Once they figured out I meant no harm, I got back in the tent and napped through rest of the night.

The following day the road climbed even further. There were some rolling hills and then mostly flat high plains. I saw multiple llamas and vicunas and similar animals along the way. They were curious and not particularly fearful, so I could get some good photos. I came to a small village of Imata, where I again expected to camp, though this time being more careful about abandoned buildings.

As it turned out, in Imata there was a small hotel. Yeah! While it was still early, I stopped here as it would let me stay overnight. I am fairly certain this evening was even colder, as water in barrels outside had a thick layer of ice in the morning. The cold early morning temperatures also meant that I waited until at least an hour after sunrise to get on the road. Not much later the temperature would go above freezing, and by the middle of the afternoon, temperatures were reasonable.

Imata was at 4450 meters (14,600 feet), and I noticed I had a slight headache that evening. The following day I cycled over the highest elevation for the trip, 4528 meters (14,856 feet). At these higher elevations I would find myself out of breath more easily on a 7% grade, but, otherwise, didn't notice many effects. Also, other than that evening in Imata, I also didn't notice anything in the evenings, s so, overall, my climbing to altitude was quick but not overly so.

Two days from Imata I reached Puno. Puno is another very touristy town on the shores of Lake Titicaca. I took a rest day there to go out to see the floating islands on the lake, which was well worth the trip. I also prepared my documents for entry into Bolivia. It felt strange again to be visiting a town with as many Western tourists. However, it also seemed nice after many days in some of these small villages.

From Puno it would be two cycling days, mostly along the lake, to reach the border of Bolivia. In a month and a half, I had cycled myself across Peru. It felt like a large transition overall from the more tropical areas of the Ecuador coast to the high Altiplano areas and Lake Titicaca on the border with Bolivia. I had enjoyed the riding, and, overall, Peru had exceeded the admittedly lowered expectations I had had before my arrival.

Bolivia

Bolivia is the one country that required a more formal visa, at least for those with a U.S. passport. Looking on the web, I found a list of 10 requirements as well as some accounts of how other cyclists had met them. Some of them, such as passport photos or a yellow fever vaccination certificate, weren't difficult, as I had the photos made in Puno and was already carrying my yellow fever card.

Three of them were slightly more difficult: a proof of departure, proof of accommodation and a typed day-to-day itinerary. As a cycle tourist I knew I was going to exit the country via Argentina but didn't exactly have day-to-day plans of where I might travel or stay. Nights camping in the tent didn't really provide paperwork. On the internet I found some cyclists had resorted to booking fake or temporary flights or travels, but that didn't quite seem right.

In the end, what I decided to do was make an online booking for my first night in Copacabana. I plotted out a list of places to stay and created a rough itinerary with dates and distances. As it turned out, during my actual trip I stayed in most of those places, with the only difference that I went quicker than the itinerary. This was because I had inserted multiple extra rest days to bring the total time close to a 30-day visa limit, because I figured it would be easier to spend less time in the country than to need additional time.

I still wasn't quite sure what to do with my proof of departure, so I ended up printing a page or two from my web side indicating my intention of cycling to Ushuaia and using my loaded bicycle and visa stamps, showing I had already traveled from Canada as evidence that I was really on my way through Bolivia.

I had all my documents, photo, application, visa fees and everything neatly arranged when I came up to the border station. After all this preparation crossing the border was remarkably easy. The immigration officers looked through my documents, sized up my bike and quickly attached a 10 year visa to the passport with the necessary stamps. I got the sense that what really sealed the deal was having a yellow fever card, not so much because it was a big risk at a high elevation, but because it demonstrated I had read and carefully followed the rules.

Just 10 kilometers past the border was the touristy town of Copacabana. The town was filled with cafes, hostels and shops for both souvenirs and outdoor supplies. However, what really gave it away were multiple places that advertised laundry by the kilogram.

From Copacabana it was two easier days cycling to the capital of La Paz. The first day cycling was extremely scenic, as I cycled up along hills overlooking Lake Titicaca. The lake had a large area to the north and a smaller area to the south, and I cycled along a narrow strip of land with the lake on both sides. At noon I came to end of this isthmus, where a sequence of small ferries crossed the water to the other side.

After crossing I followed the lake some more. At one point I must have missed a detour sign because I suddenly came to section of the road filled with people having an outdoor street celebration. There were bands, colorful costumes and many friendly people drinking beer. My bike and cycling gear were an immediate curiosity, and I received multiple offers of beer as well as curious questions as I walked through the crowds.

On my second full day in Bolivia, I cycled to the metro area of La Paz. The road started as a two lane highway, but as I neared the city, it became a full four lane divided highway. The wide open spaces and good roads reminded me a bit of crossing Wyoming on the interstate highway. Near La Paz a cable car system with gondolas stretched over the road. Apparently, this system is used as transportation to bring people from the plateau area of El Alto down into the steep canyon of La Paz city itself.

I decided I didn't need to ride my bicycle all the way down the steep and busy roads into the middle of the city but instead I could stay at a hotel in El Alto. I ended up taking a rest day there and mostly walking around the local area. I was right in the busy part of town, with multiple market streets in each direction. Many were specialized, with one selling only eggs, one fruits and vegetables, one bread and one meat.

Leaving El Alto I had two further cycling days to the mining town of Ororu. Almost all was on the shoulder of my interstate -level highway that still reminded me of Wyoming. The riding was mostly above 3700 meters (12,200 feet), but it was otherwise relatively flat and not particularly difficult. Ororu was another easy city to visit, and I spent a further rest day there before continuing on towards Uyuni and the salt flats. The Salar de Uyuni is the world's largest salt flat, and I had much anticipated visiting.

The salt flats are near a touristy town of Uyuni, another three days cycling from Ororu. I was now on a two lane road, at least half of which had been newly paved in the last few years. There were a few small towns, but I wasn't completely certain if I would find a hotel or camp outside. On the second day I came to the small town of Rio Mulato and was pleased to see a sign "Alojamiento." The price was 20Bs or approximately $3 U.S., and this was my least expensive night so far in Bolivia. It was a family run affair, and they also had a small store. One had to carefully watch the hours for these stores, since they would unpredictably close at different times in the day. There typically wasn't a big variety of things to buy, but I had learned to live from crackers, fruit where I could find it, and other basic staples.

The following day I cycled to Uyuni and came past the Salar de Uyuni for the last 20 kilometers. There was a turnoff at the small village of Colchani, where I turned right and cycled out to the salt flats themselves. There were a few fancy salt hotels there that looked much out of my price range. Some previous cyclists had written in their journal about being offered an exceptionally low rate, however, so I inquired at one hotel, only to realize it was still much out of my price range. On the salt flats I could see SUVs bringing tourists out to ride onto the salt flats.

I turned back and cycled on to Uyuni, where I found a hotel and decided to find one of these tours to take me onto the Salar. The following morning was on tour. We first stopped at an old train graveyard outside of town. Old rusted steam locomotives and train cars were parked along abandoned tracks.

After this we turned back and drove for extended time while on the salt. Off in the distant horizon, a small building appeared. There were monuments, including one with flapping flags here. There was also a small salt hotel and place where the tours stopped for people to eat lunch. We were inside by salt slab tables as we ate the lunch we had brought.

After lunch we continued farther on the salt to reach a small island of Incahuasi. The island was covered in tall cacti, each several meters high. I followed a trail up the island to the summit and then looked out across the salt. It was bright white and reminded me a bit of snow. It was now dry season, but in the summer this would be a very shallow salt lake. As the salt dried up, long intricate crystals of salt would grow in panes across the salt. It was fun to walk out on stretches of mostly undisturbed crystals and look at the intricate designs.

After visiting the island we drove back to an area that was still drying out. A small layer of water covered the salt base below. Overall, it was a great fun day trip. I had originally considered whether to ride my bike across large parts of the salt flats. I decided against it to avoid having the bike get fouled up and found that spending a day trip from Uyuni also worked for me.

From Uyuni the main highway was still under construction. Over the next 200 kilometers to Tupiza, approximately 40% was paved and the remaining 60% was dirt and gravel roads. I was hit by four flat tires in this stretch again. They seemed to mostly come from fine wires from disintegrated truck tires. This area also had some of my coldest nights yet. One of them I spent on a high overlook. There was a brief turnout filled with gravel piles used by the construction crews, and I camped on the far side of this gravel, on the edge of a large hill with a view to the valley below. It was a great place to camp even if I awoke to one more flat tire to fix.

At the bottom of this valley, I came to one of the rougher sections of road construction yet. The newly constructed route would go along the edges of the valley. While it was under construction, a temporary road had been bulldozed in the river bottom. The river wasn't very large, but the road crossed it several times, and I ended up getting wet feet walking my bike across. In sections that weren't in a river, the road often developed large corrugations that were bumpy to cycle across. After what seemed like an eternity bumping along and my fourth flat tire, I came to the small town of Tupiza. This area was known as being a hideout for the bandits Bonny and Clyde as well as a nice hiking area.

Tupiza was only one day cycling from the Argentinian border, and I had nearly crossed Bolivia. All my Bolivian cycling was at high altitude, but it wasn't as much up and down as in Ecuador or Colombia before. Areas I traveled through seemed to have some very touristy towns like Copacabana or Uyuni, separated from the smallest towns, where basic services were more difficult to find. While it was winter, this seemed to be high season, and I came across many other tourists.

I had specifically routed my trip away from the coast of Chile in order to cross via Bolivia, and I was happy to have visited. It was a slight hassle to apply for a visa, but now I had it for 10 years and could easily see coming back to explore more of the country.

Argentina and Chile until Puerto Montt

Bienvenidos a La Quiaca, Ushuaia, 5121 km. Hooray! I was pleased to cross the border into Argentina and see my first sign for Ushuaia. Only 5000 kilometers away it felt so close and yet so far still to go. It was August 5th, and I had another 3 ½ months until I would meet the TDA group in Puerto Montt. With the distance left I would only need to cycle half of the time, so I also started considering some places to explore with my extra time.

Things often change at national borders, and the transition from Bolivia was one of the biggest changes yet. Even the electrical plugs were different. However, what took the most getting used to were the long afternoon siesta hours.

Prior to this, my typical routine had been to eat some breakfast in my hotel room before departing and get on the road early. By early afternoon I would reach my destination, and I would go (a) find a hotel (b) get a shower (c) get something to eat and (d) update my blog, typically in this order. I would also then buy food for the next morning.

In Argentina, particularly in the north, most of the shops would close for a long siesta during the hours of 1 p.m. to 5 p.m., and many restaurants wouldn't open until 7 p.m. or 8 p.m. for dinner. If I arrived in a town at my customary time of 2 p.m.-3 p.m., nothing would be open, and in smaller towns it would be difficult to find anything to eat before evening. In the border town of La Quiaca, I tried five restaurants before realizing they were all closed and I needed to return at 8 p.m. About 9 p.m. was my customary bedtime, so I barely had time to eat before going to sleep.

Over time, I figured out enough places to get things to eat and was pleased that at least ice cream shops were often open during the siesta. Also, as I continued farther south, the siesta seemed to be less pervasive, with at least an occasional shop or store that was open.

On my second full day cycling through Argentina, I passed a summit marked as 3780 meters (12,400 feet). I was still on the high Altiplano, but this summit marked the start of a long descent in the following days to Salta at 1150 meters (3800 feet). This brought an end, at least until southern Argentina/Chile, to freezing overnight temperatures, as I would not climb as high during the rest of the trip. I passed signs of "hielo" and also a frozen icefall on my journey downhill.

Some of those days descending were easy cycling, but not all, as at times I encountered stronger headwinds that meant I needed to pedal into the wind, even during a sharp descent.

Towns I passed through, such as Humahuaca and Tilcara, were surrounded by colorful banded layers of sandstone, sometimes tilted on edge. This area is popular with hikers, and winter is the prime season, as the summers are sometimes much warmer. I saw considerably more tourists. In addition to being more touristy, I could also see this was a wealthier country when contrasting these small towns with Bolivian towns I had passed through just weeks before.

On my way to Tilcara, I passed the Tropico de Capricornio, an obligatory photo stop. This spot marked the maximum extent of the sun being directly overhead. As it turned out, with my timing and southerly direction, in North America the sun was almost always on my face at midday. Starting approximately 45 degrees above the horizon at Prudhoe Bay on the summer solstice, it was still in my face as I pedaled south into fall, winter and then spring. In South America the sun was almost always behind at midday as I continued south and pedaled through fall, winter, spring and eventually summer. I wasn't wearing as much sunscreen as before, but even after a year on the road, if I didn't put some on my nose, it would burn through the course of a long day in the sun.

The Argentinian roads I traveled were mostly two lane without shoulders. The roads were typically good, but traffic also sped by quickly. I missed having a rear-view mirror, which had disappeared in El Alto, Bolivia. As I approached the larger town of San Salvador de Jujay, I came to a four lane divided highway. With 300,000 inhabitants, this was one of the larger towns I had passed in a while. The downtown square had palm trees and orange trees with fruit. After many kilometers of riding past desert cactus, I was back in more tropical regions – despite having pedaled out of the tropics the day before.

The day cycling from San Salvador de Jujay was one of my most scenic rides yet. While the main four lane highway went around a large hill, there was a small road that went over the hills. Trucks were prohibited, and parts of the road were marked as having a width of 4 meters (13 feet), requiring traffic in opposite directions to briefly pause and take turns. When the road was marked for bi-directional traffic, even small cars sometimes had difficulties fitting into the lanes. The road wound back and forth through a canopy of trees as it climbed up to the pass over the hill. I also passed several lakes. Eventually, on the other side, the countryside opened up again, and it became wider as I cycled into the large city of Salta.

I took a rest day in Salta. While my bicycle was still riding well, I went to look for bicycle parts. On the top of my list was finding a new rear-view mirror that might clip on my glasses. I was also looking for spare tires, as multiple punctures made me cautious about how long it would be before I needed to swap in my one remaining spare tire. I stopped past four shops, and while all of them seemed to know about cycling mirrors, none of them had them. There were plenty of bicycle tires, but none of the more durable, tougher Schwalbe brand I was using. Less durable tires would do in a pinch but also wear out much more quickly with the weight of myself and my load. They would also be more susceptible to punctures in arid regions coming up that had many sharp, spiny plants. In Salta, as I found further north, there seemed to be a separation between shops that sold bicycles and shops that serviced them.

From Salta to Cafayate was two days cycling. The second of these days was stunningly beautiful as I came through sandstone canyon country.

The region was arid, resulting in far fewer plants to hide the brightly colored rocks. It was in this stretch that I would meet and periodically join several other cyclists as we leapfrogged each other all the way to Mendoza.

Alex was a German cyclist whom I had first met in the Baja Peninsula. He had also traveled from Alaska and was on his way to the tip of Argentina. While he rode faster than I did, we ended up staying in the same places half a dozen times as we would leapfrog each other but visit some of the same towns. Laura and Herbie were British and Irish respectively and were on their way from Seattle to the tip of Argentina. We also leapfrogged each other multiple times on our way to Mendoza.

It was fun stopping and visiting with these other riders with similar goals. Everyone does a trip like this slightly differently with different gear, a different mix of camping and hotels, different preferred areas to ride and places to visit. On my entire journey whenever I saw other touring cyclists coming the other way, we would stop and compare notes and have a brief conversation. I also ended up asking for and getting photos and ended up with photos of more than 100 other touring cyclists, many on similar trips. However, it was particularly special to spend a little more extended time traveling the same direction and stopping in same places with Alex, Laura and Herbie.

Cafayate is one of Argentina's premier wine regions, and I passed many vineyards in the countryside. This was where I first started on Ruta 40. Ruta 40 is one of the longest highways in the world and passes along the western, more arid regions of Argentina, crossing all the way from Bolivia in the north to Chile in the south. The route was mostly paved, but at times there would be longer gaps between towns and services. As a result, I had multiple occasions where I would need to pack enough food and water for two days cycling. I would camp along the way, either in roadside campgrounds or spots beside the road.

A day after I left Cafayate, I came to one of these longer gaps between towns. The distance of 118 kilometers wasn't huge, but the road had a reasonable amount of climbing and other cycling journals gave accounts of strong headwinds. To add insult to injury, I wasn't feeling 100%. As I cycled out that morning, I came to some shorter stretches of gravel road and wasn't certain how long or how rough they might be. While I could probably make it all the way to the next town, it started to feel more likely that I would end up at an abandoned house in the middle of a wide windy plain. I had learned about this house from other cycling journals.

I came into the last roadside village before a long treeless gap and started to look around for an excuse to camp. I was pleasantly surprised to see a sign to the right on a small shop that said "Camping" and had a bicycle on it. This was a sign for fresh bread, and it also had a sign for pizza.

Pizza, camping and bakery! The lure was too great, and I went to investigate. While not a formal campground, the owners allowed cyclists to camp for free right beside their shop. I had gone only 35 kilometers, and it was only 11 a.m., but I decided to stop for the day. It was well worth it, as I had some fresh baked pie, some pizza and otherwise relaxed in my tent to listen to winds pick up in the afternoon.

Later in the afternoon Alex came past and ended up also camping at the bakery. He had told me about this place earlier and had traveled farther with the intention of camping here. His bike had broken a spoke on the rear wheel. He had spare spokes with him but not the tools needed to remove his disc brakes to get at the hub. We ended up using a fiber spoke I had brought along.

The following day I cycled from the bakery to the next town of Hualfin, beyond the gap. On the way my rear tire developed a cut in the sidewall, and I swapped in my last spare tire. It now became a little more urgent to have a replacement spare, as I still had my older tire that had given me troubles in Peru but not a fresh new spare. I started to think of either finding a tire in Mendoza or even using it as an excuse to visit back to the U.S., either from Puerto Montt or Mendoza.

This region had many roadside shrines. Unlike countries farther north, with shrines commemorating road accident victims, many of these shrines had common patterns of either being painted in all red or having large numbers of plastic bottles of water in front.

As I investigated on the web, I learned the red shrines were for Gauchito Gill, a legendary Argentinian folk hero. The complete story can be found online, but apparently Gauchito Gill is a sort of Robin Hood figure, who, while an outlaw, also helped protect the needy, the poor and those less fortunate. Gauchito Gill is also a target of prayers and requests for assistance, and many of these shrines were to thank Guachito Gill for prayers answered. In one day of cycling I passed more than 10 of these shrines.

The shrines with large numbers of water bottles were to another folk hero, Difunta Correa.

Another roadside sight that became increasingly common were signs saying "Las Malvinas Son Argentinas." Las Malvinas is the Argentinian name for the Falkland Islands, and the signs are a reminder that Argentina still claims these islands, despite an unsuccessful attempt at occupying them in the early 1980's, which led to the Falkland Islands War. These signs were frequently on entrances or exits to the towns through which I cycled.

I was happy to find a municipal campground in the village of San Blas los Sauces after a long day riding. Some locals came by selling still warm, freshly baked bread, and I settled in for an early night in my tent. I was awakened by a large volume of music. It was Saturday night and, unfortunately, some other locals were using the park to host their party. I was more than 200 meters away, but the music was still extremely noisy. I got up out of the tent, walked over and asked if they might turn down the sound. It went down briefly, but then came back up five minutes later. Other than a few nights of noise, my other experiences camping in Argentina went better, and the country seems to have an abundance of municipal campgrounds.

After a noisy night of camping, I had a second long day of cycling to the town of Chilecito. It was another arid, barren region, and I was surprised to see someone next to the road packing what seemed to be a bright red tent. He didn't have a vehicle, bicycle or other means of transport. As I cycled a bit farther, I came upon a group and realized they had been parachuting, and it wasn't a tent being packed, but a parachute. We stopped and had a good conversation, and I took a few photos of the Agentinian skydiving group.

Chilecito was where I spent another rest day. It turned out that Alex, Laura and Herbie all came through, and it was fun to visit and catch up again. This was a small town right next to the snowcapped Andes, with great views. As I compared notes with other cyclists, I also made further plans. While it was still another 650 kilometers away, I booked flights from Mendoza back to the U.S.A. This would give me a brief nine-day intermission from my bike trip and also allow me to pick up some needed supplies, such as Schwalbe tires and a replacement for my missing rear-view mirror.

The second day after Chilecito I got caught in a large dust storm. The day had started clear, with wide sweeping views. It was early, and just as Alex came cycling past, the wind started to pick up. It picked up and picked up further. Soon it was gusting as strong winds as I had had thus far in the trip. The temperature also dropped by at least 5C (9F). While the route started downhill, I struggled to cycle more than 10 kilometers per hour (6 miles per hour) and stopped frequently to take a brief rest. The clear, wide skies were replaced with a haze from all the sand dust flying in the area.

Fortunately, the next town of Guandacol wasn't far ahead. This town was another good excuse for a shorter day. As it turned out, all four of us cyclists ended up in the same town again that evening.

The following morning the skies were clear blue, as if nothing had happened. Reading other journals, I've gotten the sense that it is common in this area to have such strong gusty winds, and it turned out that a front was just passing through. Another two days cycling brought me to a larger town of San Juan, from which it was only two days riding to Mendoza.

I arrived in Mendoza on August 28th and wouldn't depart until September 17th. In between I made my trip back to Colorado for a short family visit and to replenish supplies. I didn't fly my bike and all my gear both directions, but instead found a hotel that was willing to store my bicycle and belongings in return for an extended stay. I also brought my bicycle in for service and spent some relaxing days wandering through town.

Mendoza is a nice, relaxed city. The downtown area where I stayed has a huge square surrounded by four smaller squares a few blocks away. There are multiple streets with shops of various types as well as restaurants. Unlike Salta or many smaller towns farther north, the town didn't come to a standstill for an afternoon siesta. It was a nice place to spend some time reading, writing and visiting rather than moving each night to a new place.

From Mendoza to the next intermediate point of Bariloche was another 1500 kilometers along Ruta 40. While elevations along the way didn't exceed 2000 meters, it was gradually becoming colder as I went south, and it was still early spring. This was an arid region without larger trees and occasionally stronger winds. There were small towns along the route but also gaps as big as 250 kilometers between services.

I was fortunate to still have over two months before I would meet TDA in Puerto Montt, Chile. I briefly considered cycling all the way south to southern Patagonia but then decided instead to spend a few weeks at a Spanish language school in Bariloche.

The ride from Mendoza started along flat agricultural plains with snowcapped peaks of the Andes to my right. It reminded me of Colorado, although there was less corn and wheat and more grapes and olives. At the end of this agricultural region was a small town of Tunuyan, where I stayed for the night. It was nice to be back on the road.

From Tunuyan I started a pattern I would repeat multiple times,.one day of cycling mostly through scrubby arid regions and then camping along the road, followed by a second day of cycling into the next town. This first night and several others were in a roadside pullout, where I had company from truck drivers who also parked there overnight. This brought me first to San Rafael and then to Malargue. Malargue was a ski town with ski resort of Las Lenas a little ways north in the mountains. It was still the end of the ski season, and shops were open to rent equipment. The town had a good selection of inexpensive hotels and restaurants and was a nice spot to spend a rest day before cycling across wide open spaces farther south. It would be another four days cycling before I next had a hotel fancy enough to have a wifi connection. One of those nights I camped in a gravel pit, and the other two nights were in very basic village lodgings.

This section also included slightly over 100 kilometers of gravel road. Approximately half of the gravel was somewhat smooth and graded and not much more difficult than cycling on pavement, although my speeds were a bit lower. The rest of this gravel included some rough sections that either had ugly washboard bumps or had a lot of soft, loose gravel. At times the route had both rough washboard and soft gravel. My average speeds slowed considerably. Cars would come by raising clouds of dust, but fortunately these were also less frequent than before.

Near the end of this stretch, I crossed into Neuquen Province. This also marked the boundary of the Patagonia region. Once again it felt both close and far, as I had now reached the last region of my journey but also still had many kilometers to go. I was happy to reach the small town of Buta Ranquil. This small town had a central square and even a bank with an ATM. Unfortunately, here as in many of these small towns, the only ATM gave a cryptic message and didn't dispense cash. I liked to do most of my daily spending using cash, but there were several reasons Argentina made this more difficult. There was always a fee of slightly over 100 pesos (~$6) charged, and the maximum withdrawal limit was 2000 pesos (~$120). Furthermore, perhaps half of the ATMs wouldn't work to withdraw funds. I think the withdrawal failures were likely because they weren't always filled up, but the error messages were generic. As a result I tended to carry more cash than normal and try ATMs in many of the towns through which I passed.

From Neuquen it was one day of cycling to Chos Malal, and then two days farther to Zapala. In between I found another great little campsite. It was not far from the highway but hidden behind a large hill. It overlooked a valley but was also sheltered from the wind. In this part of Argentina, I was frequently getting on the road not long after sunrise in order to beat some of the winds that tended to pick up in the afternoon.

I came to the town of Zapala through one of these headwinds and was ready for a rest day. As I looked further at the weather forecasts, they looked more daunting, with high wind warnings and a forecast of winds of 80-100 kilometers per hour (50-60 miles per hour). After Zapala was a gap of more than 200 kilometers. With such strong headwinds it would be three tough days of cycling a distance n I might otherwise be able to cross in two days. I decided to wait out the worst of the wind and ended up spending six days in Zapala.

As I cycled on from Zapala, I was happy to have waited out the wind, as the region was very open. Towards the end of this first day, I climbed over a low hill and descended to a road junction. There was an abandoned store at the intersection, and I decided to camp beside a low rock wall. Several police officers were nearby, and one came over to check out my passport and documentation. All was well, and he let me know he would be 20 kilometers down a gravel road if I needed assistance.

Checks along the route were more common in Argentina than in any other country. At perhaps half of these, they would ask to see a passport, and at the other half I would be given a quick verbal check to see where I was going. The police were always friendly, though I wondered what purpose these checks were serving.

Junin de los Andes was a town on other side of the gap from Zapala. This was the start of the lakes region and a dramatic contrast to the earlier windswept plains. In addition to clear blue lakes, this area also had more trees. The towns had a resort feel to them, though high summer season wouldn't start for another few months and the winter ski season was just drawing to a close. I got the sense this was also an area to which Argentinians from more populated parts of the country came to vacation.

The next of these towns was San Martin de Los Andes. The Chapala ski area was nearby. In addition to skis, the town also rented mountain bikes, and I got the sense one could almost do both. One could ski in the snow of the mountains above and go mountain biking where it was already spring below. On my touring bike I went over some of the low passes in weather that was just on the edge of snowing. One evening the private campgrounds weren't yet open, and I ended up being the only one camping in a rainy public campground. It was great scenic ride, and I had only three days left to reach Bariloche.

Bariloche was home of La Montana language school. The school offered lessons by the week, and I had signed up for three weeks. On my first day they did a quick assessment and put me in a group with one other student. Our classes were held for four hours during weekdays. Twice a week we had some type of afternoon excursion, and the rest of the time, I explored around town or relaxed. Each week new students might arrive, and others would finish. As a result my classes also varied but were small, with a lot of individual attention.

I had picked a "homestay" option and was placed with Marelia, Jose and their two daughters. Their house had a large attic area fixed up for guests, and it was a very nice place to stay. Each morning I'd get up and catch breakfast before everyone left, and in the evenings we might have dinner together. Overall, they were very patient as I struggled to practice my Spanish with them. I enjoyed it more than if I had spent time in a hotel.

During this time I also brought my bicycle to a bike shop for a good service. When I went to pick it up, I got a rather big surprise. The shop owner showed me a crack along the right chainstay. Aluminum frames are tricky to weld, but I asked if he could he fix it. He thought so, and so I gave the go-ahead. I also thought a bit further about my options. I still had a spare mountain bike in storage in Austin, Texas, and just enough time to fly from Puerto Montt to the U.S. to retrieve it. In the end I decided to keep this option open, but otherwise (a) to stress the bike with local rides around Bariloche and (b) to ride with all my gear to Puerto Montt to arrive early and hitch a ride if necessary. As long as the bike still looked good in Puerto Montt, I wouldn't exchange it for my spare bike. Once I was with TDA, if the bike failed, at least I would be on a supported ride and not as completely stranded in the middle of nowhere.

My time in Bariloche passed quickly, and soon it was already time to cycle on to Chile. I spent one day backtracking to the lakeside town of Villa La Angostura before riding up and over the pass into Chile. On one side of the pass was the Argentinian border post, and 39 kilometers farther was the Chilean border post. In between there was a higher pass with deep snow still along the road.

As I reached the Chilean border, they handed me a slip of paper with places for stamps to mark three steps. First, I came to Immigration, where I got an entry stamp. Next, I went to Customs. At Customs, when I told them I had a bicycle, they stopped to write out a document describing my bicycle. I was given this document to provide if necessary when I left Chile to prove that I wasn't exporting my bike. The third stop was the inspection station.

I had indicated agricultural products on my customs form because their description included cheese. I had already eaten my bananas but had a good portion of bread and cheese for later. I was told I couldn't bring this cheese into Argentina but would be allowed it eat it at the border post. So, I stopped and had a much larger lunch than I otherwise would have had. I then continued on until a campsite near Lago Puyehue.

This area was still the lakes district, but now in Chile. Similar to areas of Argentina, this also seemed to be an area for vacationers. It was also still a few months before peak summer holiday camping, so it wasn't difficult to find lodging. On my way to Puerto Montt, I camped in Puerto Octay as well as Lago Puyehue. In contrast to my Bolivia/Argentina crossing, there were fewer noticeable differences across the border. I was pleased that the ATMs seemed more reliable and had lower fees. I also was happy to find many fewer shops closed for the siesta.

I reached Puerto Montt on November 11th. My frame had held! I still had ten days before the TDA group would arrive, and I didn't need to use this time to fly back and retrieve a bicycle.

Puerto Montt was both an end and a beginning. I had traveled 24,750 kilometers (15,379 miles) carrying all my gear on my bicycle and traveling alone or parts with David or Bert. I had now reached the end of the loaded touring part of my trip and had another 2475 kilometers to go. As a supported ride with a fixed agenda, my focus would narrow more to cycling the route each day while others worried about routes, water, lodging and other logistics. I would also now be one part of a much larger expedition as we cycled to the end of South America. I looked forward to the change.

Chile and Argentina, riding with TDA to Ushuaia

"Here is your envelope. Inside the white envelope are 3300 Chilean pesos for the ferry." All of us riders were handed envelopes as Emily presented the white board with the route to Hornopiren. I'm not sure why, but somehow I found it an amusing introduction to how the next month of cycling would differ from the last 17 months.

The route on this first day had a ferry at the midpoint, and TDA staff had investigated both the cost and timing of the ferry. Each of the riders would cycle at different speeds, and the ferry wouldn't allow fares to be prepaid. Hence, TDA staff provided each rider with exact change and had also arranged to have empanadas at the ferry dock. It was a nice and caring touch.

It also symbolized some of the largest differences since just a few weeks before. On my own tour I would have just cycled to the ferry and waited to sort things out or perhaps read a previous account on a web journal. Now a lot more things were being taken care of for me: carrying my baggage, cooking meals, determining routes and even counting out change for the ferry.

I fell into the TDA rhythm fairly easily. It was still familiar from my TDA ride across Africa four years prior. Despite the differences in continents and total size of the group, many of the practices were similar. I even ended up doing my turn on pot duty that first evening. Many of the patterns were influenced by the timing of meals. In the morning breakfast typically would start at 7 a.m. and not a minute earlier (except for those on the trucks). I'd eat porridge and granola and also prepare some sandwiches and fruit for snacks along the way. In the evening the dinner would be preceded by a rider meeting to review the route for the next day. It was then early to bed and early to rise in a pattern that was repeated until the next rest day.

At times I was asked, "Which do you prefer, self-supported riding or the TDA trip?" My response to them but also partially to myself was "They are just different." I had very much enjoyed my riding before Puerto Montt and also the sense of freedom of going where and when I wanted. However, it was also nice to ride with a group and have more social interactions. The extra support was particularly helpful in places with multiple ferries and longer distances and extreme winds. I had chosen to ride this part with TDA because it would let me see more of the Carretera Austral route when my cautious nature would otherwise have dictated that I stay on the Argentinian side of the Andes Mountains. One of the things I most enjoyed later were visits we made to El Chalten and Torres del Paine Parks. On the other side perhaps one of the most frustrating things for me were days when the total distances were just a bit too long, and I took the bus to get into camp on time.

Our first day to Hornopiren was a scenic ride, first along the coast and then, after our ferry crossing, over a larger hill and through a construction zone with steep sharp hills. Without too much difficulty, I arrived at camp, though I was the last cyclist in that day. Dinner was excellent, a pattern that would continue for the rest of the trip.

Riders were presented a choice for the following day. Most of the day would be spent on two longer ferry rides, but there was a 10 kilometer separation between end of the first ferry and the start of the second. The second ferry departed 30 minutes later, with another passage 30 minutes after that. This left only an hour to cover the 10 kilometer distance, less if one wanted some buffer time for loading and unloading. Approximately half the group, including myself, picked an option to take a van across this gap, while the remaining cyclists decided to ride.

It was interesting to watch the ride/race. The route had some gentle hills, but the biggest factor was huge clouds of dust raised by all the vehicles on the road racing between the ferries. It turned out the departure times weren't as tight as we had anticipated, but I was still happy to have made an easier choice.

Wow! It was on our third day cycling when I really thought to myself, "I'm now on the Carretera Austral." Some of this came from our start on an isolated end of the road location, camped not far from the ferry landing, but, otherwise, from only seeing vehicles a few times a day. However, more significantly, the gravel road started immediately and had a lot of climbing. The route wasn't difficult to ride but had considerable hills, and after two hours I was only 20 kilometers down the road. The weather was overcast, just on the edge of rain, and thick foliage encroached on the road. Later in the afternoon some of the clouds would lift, and we would see snowcapped peaks nearby.

After passing through another construction zone, I was back on pavement as I made my way into small town of Chaiten for lunch. Afternoon cycling was a sharp contrast to that of the morning, with both a smooth paved highway and a light tailwind. This brought us to Lago Yelcho. There was a fancy lodge here, but I opted for the campground, which was also nice.

There was rain on the roof the following morning as we broke camp. I was up by 6 a.m. and had my tent and gear all packed away in time for the 7 a.m. breakfast. By 7:30 a.m. I was on the road and climbing up a hill before a sharp descent into the village of Santa Lucia. Sadly, this village would be wiped out by a flood three weeks later after a rainstorm of more than 11 centimeters (4.5 inches). At least five lost their lives. However, as we passed through, Santa Lucia was still a little town with an old yellow church.

By afternoon the sun had come out, and after another longer section of road construction, we had smooth pavement to our camp. We were camped on a farm, where the owners provided a lamb-on-a-spit dinner and entertained with songs afterwards.

Ice on my rims and a cycle computer that read minus 1 Celsius were the start of our next day riding. After it warmed up, it was both pleasant and scenic cycling, though I was almost numb to the spectacular views. Our route climbed up and over a steep hill for 400 meters within not very many kilometers. As I approached the hill, I thought, "I could climb this hill, but it would be at least as pleasant to get a lift over the other side." At least as much a concern for me as the climbing was a steep descent on gravel. I ended up in the bus for a short stretch for the first time, though what would not be the last time on the trip. Even with the extra lift, there were still 1300 meters of climb that day, and none of our riding on the Carretera Austral those first weeks was less than 1000 meters a day.

The sixth day cycling was posted at 146 kilometers but expected to be entirely on pavement. It was a long and tough day, and I was the last cyclist into camp. If possible, however, it was even more spectacular than the previous days, with snowcapped peaks now augmented with purple lupine flowers along the way. This brought us to Coyhaique, the largest town in this region and site of our first rest day.

Just as riding days have a rhythm to them, rest days on TDA also have some patterns. First on my list was finding a place to do laundry. I had some of my own laundry soap, but it was also convenient to find a place that would really get my clothes clean. Meals are not provided on rest days, and this gave me a good opportunity to sample local restaurants. I also found my way to the large grocery store for some additional snacks for my riding days.

Rest day was also an opportunity to rest, as the following five days to O'Higgins were mostly over gravel road. I would end up taking three half days cycling, as the distances were otherwise just slightly too long for me to finish in a reasonable time.

Our first day wasn't too difficult, as except for the last 12 kilometers, it was entirely on paved roads. We started through wider, more open areas, but by lunch our route climbed up and over a low pass. On the other side was a long descent, with sweeping turns into Cerro Castillo. Cerro Castillo was at the end of the paved route, and our campsite was a little ways farther down the road. At camp that evening were Linda and Mike Stuart, whose blog I had followed on my own riding across Bolivia. It was nice to compare notes.

The following day the route started out tough, with a lot of loose gravel graded onto the road. This was still a construction zone, though other than the gravel, we didn't see signs of ongoing construction. Fortunately, after 20 kilometers the road narrowed and became easier to ride. I climbed up and over the hills here and was happy to see a TDA bus parked with lunch. Our TDA trip had two buses. One bus, named the dinner bus, would be the last to leave and then drive straight through to the campsite at the end of the day. The other bus, the lunch bus, would park at a pre-designated spot and have tables with fixings for sandwiches for lunch. These two buses thus also made it somewhat easy to ride partial days either to or from the lunch spot. I was the last cyclist into lunch, and, with a little reluctance, decided to take the bus for second half of the day.

The following two days were billed as some of the toughest yet, with longer distances, gravel roads and a reasonable amount of climbing. The route was small gravel road and, with some smaller exceptions, was generally reasonable to ride. These brought us to Puerto Yungay, a small settlement on a fjord. There wasn't much to the settlement, and a big portion seemed to have burned down recently. However, there were a small café and a place to camp along the beach.

The following morning we took the first ferry at 10 a.m. After an hour ride we were on the other side, with still 100 kilometers to ride to Villa O'Higgins. The road was small and hadn't been constructed until 2000. The only crossings from Villa O'Higgins were on foot or bicycle, and hence we really were coming to end of the road. This also meant many fewer cars or motorcycles passing.

At the 16 kilometer mark, the road banked slightly on a curve. I was pushing hard, and before I knew it, my front tire slid out from under me, and I was on the ground. Fortunately, I suffered only a scraped knee and some wounded pride. My palm and elbow also had some pains but were fine by the next day. After checking everything I rode more carefully after that.

It was a pretty ride, with waterfalls along the way and a large lake. I'd eaten an early lunch, but it was still nice to make a brief stop at a TDA vehicle parked at the 50 kilometer mark. The lunch bus had departed the previous evening because it was taking a long detour around the previous automobile crossing to meet us after we came from Villa O'Higgins. It was already late in the day, but calculating my speed, I knew I would make it before sunset, though not necessarily before the start of dinner.

It was already 7:30 p.m. when I arrived at Villa O'Higgins. I was the last rider in that day, and dinner had been served. Somewhat to my embarrassment, other riders gave me an ovation coming into camp. Some food had been saved, and I was happy after a long day riding.

The crossing from Villa O'Higgins to El Chalten, Argentina, is for bicycles and pedestrians only and one of the more interesting crossings I had made. It was also a place where I was grateful to be on a supported ride, with TDA working out more of the logistics. We started the day with a short 8 kilometer ride to a ferry terminal, followed by a three hour ferry ride.

This brought us to a narrow gravel road. Steeply uphill another kilometer was the Chilean border post. I waited with others for my turn and an exit stamp to leave Chile. While I officially had left Chile, there were still another 20 kilometers to the actual border. Most of this was a narrow, two track jeep trail.

At the border the fun began, as crossing into Argentina we were on a narrow single-track trail. It was steep, with some deeper water crossings. The trail was rough enough and steep enough that I ended up walking most of the next 6 kilometers. On one short stretch I was following other cyclists, only to realize we had gone off-route and needed to backtrack along a steep hillside.

The tracks ended at the shore of a lake with both an Argentinian border post and a ferry crossing. We waited with the group for another hour and then took the ferry across the lake. Exiting the ferry I was eager to get on shore and accidentally stumbled. My handlebar bag popped out of my hands and was on its way into the lake when I caught it just in time. With my passport and camera in it, losing it would have been a big deal. Fortunately, other than some embarrassment and pride, all was fine. After the ferry we had another 34 kilometers to cycle into El Chalten. It ended up being one of my longest riding days yet, as I arrived just before sunset.

We had three rest days in El Chalten. This gave sufficient time for our support vehicles to make it all the way around via an earlier Chile/Argentina border crossing. It also allowed for some contingency days in case winds prevented the ferry from running. As I read accounts from other cycle tourists later that summer, the reliability of the ferry was a big issue at times, with cyclists often waiting multiple days.

El Chalten is a very touristy area and well known for hiking. I took one of the rest days to make a longer hike up to viewpoints of Mount Fitzroy but otherwise relaxed. I was also happy to have completed the Carretera Austral route from end-to-end.

The following week from El Chalten to Torres del Paine was mostly spent cycling through Argentina. This was the dry side of the Andes, with much less vegetation but also more wind. We had great tailwinds on our first day cycling to La Leona and then increasingly strong cross-winds cycling to the road junction of El Cerrito. At times the winds were strong enough that I found myself unexpectedly cycling on the left side of the highway.

El Cerrito wasn't really a village, but instead was a road department building. When I arrived, most of the group was huddled in an alcove. A rider who was no longer on the trip had worked with one of the other riders to provide some wine and crackers, and this was a nice touch. The winds were strong enough that people waited until they were expected to die down before putting up tents. That evening I found an alternate building in which I pitched my tent.

It was one day cycling from El Cerrito back to the Chilean border and then crossing to Cerro Castillo. The day started with 65 kilometers of gravel road. The construction workers told us that despite being gravel, it was a good road, with the roughest parts at the beginning and end. While the road wasn't too bad, we did have a stretch with large river pebble-sized rocks in the middle that made me wonder what the construction workers thought was a good road. By lunch I had had enough, and as the route turned into a stronger wind, the lunch bus steadily picked up other cyclists as well.

We got to the Argentinian border crossing, where the border officials decided if cyclists entered the country riding their bikes, they also needed to leave on bikes. This was not a big issue, although just as we got to cycle the last bit, a strong, cold downpour made everything wet.

The following day was a shorter ride into Torres del Paine Park. We expected a route with almost entirely gravel road and were thus surprised when the majority was paved. About half way, we rounded a bend, and I got my first sight of the tall peaks. Wow! It was a spectacular sight, made even more interesting as the next 30 kilometers kept bringing us closer. I took many photos that day as each time I came around a bend, I saw another view.

At Torres del Paine we were given a choice of staying either in a campground or in a hostel. There had been a mixup, and hostel reservations had accidentally not been cancelled. I decided I would be at least as happy in my tent as in a room with half a dozen others. Both nights we had some strong winds and the second night there w also heavy rain. However, my tent held up well.

On our rest day in Torres del Paine, I made a hike up to the viewpoint at the base of the peaks. The weather was on the verge of a storm, but it was otherwise a great hike.

From Torres del Paines to Punta Arenas was three days cycling, including one of my coldest days on the trip. What made it cold wasn't just the temperature but also a cold, wet wind. By the time I reached our campsite, I was shivering. Fortunately, after a warm meal and a brief visit inside a nearby store, I felt much better.

Punta Arenas is a city of 100,000+, a large center for southern Chile. We took a rest day here. Punta Arenas is also the port town for a ferry across to Tierra el Fuego. The group had been counting down the days for a while, but now with only four days left, it really hit home that the trip was ending. Many on the trip were eagerly anticipating Christmas holidays, warmer weather and the comforts of home. While I shared in those, I was also sad that the trip was rapidly coming to a close.

Our first day from Punta Arenas started with a longer ferry ride. As during the day to Villa O'Higgins, this meant a later start on the road, and once again I was into camp just past dinner. However, by now the approaching summer and our southern latitude meant for long days of daylight. A good portion of this ride was on gravel roads, where we had a glorious strong tailwind.

The following morning we made our last border crossing, from Chile into Argentina. I exchanged the last of my Chilean pesos for Argentinian and then followed the mostly paved route to the town of Rio Grande. After Rio Grande the landscapes changed from wide open, windswept areas to having more trees. We also had more hills in this stretch. Even with the trees and hills, we encountered strong winds, including that day riding into a camp at Lago Fagano.

It was our last night on the road, and the TDA staff had prepared wine and crackers and fruit. They also had an informal awards ceremony. Riders were presented informal awards that were generally fun and in good taste, for example, awards for the rider with the most exotic food tastes or the one with most visits to medical. I received a "Dr Doolittle" award for talking to animals. I think this came from my habit of mooing at cows and baaing at sheep as we passed.

We received jerseys, and the following morning we took photos before breakfast and the start of our last day cycling. Throughout the day, the signs for Ushuaia showed decreased distances. It still wasn't easy cycling, with several larger hills to climb, but the adrenaline and finish line spurred me on.

As one of the slower riders, I would often be followed at end of the day by a staff member who was riding sweep. The route that day went directly to the finish hotel. Somehow as I had thought about things the days before, that wasn't quite how I wanted my trip to end – with a rush to a hotel and then quickly taking apart the bike. Instead, I wanted a chance to savor the end of the trip as well as ride into the downtown waterfront area in the middle of town. While it marked the end of the TDA route, it was also the end of my own journey from Alaska, 90% of which I had cycled before joining the TDA route.

Hence, I'd informed the staff I would go off-route and cycle in on my own to arrive at the hotel later. I watched the sweep pass and then found my own route along the shoreline. I saw the city center from a few kilometers away and pieced my way through a construction zone. Before I knew it I was at the city center, and my trip was complete. After 18 months and more than 27,000 kilometers (16,800 miles), the ride was now complete.

Conclusion

I spent the next few days in Ushuaia as a tourist. I also wrote up the following overall summary of lessons learned and posted it to my blog.

After completing a trip, I find it helpful to reflect on what worked, what broke, what I enjoyed more and less. I believe there are many different ways to do bicycle touring – and not one single "right" method – but instead a set of preferences and things that work differently for different people. However, also I write this down if it might help others thinking of a similar trip.

Bicycle

On previous long trips, I often bought a new bicycle especially for the trip. In contrast, for this ride I decided to take four of my existing bikes prepped as necessary: two Trek 4500 mountain bikes (one of which I had used to cycle across Africa) and two Trek 520 mountain bikes (one of which I had cycled on across Europe and Asia). This gave me both a primary bike and a spare of each type. I cycled most of the way to Banff on my touring bike, and, after that, the rest of the trip on my mountain bike.

None of these bikes are particularly fancy or expensive, but I updated them to get stronger wheels and a leather saddle. I also put a front rack on my mountain bike.

Reflections

Disc brakes: I have become a big fan of disc brakes – mainly because of a failure I didn't have. As a rider who is both heavier than average and cautious, I wear through brakes. On previous trips this also eventually meant a failure on the rear rim. This didn't happen on this trip. I replaced rotors once and brake pads many times but didn't have any rim failures.

Hubs/Wheels: I had two hub failures, both with a Phil Woods hub and the pawls sticking down and the hub spinning freely in both directions. After that I had Sugar Wheel Works build up a different wheel around a DT Swiss 540 tandem hub. I took an extra ratchet mechanism and grease with me, but the hubs worked without a problem. In my experience, while Phil Woods makes a strong hub, it seems as though it is also important to get the mechanism opened, serviced and cleaned, and that is difficult for me to do on the road. After four Phil Woods failures, two prior to this trip and two on this trip, I am more shy about using them on other trips. Through the failures I was pleased with service I had from Sugar Wheelworks.

Frame: The right chainstay of my aluminum Trek 4500 bicycle was cracked in Bariloche and welded. There is sometimes a debate about the suitability of aluminum vs. steel on touring bikes. Despite the failure I am still undecided on the debate.

Derailleur: My rear derailleur twisted off the bike in the mud of the Dalton Highway. For now I still think of this as a fluke that happened only once in many cycling miles.

Tires: I used three different models of tires during the trip: Schwalbe Marathon Plus, Schwalbe Marathon Mondial, and Schwalbe Marathon Supreme. The first two are heavier but also are extremely durable tires that served me well. The Supreme tires are considerably lighter (and hence faster). They held up well enough, though I did eventually have enough punctures that I ended up picking up new tires from the U.S.A. Once I got past Mexico, I didn't see Schwalbe tires in bike shops I passed along the way. They might be there if one searches more.

Tubes and tire sizes: Through Latin America, I had 26" wheels but with Presta tubes and not the more common Schraeder valve. There is also a debate in cycling community about 26" vs. 700c in Latin America. I carried enough spare tubes, and in my experience, the odd sizes I had were not an issue.

Overall, I thought the bikes served me well enough from a reliability and durability angle. Some choices made for a slightly slower ride on my mountain bike. That wasn't a big deal when I was doing self-supported touring and was a minor factor in the group riding.

Self-Supported riding vs. a TDA supported ride "They are just different." I found myself saying this statement a few times, partially in answer to conversations I had about which I enjoyed most, and also partially as a reminder to myself that on the TDA trip I should focus on that ride (going on a TDA ride focused on all the ways it isn't the same as self-supported touring is a setup to be unhappy).

In general the largest tradeoffs I found were as follows:

On the TDA supported ride, one has support, with cooked meals, your gear carried and the security of a medic and bike mechanic along the way. The food was excellent, not just in my opinion but also in the opinions of other riders.

On the TDA supported ride, one has the social interactions of traveling with a group of riders. For example, it was interesting that when we met solo-supported cyclists along the way, they seemed eager to talk with us as other cyclists.

The TDA ride essentially has a fixed agenda and fixed route. Each riding day one checks a whiteboard and copies down the route instructions. During the day riders go at their own pace and stop when/where they want but generally follow route instructions or "flagging tape" to figure out where to go. On my self-supported riding, I would adjust my distances and routes as I went along and also take rest days when it made sense for me.

The alternatives to cycling the daily TDA route and distances are essentially to be on the bus or other transport. After cycling every inch from Cartagena to Puerto Montt, I had some long days of gravel riding where I ended up on the bus.

Overall, I planned my trip for 2016/2017 to give myself an option of riding with TDA through some/all of South America and ended up exercising the option to do the last month with TDA from Puerto Montt to Ushuaia. This gave me a fixed end date for completing the trip and support through some difficult parts of the Carreterra Austral as well as some of the most remote parts of South America.

In hindsight I think this was the right choice. While I could have cycled on my own for this last section, I would have chosen to ride via the Argentinian side and also would not have taken the extra time for hiking at El Chalten or Torres del Paine. I would have also missed the interesting border crossing at O'Higgins.

I've now cycled with TDA three times: once through China, once across Africa and once in South America. Given the tradeoffs above, I don't expect to ever be a TDA customer for their tours in "tamer" parts of the world, e.g. North America, Europe or Oceania, and I'll prefer touring self-supported on my own. However, in those places where language/geography/weather make things more extreme, I'll choose TDA for a supported ride again.

Other equipment

Tent: My REI Quarterdome tent served me well enough. It started new. There are some holes in the floor and also now one in the rainfly. One of the poles is slightly bent. One zipper is starting to stick. It held up well enough in the wind and other weather. Hence, it is starting to get "worn out" but will be fine for more local trips.

Sleeping Bag: My sleeping bag was rated for -8C/17F. Except for a few nights in Peru/Bolivia, this was warm enough for the trip. I had many days of temperatures just below 0C, but only a handful in the -15 C to -5C range. I had a second light sleeping bag for the Altiplano region of Bolivia and Peru and was warm enough. For most of Mexico, Central America and coastal Colombia, it was much warmer even at night.

Thermarest: My thermarest developed a hole in it from camping with thorns in Baja California. I was able to patch some of the leak, but it still leaked slowly enough to deflate halfway through the night.

Cycle Computer: My Garmin cycle computer worked through the trip. The rechargeable batteries run down after a day of riding, so I found an extra battery pack helpful. I stayed in hotels often enough that other charging e.g. dynamo or solar wasn't necessary.

Worn out: The following things wore out during the trip: one pair cycling gloves, two handlebar bags, one broken pannier, one Camelbak. I also lost two cycle mirrors and one little thermometer.

Trailer: Originally I didn't have a front rack on my mountain bike, but I did have an Extrawheel Trailer. I somehow misordered and discovered I was missing the hitch and then later purchased a front rack. I think that was a blessing in disguise as having front rack ended up working better than I expect the trailer would have.

Overall, other equipment held up well enough along the way.

Routing Choices

As the trip progressed, I largely picked the route based on what I wanted to see and where I wanted to go. I didn't ride "both" alternatives, so I won't necessarily have a scientific comparison, but the following were my perceptions of some of the major choices as I made them from north to south:

Cassiar Highway vs. Alaska Highway: In 1997 I had cycled the Alaska Highway all the way to the end. This trip I cut off on the Cassiar instead. I enjoyed the choice and found the Cassiar was still more "rugged." The cleared areas on both sides of the highway are less, the short grades occasionally steeper, and I saw more wildlife in this part of the Cassiar than I did previously on the Alaska Highway.

Icefields Parkway: The Icefields Parkway was stunning and a highlight of the trip. It also ended up being crowded enough that I needed to make reservations in advance for camping and hostel sites. I'm glad I made the choice to ride this section rather than going back via the U.S. Pacific Coast. The Pacific Coast is also nice, but I've previously cycled most of it three times.

Great Divide Route vs. Paved roads: I cycled just some parts of the GDMBR before riding most of the distance on the paved highways going through the same areas. I expect this is one of those personal preferences, where some prefer the more rugged/wilderness aspects of a wilderness road and others prefer better road quality/small towns of a busier highway. I am more in the latter camp. I enjoyed the parts of GDMBR I cycled, but overall am at least as happy on paved roads.

Baja California: I enjoyed Baja. I had picked Baja as a "gentle introduction to Mexico" and found the riding not difficult. There is only one highway, and in a few sections, the road is narrow, with not quite enough room for two trucks and a bicycle to pass. There is also a moderate amount of traffic. However, I enjoyed the overall desert terrain and occasional small Mexican village. It also was easy cycling that helped my confidence in starting my trip to Latin America.

Highlands of Mexico: Elevation matters. Even in December/January, the lower coastal areas of Mexico were surprisingly hot. I'm glad I was able to ride through highland areas, where it was significantly cooler.

Toll roads vs. Free roads: I crossed a good portion of Mexico on the toll roads (cuota) rather than the other (libre) roads. Some of this choice was for better roads, including shoulders, and in some cases the travel advisories suggested they might be safer. This worked well enough for me. However, I now also have additional confidence that I might make more of a mix of both roads types on a future trip.

Highlands in Guatemala and Honduras: Elevation matters. As in Mexico, traveling at higher elevations is cooler cycling at the expense of having more hills to cross. I would make the same choice in the future.

Pan American through Panama: A good portion of my cycling though Panama was on the major highway. The road was good, and there usually were good shoulders. However, traveling a busy highway through an area that was fairly hot was not a highlight of the trip, and I might look for other alternatives on a future ride.

Cartagena/Medellin/Popayan/Pasto: I took the major road via the west in Colombia. Overall, I enjoyed this route and Colombia as a whole was one of my favorite countries.

Coast of Peru: I cycled more than 2000 km. along the coast of Peru. There is a definite tradeoff in Peru between the coastal areas, which are flat, and the highland areas, with poorer roads, many more hills, and smaller towns. Average distances in the mountains would be significantly lower than along the coast. The coast was surprisingly cool, with the Humbolt Current creating temperatures rarely below 12C or above 20C. Farther south it also brought headwinds. While not the most exciting part of my trip, it was an expedient route that I would do again if I were crossing all of Peru.

Lake Titicaca, Bolivia, Altiplano, Salar: While I could have kept going south into Chile, I really enjoyed my time cycling up at the higher elevations. Lake Titicaca is beautiful and going via the salt flats was a highlight of the trip.

Argentina vs. Chile, particularly south of Mendoza: My perception is that the tradeoff is that Argentina is drier and windier, while Chile may not be as windy but a lot wetter. As a whole I found the riding via Ruta 40 to be interesting and enjoyable. Once I got close to Bariloche, it became rather beautiful as well.

Carreterra Austral: Already covered in the TDA section above, but I also found the Carreterra Austral to be a highlight of r the ride.

Overall, I followed relatively common routes mostly along the Pacific Coast of South America; in other places there wasn't as much choice.

Miscellaneous:

Spanish: I had enough "survival Spanish" to do the trip but found extra times I spent in Oaxaca and Bariloche to also be valuable. More Spanish generally helped more with my interactions with locals and further conversations than with purchases or hotel stays.

Six Trips:

This trip is my sixth long bicycle ride and completes rides across six continents. Some might inevitably ask, "Which was your favorite and why?" My general response and advice is generally twofold: (a) my recommendation is always to "do your own country first," e.g. Americans cycle across the U.S.A., Canadians across Canada, Europeans through Europe, etc. The reason is that one has extra connections to people, history, and language in his/her own part of the world. Hence, my first ride across the U.S.A. (in 1992) was also special. (b) If I have to pick a favorite, I'd probably select time in Australia. I really enjoyed the outback areas and being in the country long enough to get a feel and sense for what it is really like. English-speaking made travels a bit easier as well.

With that said, I really enjoyed my cycling these past 18 months through Canada, the U.S.A. and then Latin America. There has been an interesting phasing of regions and variety going from country to country. I also like the "newness" of seeing a different part of the world and found travels in this Spanish-speaking area to be relatively easy. I'm not sure what or where my next trips might take me, but I've seen enough of Latin America that I'd love riding through the areas again.

Overall, I really enjoyed my ride, and I am happy and grateful I was able to do it. I would make many of the same choices if I were to do the same trip again. One might also ask, "What next?" and for the first time in a while, I don't have another cross-continental, multi-month trip already in my plans/dreams. I'm sure I'll keep doing other shorter rides and tours.

Selected Photos

Many more photos are in my blogs for each of five major trips:

- 1997 – http://www.bike1997.com
- 2001 – http://www.bike2001.com
- 2007 – http://www.bike2007.com
- 2013 – http://www.bike2013.com
- 2016 – http://www.bike2016.com

1997-- cycling across Canada with a spare wheel on the back of my bicycle

2001 - St. Augustine, Florida, after riding across America for the second time

2001-- at the finish line after cycling one lap around Australia. Fellow cyclists Brendan and Wendy also cycled around Australia and came to the city to help me celebrate.

2001 - New Zealand, a mechanic taking apart my hub. It still failed a week later as would other hubs in 2007 (Thailand) and 2016 (Canada and the U.S.A.)

2002 – India, newly shaved head after tonsure

2006 – Pensa, Russia. My brother Bert and I made a shakedown bicycle ride through Ukraine and Southern Russia a year before my cross Russia ride.

2007 – Russia. Each day we had our water ritual where we ask the locals where to get water for drinking, cooking and cleaning.

2007 – Mickey and I cycled across Russia together. The bugs were bad enough on the West Siberian Plain that we would put on our rain gear and mosquito nets before setting up camp.

2007 – Finish line in Vladivostok

2007 – At the end of the silk road. TDA bicycle trip finish in Beijing.

2013 – Ready to bicycle across Africa

2013 – Capetown, South Africa, with Table Mountain in the background after almost finishing the ride across Africa.

2016 – Campsite on my first night in northern Alaska. The outhouse door was welded shut and I couldn't get my tent drawstring open at first.

2017-- David and I cycled together for six weeks through southern Mexico, Guatemala, Honduras, Nicaragua and Costa Rica.

2017-- Panama City was the destination for for the finish of my North American cycling. I next flew from Panama City to Cartagena, Colombia, by way of a trip back to the U.S.A.

2

017 -- In Peru I spotted a somewhat familiar vehicle, the TDA support van. This was five months before I would join the trip in Puerto Montt.

2017- In Arequipa, Peru, I was "doored" and my pannier split right open. Fortunately, I found a shop that could repair things.

2017- Welded frame after it cracked

2017- Ushuaia, end of the trip across the Americas

Epilogue

Six trips, six continents, 60,000 miles and 36 countries. It has been a fun ride in more ways than one.

After flying back from South America, I moved back to my townhouse in Austin, wrote out this memoir and looked for my next employer and work assignment. I have also continued with shorter bicycle tours in the US including a round trip to Houston and a one-way from El Paso back to Austin.

I still never expect to ride on, let alone across, Antarctica. I've seen recent explorers starting to make these journeys but this is really a class of adventure beyond my skills or interests. While there isn't a seventh continent I will ride, I expect more shorter tours. The real question is what duration for these trips. My longest three trips were 18 months (the Americas), 12 months (Australia) and 10 months (Russia) and it is hard to foresee a trip of quite that duration. However, I could see a shorter trips closer in duration of my first cross-USA trip. No plans yet!

Writing this book has been an interesting experience. It takes a different approach than a blog. It has been fun to review these past trips and try to capture the essence of the travels. I don't know how well I've succeeded, but welcome corrections or updates.

Finally, a salute out to the bicycle tourists out there and wish you tailwinds and safe journeys. It is a wonderful way to travel and to see little slices of the world. To the motorists out there who see us on the road, thank you for your courtesy and be careful as the next cyclist you pass could be someone like me.

Mike Vermeulen, May 2018

Alphabet and acknowledgements

A is for Adventure Cycling Association. I followed Adventure Cycling routes and used Adventure Cycling maps in both 2001 and 2016. I am a life member of this organization.

B is for brothers Rob, Bert and Tom. Bert cycled with me in short parts of some tours and helped me with logistics in others.

C is for Cannondale T-1000, Trek 520 and Trek 4500, the bicycles that carried me on these tours.

D is for Digital Equipment Corporation, an employer in college whose location 26+ miles away helped me with long-distance bicycling.

E is for editors who helped clean up the text. Remaining problems are mine.

F is for 51 months bicycle touring described in this book.

G is for Gretha and John, my parents who helped me with my trips both little and big ways, e.g. web sites, US postal mail,...

H is for Hewlett-Packard and AMD, two employers whose leave policies I used in four of the six tours described herein.

I is for Internet a valuable research tool. Of particular note were bicycle touring forums and crazyguyonabike.

J is for Jacksonville, my destination on my second trip across the USA.

K is for Kaapstad, Africans for Cape Town and destination on my trip across Africa.

L is for Loveland, and particularly the Loveland bicycle club, PEDAL

M is for Mickey, my cycling companion on the ride across Russia.

N is for Newfoundland, my destination on my trip across Canada, and because **S** for St John's is already taken.

O is for Oaxaca, Bariloche, St Petersburg language schools for Spanish and Russian. Particularly enjoyed time with my host family in Bariloche while studying Spanish.

P is for Portland, destination of my first trip across the USA and part of the overall Portland to Portland theme.

Q is for Quarterdome, the tent that brought me across both the Americas and Africa.

R is for Roff Smith whose 1998 articles in National Geographic were inspiration to do my own trip around Australia.

S is for the Sydney Harbour Bridge, the start and finish of my trip around Australia.

T is for Tour D'Afrique and TDA Global Cycling. I traveled with TDA across Africa, across China and in southern parts of South America.

U is for Ushuaia, destination of my trip across the Americas and my screensaver for several years prior.

V is for Vladivostok, destination of my trip across Europe and Asia.

W is for wheels, the bike system I seemed to stress the most. Sugar Wheelworks built strong wheels that carried my across Africa and Latin America.

X is for cross as in X six continents.

Y is for Youth Hostels. Hostels on Cape Cod were a big help in my college touring experiences.

Z is for 26 because Z is the 26th letter and it has taken me 26 years since my first trip across the USA to write out this book.

Manufactured by Amazon.ca
Bolton, ON

17744451R00185